PARASITISM and SUBVERSION
The Case of Latin America

PARASITISM and SUBVERSION

The Case of Latin America

STANISLAV ANDRESKI

PANTHEON BOOKS

A Division of Random House • New York

ACKNOWLEDGMENTS

My Latin-American friends will perhaps recognize in the book the ideas which have emerged during our long discussions; and I can assure them that I have not forgotten it, although for reasons of prudence I have not mentioned them by name.

My thanks are due to the authors from whom I have taken the quotations, as well as to Mr. Cornelius Chikwendu (Port Harcourt, Nigeria) and Mrs. Audrey Savin (Reading, England) for their work on the typescript.

The first draft of this book was written during the most difficult period of my career, and I should like to express my gratitude to Ernest Gellner, A. H. Halsey, Hugh Seton-Watson and Michael Young for their help at that time.

The biggest share in whatever merit the present work may have belongs to my wife, without whose help, encouragement and fortitude it could not have been written.

CONTENTS

FOREWORD

THIS is neither an encyclopaedic treatise nor an elementary introduction to Latin American affairs. It is an attempt to interpret and explain certain specific features of the structure of Latin American societies. My aim has been to provide new insights into causal connections rather than to present hitherto unrecorded data, although some factual information given has not been brought to light before. Though it is primarily concerned with analysing and explaining the present predicament of Latin America, this book contains a great deal of comparative analysis and is intended as a contribution to general understanding of the factors which foster or impede the progress of human societies towards a decent social order – that is to say, towards the elimination of poverty, ill treatment and violence.

A medical report does not give a well-rounded picture of a person's body since it entirely omits its aesthetic qualities. In the same way the contents of the present study do not add up to a well-rounded picture of Latin American societies and cultures. I have restricted myself to the analysis of certain social mechanisms, and tried to disentangle the causes and effects of the economic difficulties and political troubles which afflict Latin America. The view appears rather sombre because it is focused on phenomena generally regarded as evil. One could provide a much more attractive picture of Latin America by concentrating on the arts, literature, music, forms of entertainment or manners.

As widespread social evils are seldom unconnected with the selfish and brutal behaviour of powerful groups and individuals, an honest study of an afflicted society must perforce contain a great deal of muck-raking. Moreover all groups create and cherish myths, some of which are fairly innocuous, others highly pernicious, whilst deliberate misrepresentation has always been used for bolstering power, though in varying measure. So merely by telling the truth about important issues, a writer cuts himself off from a position of comfortable neutrality and exposes himself to the wrath of both naïve believers and the manipulators who cynically delude the public.

Latin American intellectuals, forced by the lack of academic posts with decent salaries and security of tenure, to seek their incomes from various sources are often dependent on charity with strings from institutions, ostensibly neutral, but in fact controlled by vested interests. They must thus either avoid controversial issues or follow the line of one of the power blocs. Though many of them have courageously exposed the evil actions of one or two institutions or groups, none of them can afford to offend all the big battalions by a comprehensive and truthful analysis of the mechanisms of exploitation and strife.

PARASITISM and SUBVERSION

The Case of Latin America

CHAPTER ONE

THE PREDICAMENT

*The Traditional Society and its Waning**

UNTIL the end of the nineteenth century the economic life of the Latin American republics was little different from what it was during the early days of the Spanish and Portuguese empires. The most inaccessible areas were (as a few still are) occupied by independent Indian tribes. The areas of very difficult access, though not entirely inaccessible, contained Indian village communities which retained some self-government in spite of being constrained to render dues in labour or kind. The rest of the inhabited land was divided into large estates, called *fazendas* in Brazil, *estancias* in Argentina, *haciendas* in Mexico, *fundos* in Chile.† Whatever their name, they differed little in social structure: whether the labourers were slaves or serfs or legally free wage earners, the owner of an estate was *de facto* their absolute master. The only important difference between the various kinds of estate was that which existed between self-sufficient manors and plantations growing crops for export; but this did not materially affect the treatment of labour. In fact where this distinction existed it was to the disadvantage of those plantations which were normally devoted to cultivating a single crop such as

---

* When writing about countries of the American continent, one cannot logically speak of 'the Americans' in the sense of the citizens of the USA. For this reason I have decided to use the term Northamericans, following the usage current throughout Latin America. Joining the words 'North' and 'Americans' is necessary because even if one follows the cultural rather than physical geography, and decides that North America begins at Rio Bravo (otherwise known as Rio Grande) one cannot exclude Canada. So, according to this usage, the North Americans are divided into Northamericans and Canadians.

† Beyond the areas of permanent settlement, however, there were grasslands inhabited by nomads who lived by varying combinations of cattle-breeding, slave-hunting, gold-digging and banditry.

sugar or coffee, where the labourers had less opportunity to find supplementary foodstuffs. Until the advent of steamships and railways, plantations producing crops for export were confined to the Caribbean islands and north-eastern Brazil; and their only important product was sugar. Later, improvements in transport led to a great expansion of the production for export.

The cities of traditional Latin America had all the characteristics of consumer (as distinct from producer) towns: they were places where officials and absentee landowners lived with their retinues and garrison, the rest of the population consisting of merchants and the artisans who worked for them. The relationship of the towns to the villages was purely parasitic: they consumed agricultural produce without supplying the villagers with anything in return.

The mining camps constituted the third principal element of the traditional economy of Latin America; and it was there that the exploitation was the most cruel. Herding the Indians into these camps was one of the causes of depopulation in Peru and Mexico during the first two centuries of the Spanish rule. In Brazil since gold had been discovered in a sparsely populated region of the interior, mining did not cause depopulation, but it used up a large number of imported slaves.

The gold and silver extracted from the soil of America proved to be a doubtful blessing to Spain and Portugal but it benefited the colonies even less. In Spain and Portugal the influx of precious metals drove up prices and crippled industries by making them unable to compete with imported wares. In America the same effects were further aggravated by the mercantilist policies of the Crowns, which prohibited all manufactures in order to preserve the markets for the metropolitan industries. In fact, however, it was the products of northern Europe which were transported by Spanish merchants to the colonies and sold there with tremendous profit. A calculation of the amount of labour which the enslaved Indians had to put into extracting a pound of gold would show that mining of precious metals was thoroughly bad business for the colonies; their inhabitants would have been much richer if they had dedicated themselves to manufacturing industries. The activities connected with mining formed pipelines leading straight to Spain and Portugal with a minimum of leakage. The merchants of Seville, who had a monopoly of trade with the American colonies of the Spanish crown, followed the policy of enormous profit margins on small turnovers; and, although the English, Dutch and French smugglers did more trade than the authorized merchants, the amount of trade was trifling.

The first commodities to be exported from Latin America were, apart from precious metals and sugar, guano and nitrates from Peru. From 1879 onwards the nitrates became the speciality of Chile, which wrested from Peru and Bolivia the areas containing them. Later, coffee began to be exported from Brazil, tropical fruit from the area around the Caribbean, and oil from Mexico and Venezuela. The seemingly trivial invention of barbed wire added to the advantages of steam navigation, refrigeration and the railways, enabled Argentina to become the biggest exporter of cereals and meat in the world.

The presence of exportable commodities attracted foreign capital. British financiers entered the field first, opened banks and advanced capital for the construction of railways throughout the continent. They also invested in Chilean nitrates, Peruvian guano, in the silver mines of Mexico and in many other ventures. British capital and business had almost complete monopoly until about 1880, when Germany and the United States entered into competition, and it retained the predominating position until the First World War. The Germans made rapid progress but suffered severe setbacks because of their defeats in the two world wars. Northamerican business and capital, on the other hand, continuously improved its positions, and gained an ascendancy over its competitors during the First World War which became complete during the Second.

Until 1914 the countries of Latin America imported nearly all the manufactured products which they consumed, paying for them by exporting raw materials. The first movement towards industrialization began during the First World War owing to the inability of the traditional suppliers to deliver the goods. The second impetus came from the collapse of export markets during the thirties, which forced the Latin Americans to try to produce those commodities which they were no longer able to buy. It was, however, only during the Second World War that industrialization became really rapid – at least in Mexico, Brazil, Argentina and Chile. As usually happens in capitalist economies,

3

industrialization began with light industries, and only recently have heavy industries begun to spring up. So far, however, the industries produce only for the internal market, and exports consist only of raw materials.

Industrial growth has been very rapid in most countries in Latin America: between 1945 and 1958 the output of the manufacturing industry increased by about 90%. Agricultural production has increased substantially in Venezuela, Nicaragua, Mexico, Ecuador, El Salvador and Brazil, but this is due to the expansion of the production of commercial crops, principally cotton, while the production of food has not kept pace with the growth of population, except in Ecuador where the production of bananas jumped from 18,000 tons in 1945 to 424,000 tons in 1952. Moreover, these increases in agricultural production were not due to better methods of cultivation – as a matter of fact, the productivity of agricultural labour remained the same – but to the utilization of hitherto uncultivated areas. In Mexico this required large-scale irrigation, whereas in Brazil and the other countries the much less expensive investments in roads were sufficient to stimulate the extension of cultivation. However, this method of increasing agricultural output cannot be followed much longer because only Brazil still has large reserves of cultivable land.

The table opposite, based on the calculations of Jorge Ahumada of the United Nations Economic Commission for Latin America, provides approximative indication of the annual rates of growth of total national products in real items (i.e. allowing for changes in prices) over the period 1945–58 in relation to the rates of growth of the population.

These indices show that some countries of Latin America have made substantial progress, but they do not necessarily indicate a radical improvement in living conditions. It is the peculiarity of economic statistics that they magnify the increments of real income in economies which are undergoing a transition from domestic self-sufficiency to production for the market. In the first place, when production is becoming more 'round-about' the total amount of goods produced increases faster than the amount of goods produced for consumption: the production of goods used in producing others does not directly provide

Country	Total product % p.a.	Population % p.a.	Product per head % p.a.
Venezuela	9·0	3·0	6·0
Nicaragua	7·7	3·3	4·4
Mexico	5·7	2·6	3·1
Ecuador	4·4	2·9	1·5
El Salvador	5·8	3·3	2·5
Brazil	6·2	2·5	3·7
Peru	3·7	2·1	1·6
Colombia	4·3	2·8	1·5
Costa Rica	5·7	3·4	2·3
Panama	3·9	2·7	1·2
Cuba	1·8	2·1	−0·3
Uruguay	1·9	1·7	0·2
Honduras	4·2	3·1	1·1
Paraguay	2·7	2·4	0·3
Chile	2·8	2·2	0·6
Guatemala	5·1	3·1	2·0
Argentina	1·7	2·1	−0·4
Haiti	2·1	1·3	0·8
Bolivia	0·6	1·3	−0·7
Western Germany	7·4	1·1	6·3
Britain	2·2	0·3	1·9

anything for consumption. Furthermore, product and income statistics are swollen by the effects of the transition from autoconsumption to buying and selling. For example: when a wife, instead of preparing good meals, goes to work and earns just enough to pay for bad meals in a restaurant for herself and her husband, she raises the income (including the national income) without in any way raising the standard of living. If a man, instead of walking a short distance to work, takes a job farther away for a pay increment equivalent to what he will have to spend on travelling in discomfort, he in fact loses in terms of well-being, although again he adds to the national income. Even the statistics of consumption must not be taken as depicting exactly the level of material well-being, because a rise in consumption may be entirely due to a wider use of inessential gadgets combined with a decline in consumption of essential foodstuffs. Certain strictly material aspects of existence which affect health and well-being – such as space, clean air and freshness of the food – do not come within the purview of economic statistics at all. This does not mean, of course, that such statistics are useless, but only that they must be taken as very rough approximations. In very poor countries the most important index of social wealth is the *per capita* consumption of food and clothing; and in this respect progress in Latin America has been very slight in the countries with high rate of growth and non-existent in those with moderate rates; while in those where these rates were insignificant there has been a decline in the standard of living.

Taking the years 1945–7 as the base (= 100), the indices of real salaries between 1955 and 1957 stood at: Argentina, 88·6; Brazil, 99·4; Chile, 88·0; Venezuela, 124·0.

Thus only in Venezuela has the situation of the working class improved, whilst even in Brazil it declined slightly in spite of the remarkable rate of industrial growth. In Argentina and Chile the decline was very noticeable. In the Colombian capital, Bogota, the real wages declined by 23% between 1950 and 1954.

With the exception of the few smaller and poorer states, the countries of Latin America are not uniformly undeveloped in the way that the new African states are: the most conspicuous feature of Latin American societies is the juxtaposition of incongruous elements. In no other aspect of social life is the incongruity of the elements more evident than in the combination of a high degree of urbanization with the extreme backwardness of the agricultural areas.

The southernmost and northernmost parts of Latin America are among the most heavily urbanized areas of the globe. In Argentina, Uruguay and Chile more than 60% of the population live in towns, and in Mexico over 40%. Buenos Aires with a population of 5½ million and Mexico City with 4½ are enormous conurbations, as are Rio de Janeiro and São Paulo with their 3 million each. Bogota in Colombia, Santiago in Chile, Montevideo in Uruguay are also large cities. In addition to standing in sharp contrast to the uniform backwardness of the rural areas, the big cities themselves harbour most incongruous elements.

In some ways they are more modern than London or Paris, but they have slums which are bigger and much more primitive than anything that can be found in Europe. True, there are some very primitive slums in southern Italy and Greece, but as the cities in which they are found are smaller and more provincial than the Latin American capitals, the contrasts are not so striking. In Caracas, for instance, an impressive avenue, no narrower than Les Champs Élysées in Paris, has on one side the sumptuous building of the Officers' Club, and on the other a wide area covered with hovels made of discarded boxes where thousands live without running water or sanitation. In Bogota one can see from the windows of an air-conditioned hotel rats searching for refuse on an unpaved street.

Proliferation of slums, breeding every conceivable vice, is not entirely due to the inefficiency or lack of conscience of public authorities. The problem has become unmanageable: the cities are growing at the cumulative rate of 5% per year, owing to the high rate of natural increase of their populations coupled with intensive migration from the rural areas, which amounts to the transfer of 1% of the total population every year. It might be said that such growth merely requires an effort equivalent to that made by Western Germany during the decade when it had to provide housing for refugees from the east. It must be remembered, however, that the Germans expelled from the eastern territories did not differ in occupational skills or composition from the inhabitants of the Federal Republic, so that their absorption was easy and they could contribute immediately to the expansion of the economy, whereas the migrants into Latin American cities are illiterate peasants for whose unskilled labour there is very little demand. The exodus is due less to the attraction of the city than to the disastrous conditions of rural life, and it amounts largely to a transfer of unemployment from the countryside to the cities.

The rural exodus is not on the whole due to the mechanization of agriculture and the rise in productivity. Given the type of land tenure which prevails throughout Latin America, there is very little incentive to expand agricultural production, and consequently the natural increase in the rural population produces chronic unemployment and underemployment. This permanent and general factor is reinforced in some cases by special circum-

7

stances: the exodus from northern Brazil has been aggravated by a series of droughts, while in Colombia thousands of peasants fled to the cities in search of some security from the terror deployed by the police and the warring bands.

Even where the industries are growing very fast (as, for instance, in São Paulo), it is the demand for skilled workers that grows most quickly, while the demand for unskilled labour lags behind. Naturally the firms train some employees but only training schemes organized on a truly massive scale could change the situation radically.

The cities of Latin America are burdened not only with masses of miserable paupers, but also with the low productivity of those inhabitants who are employed. To judge by the indices of urbanization, Argentina, Uruguay, Chile and Mexico should be highly industrialized nations; but this is not yet the case. Buenos Aires and Mexico city have many factories but their production does not approach that of the Parisian conurbation, which is of comparable size. Urbanization has outrun industrialization not only because of the influx of rural paupers, but also because of the hypertrophy of personnel engaged in commerce and administration. Consequently the cities are to a large extent parasitic: they live upon the countryside without contributing much to its welfare. This is particularly true of the capitals with their absentee landowners, generals, politicians, clergymen, officials, troops, lawyers, students and the enormous numbers of servants attending to the needs of all these categories. The situation is slightly different in São Paulo which, not being a national capital, is the most productive large city in Latin America. However, in the chief industrial towns of Colombia, Barnaquilla and Madellin, the workers constitute only 30% of the population, whereas office workers constitute 40%.

The parasitic character of the cities reveals itself in the smallness of their contribution to the consumption of the rural population. The villages are mostly self-sufficient, and their inhabitants buy only a very small part of the products of the urban industry, although they have to surrender to the townsmen most of their produce. In other words, though fed by the peasants, the towns consume almost the entire output of their industries. Later we shall examine in detail the mechanisms of parasitic suction which make this possible.

8

Strife and Disorder

Proverbially Latin America is the land of revolutions. This reputation is not without foundation but, to keep the matter in proportion, one must remember that few parts of the world have enjoyed internal peace for long periods; and that although armed strife has been extremely frequent in Latin American states, it has seldom attained the massive dimensions of the Northamerican Civil War or of the Spanish Civil War or of the fighting in post-revolutionary Russia. Moreover, the records of the various countries differ greatly: Chile, which suffered fewer interruptions of legality than any other country of Latin America, compares favourably in this respect with most countries in Europe. In contrast, in Mexico there were over a thousand armed uprisings between 1800 and 1940. According to another calculation over 130 revolutions took place in Bolivia. These calculations are fairly arbitrary, because there is a wide spectrum between revolts and ordinary banditry, but they do illustrate the prevalence of violence in Latin American politics. Even when there is no open fighting the governments rest either entirely or partly on naked force: everywhere there are important sections of the population which would disobey or even overthrow the government if they were not forcibly restrained. Only the political systems of Uruguay and Costa Rica can be said to rest upon popular consent but even they are far removed from the democratic stability of Sweden or Switzerland: in Uruguay there was a revolution in 1933 which established a dictatorship – short-lived, it is true – and in Costa Rica a relatively bloodless civil war took place as recently as 1948. The extraordinary record of legality in Chile is the product of a consensus within the ruling class, whilst the lower classes have been kept in order by the police. The same is true of the peace which has prevailed in Mexico since 1938 when the last military revolt was put down. Regimes like that of the Somozas in Nicaragua, of Perez Jimenez in Venezuela, or Trujillo in the Dominican Republic, or of Duvallier in Haiti rested (or rest) upon terror.

Economic progress requires peace and order. Planning, saving and investment become unprofitable if nothing is secure. Strife impoverishes and may ruin a country, if it is sufficiently serious. On the other hand, it is equally clear that generalized poverty,

9

and sudden impoverishment especially, generate strife and disorder – a vicious circle which can maintain a country in a pitiful
condition. However, the relation between economic conditions
and ruinous strife is complicated by the influence of the strength
of the political structure: a gust of economic adversity which
may break a weak political structure would be powerless against
a stronger structure

Widespread poverty greatly aggravates the effects of a system
of graft. In the United States the offices which in most countries
of Europe are reserved for permanent civil servants are distributed among its supporters by the party which wins at the polls.
The extent of this practice varies greatly according to region
and the agency but it always affects a large number of even relatively minor officials. In the United States the spoils system has
been receding during recent decades because of the growing
demand for professional administrative training, and of the desire
to recruit capable administrators by offering them security of
tenure, but such a trend has been much less marked in the
countries of Latin America where the regulations concerning
promotion and security of tenure are rarely taken seriously.
In reality, the spoils system now affects far greater numbers –
both absolutely and proportionately – than it did under the conditions of simple rural life. Not only has the number of dispos-
able posts increased, but also the economic stakes have become
more important, owing to the expansion of governmental control
over economic affairs which has created new opportunities of
making money by political means.

The decisive difference between the North and Latin American spoils systems resides in their relative importance to other
avenues to wealth. In the United States the proceeds obtainable
through politics have always been and remain negligible in comparison with success in business. The rich of Northamerica are
not the successful politicians but the successful businessmen and
their descendants. Although few Northamerican presidents
followed the legendary route from log cabin to the White House,
most of them were not very wealthy, and continued to live fairly
modestly after the expiry of their office. The captains of industry
and finance might bribe or blackmail politicians and officials
in order to twist the law to their convenience, but they seldom
entered directly into politics, which they were content to leave

to Irish demagogues who could not make money in better ways. In contrast, throughout Latin America political power has always been the surest and quickest way to wealth; and more often than not it was the only way. Once a society is pervaded by parasitic exploitation, the choice is only to skin or be skinned. A man may combine the two roles in varying measure but he cannot avoid them: he cannot follow Candide's example and till his garden, relying on hard work for his well-being, because he will not be left alone: the wielders of power will pounce upon him and seize the fruits and tools of his labour. In certain countries – most notably in Argentina, Chile and Colombia – an estate owner could at least confine himself to his own sphere of private exploitation, and shun the political arena. In other countries – such as Venezuela, Paraguay, the Dominican Republic – nothing was safe from the conquerors of power, who grabbed the estates of those who did not belong to their band. This difference was rooted in the distinction between the bright periods of urbane politics in the former countries and the perpetually cut-throat politics of the latter. These facts fit the general principle that the ferocity of a struggle depends on the importance of the stakes – that is to say, on the expectations of what can be lost through defeat or gained through victory.

The greater and more general the poverty, the more important the stakes of political contests. In an opulent country a man who is thrown out of office can usually find decent employment elsewhere, but in a poor country, full of paupers and genteel semi-paupers, a loss of office usually means ruin for anybody who has no private wealth; and even the people of the latter category are safe only in so far as the rights of property are respected. In consequence, the fight for office is a matter of life and death for all the minor figures who cannot place large funds in foreign banks, and becomes a struggle for existence fought with every available means and without regard for law or convention.

In such circumstances politics tend to oscillate between despotism and anarchy, because a constitutional parliamentary government cannot function without a readiness to compromise and to observe the rules of the game. This applies even to oligarchy, but it can be stated as a general rule, to which no exception has yet been found, that a democracy can function only in a society which is fairly prosperous, and in which privileges obtained through political influence are not indispensable for making a decent living. Despotism, however, cannot ensure peace for periods exceeding the length of one reign unless it is based on an undisputed rule of inheritance. With a few partial exceptions, in Latin America the republican ideology could not bring forth viable democracies, but it was too strong to permit the establishment of national monarchies, or even the continuation of the one which existed in Brazil until 1889.

Poverty as a Stimulant to Parasitism

Parasitism exists in all human societies: everywhere there are people who succeed in obtaining a large share of wealth without in any way contributing towards its production. There are, however, differences of degree which are of decisive importance; in some societies it is a residual phenomenon whereas in others it pervades the whole social fabric. Generally speaking, parasitism constitutes the most powerful brake on economical progress by destroying the link between the effort and the reward.*

The idea that parasitism is inimical to economic progress is not new: Adam Smith broached it, and in 1826 Charles Comte – one of the great founders of sociology, unjustly overshadowed by his namesake Auguste – published four volumes devoted entirely to the elaboration and verification of this principle under the title *Traité de Législation, ou Éxposition des Lois Générales Suivant Lesquelles les Peuples Prospèrent, Dépérissent ou Restent Stationnaires*. This great work still remains the most exhaustive survey of parasitism and class oppression. Karl Marx and Charles Comte complement each other: Comte deals with pre-industrial forms of exploitation whereas Marx concentrates on the fate of the factory workers. Since they studied different forms of exploitation, they differed in their assessment of its effects: Comte regarded it as an insurmountable obstacle to the growth of wealth, whereas Marx viewed it as essential to accumulation of capital, and, therefore, to the progress of capitalism. These views, however, are not really contradictory because a reduction of the workers' share in the fruits of their labours has different effects

* This point is treated in greater detail in my *Elements of Comparative Sociology*, Weidenfeld and Nicolson, 1964, Chapters 11, 15 and 16.

according to whether the resulting surplus is consumed by the parasitic classes or used for increasing production. Marx has exaggerated the roles of exploitation and accumulation of funds as the causes of the rise of industry. Obviously, capitalism could not have developed without the accumulation of capital. But with the slow population growth, the simplicity of early machines and the relatively slow progress of inventions, the amount of capital necessary to assure a moderate rate of development was not large, and there were already sufficient funds in most large societies. The factors which were crucial in producing industrial capitalism were those which canalized an important fraction of available wealth into improvements of productive equipment. An influx of capital into a country whose social structure fosters its wasteful and parasitic use, far from stimulating economic progress, can ruin it, as can be seen from the decline of Spain.

The implications of the foregoing propositions, in so far as they concern Latin America, will be treated in greater detail in later chapters, and the remaining part of the present section will be devoted to elucidating the important fact that the causal relationship between parasitism and poverty is not unilateral but circular. The principle of the circular causation arises from a combination of Charles Comte's tenet that parasitism causes poverty and the principle that in a fairly complex society poverty fosters parasitism. The qualification concerning complexity is necessary because poverty has no such effect in simple unstratified tribes: parasitism can flourish only in societies in which there are differentiated groups, some of which can exploit others. Instead of 'causes' the word 'fosters' is used in the second component because the effects of poverty upon parasitism are less immediate than the effects of parasitism upon poverty, and can be temporarily counter-balanced by such factors as ideological fervour or the power of an austere despot: in Russia under Lenin there was more poverty than under the tsars but less parasitism.

The assertion that poverty produces parasitism does not imply that parasitism cannot grow in its absence. Actually, bureaucratic parasitism is growing in the wealthiest countries and, although it is probable that eventually it may bring about the arrest of technical progress, at present it is stimulating progress by preventing crises of over-production, such as the one which nearly destroyed capitalism in the thirties. In order to clarify the issue we must make a distinction between a relatively benign parasitism in opulent societies, where a parasitic existence of a fairly large number of people does not necessitate severe deprivation of the rest, and more malign forms which occur in poor societies where the unproductive and comfortable existence of a minority can be secured only by the ruthless exploitation of the majority. In medical terms, we can say that tolerance of parasitism (that is to say, immunity to its deleterious effects) depends upon wealth. The medical analogy is exact: a dose of bacteria which may be fatal to a debilitated body may scarcely affect a strong one, but nearly every illness increases the body's vulnerability to other diseases.

Granted that poverty in complex societies is in the long run invariably accompanied by parasitic exploitation, it may be argued that this correspondence is accounted for by the principle that parasitism breeds poverty. There are, however, examples of impoverishment caused by extrinsic factors stimulating parasitism, which then produced further impoverishment. This was notably the case in Italy at the end of the Renaissance, when a shift in the trade routes reduced commercial opportunities and stimulated the conversion of enterpreneurs into landlords and *rentiers*. Further, if the relationship between poverty and parasitism were in the nature of one-way causation, then it would be much easier to abolish them: it is because they are enclosed in a vicious circle, entangled with other vicious circles, that this is so difficult. (We can deduce from general principles of cybernetics that in a system of interdependent variables, containing stochastic elements, only those variables can be consistently maintained at a maximum or minimum which are included in positive feedbacks, i.e. vicious or virtuous circles.) In addition the social mechanisms through which poverty produces parasitism can be traced.

These mechanisms exemplify the principle of the least effort: all men seek the wealth necessary for the satisfaction of their basic needs, and everywhere where wealth can be conserved there are men who amass it in order to gain more power and glory. If the easiest or quickest road to minimal prosperity as well as to riches leads through participation in activities which add to the collective wealth, then men will put their energies into socially useful occupations. If, owing to circumstances among which general poverty usually occupies a prominent place, productive activities are unrewarding, then men will concentrate on devising ways of wresting from their fellows such wealth as already exists. In other words, the energies which in an expanding economy will be applied to production, will be canalized in a stagnant or contracting economy into open or covert predation. Naturally, there are people everywhere who will always opt for parasitism and predacity, and others who will never do so; but the great majority can be swayed by the relative advantages of these alternatives.

The social mechanism in question offers an analogy to the mental mechanism brought to light by Freud (with whose detailed interpretation we need not agree): when the basic propensities of human nature find no outlet, the mental energy turns inward to consume itself in internal conflicts. In the same way, when social energy finds no outlet in constructive activities, it is used up in social conflicts.

Another mechanism of conversion operates between internal and external conflicts. It has been analyzed at considerable length in my *Military Organization and Society* (London, 1954) and in Chapters 7 and 8 of my *Elements of Comparative Sociology*. It can be succinctly described as follows: external and internal conflicts represent alternative manners of predacity; they constitute alternative and mutually compensatory releases of population pressure, as they are alternative methods of organizing emigration to hereafter; finally, by displacing resentments and aggressiveness towards the outsider, an external conflict helps to smooth internal quarrels, and *vice versa*. Thus social energies can be regarded as having three main outlets: construction, internal strife and external conflict. The relationship between them is such that a blockage in any of them produces an increased flow through the others, whereas a widening of one tends to drain off the flow through the other channels.

The relevance of all this to Latin America is obvious: a combination of economic distress with international peace has exacerbated internal predacity. The growth of the population has nullified the benefits of increased production, creating new needs and multiplying energies without providing for them enough outlets other than predation and strife.

15

The Curse of Numbers

The economic difficulties of Latin American countries have been rendered unmanageable by the tremendously fast population growth. (The only exception is Uruguay, where the rate of population increase is not far above the western European level.) This extraordinary increase is due to the lowering of the death rate without a corresponding lowering of the birth rate, which imbalance condemns most of the world's population to misery. In Latin America it is greater than elsewhere, although its impact is slightly softened by the greater amount of unused resources in Latin America as compared with Asia. Its population growth is higher than that of any other continent and is itself increasing. Between 1935 and 1955 the rate of growth of the total population of Latin America rose from 2·2% per year to 2·6%. Uruguay and Argentina constitute the only exceptions to this trend. During the same period the rate of growth fell from 2·0% to 1·7% in Argentina, and from 1·3% to 0·9% in Uruguay. On the other hand, in a number of countries the acceleration of growth was due not only to the decline in the death rate (though this was unquestionably the primary cause) but also to the rise in the birth rate. In Mexico, for instance, the birth rate was 32·0 per thousand in 1910, but 47·3 in 1957.

In 1955 the rates of population growth of the republics were as follows:

Costa Rica 3·3; Dominican Republic 3·2; Guatemala 3·1; Venezuela 3·0; Nicaragua 3·0; Colombia 2·9; Mexico 2·9; Ecuador 2·8; Panama 2·8; Peru 2·8; Honduras 2·7; El Salvador 2·7; Brazil 2·5; Chile 2·4; Bolivia 2·4; Haiti 2·2; Paraguay 2·0; Cuba 2·0; Argentina 1·7; Uruguay 0·9.

Death rates are still falling, and if they dropped to the Northamerican or western European level, the population of Latin America would double itself every twenty years. If that were to happen, within 300 years it would become so large that there would be more than one human being per square metre (that is to say, standing room only) even if lakes, rivers and swamps were made habitable. Clearly this situation would be disastrous and the birth rate must fall or the death rate rise to a level commensurate with the birth rate. In other words, either birth control will spread or what Malthus called repressive checks – war (whether international or civil), famine and pestilence – will come into operation with sufficient force to bring the demographic explosion to a halt.

In the prosperous countries of western Europe the decline in fecundity occurred spontaneously, without any encouragement from the governments, as the result of the rise in the standard of living and the spread of a rationalistic outlook. It must be remembered, however, that this happened in Europe when wealth grew more rapidly than the population, which is not the case in Latin America of today. At the time when the birth rate began to decline, the population of Europe grew by only 1% per year – that is to say two and a half times less than the present rate in Latin America. True, at the turn of the century Europeans did not have at their disposal the technical knowledge of today, but they had ample outlets for emigration, and above all they could become providers of manufactured goods for the rest of the world from which they imported raw materials. Those who regard industrialization as an automatic cure for poverty forget that it is impossible for all the countries of the world to become 'workshops of the world' at the same time. Britain, Belgium and Western Germany are prosperous today because they can import food and raw materials, but they would become poverty stricken if every country in the world had to do the same. When the food supplies are inadequate indices of growing total production indicate only an increased use of mechanical gadgets by the rich. And as far as food is concerned, the position of Latin America (with the exceptions of Argentina and Uruguay) is grim. According to the Food and Agricultural Organization, the production of foodstuffs per head in Latin America in 1956 was only 94% of the 1938 figure, although the total quantity produced in 1956 amounted to 142% of the production in 1938.

A spontaneous decline in the birth rate cannot take place in a country where the majority of the population is plunged in such misery that have neither an incentive nor even the material possibilities of practising birth control, and are too superstitious and improvident to care. Another important fact is that sexual intercourse is the only pleasure which the very poor can afford. As on the other hand the standard of living cannot be raised so long as the population grows so fast, we have here a vicious circle out of which it is very difficult to break. It is usually said that the remedy is to accelerate the growth of wealth until it overtakes the increase of the population, but apart from other difficulties we encounter here another vicious circle: an excessive growth of the population is not only difficult to catch up with simply in virtue of its speed, but it also acts as a brake on accumulation of capital.

In a rapidly growing population a large number of children have to be supported. In Latin America as a whole young people under 15 constitute 45% of the total population, while persons aged 65 and over make up 3%; thus only 52% make up the economically useful age group. For every 100 persons aged 15–64 years there are 90 in the dependent age groups. Uruguay, where the age composition resembles that of the countries of western Europe, and Argentina, in which it is similar to the United States, are the only exceptions.

If all other conditions were equal and the average output per worker in Argentina and Brazil were the same, the Brazilian output per inhabitant would nevertheless be smaller because in Brazil there are 181 persons of all ages for every 100 persons of working age (15–64), whereas in Argentina there are only 155. If Argentina's output per head were 100, that of Brazil would be only 86.

Owing to their unfavourable age composition, the countries of Latin America suffer from the following disadvantages in comparison with countries with lower birth rates: (1) relatively fewer persons in the population are of working age; (2) fewer women can undertake work other than the care of children; (3) the resources which could be applied to raising the standard of living have to be devoted to the struggle to maintain it.

As a more numerous generation replaces the one preceding it, the current level of consumption can be maintained only if the amount of productive equipment is increased at least in proportion. In other words, investments must be made merely to prevent a deterioration in the standard of living. On the basis of certain not unrealistic assumptions it has been calculated that, if a population grows by 1% a year, about 4% of the total national product must be allocated to investments – called demographic investments – which merely counteract the effect of the growth of the population. This means, of course, that, given the rate of saving, the faster the growth of the population, the fewer are the resources which can be used for effecting an improvement. Unfortunately, however, even the rate of saving is not exempt from the influence of demographic factors. In a poor society with a low ratio of workers to dependants saving is difficult and therefore capital available for investment is scarce, which means that the necessity for making heavy demographic investments rules out (or at least slows down) economic progress.

The vicious circle of poverty and demographic imbalance is even more difficult to break than the foregoing purely quantitative considerations indicate because, as we saw in the preceding section, economic distress fosters parasitic tendencies and institutions, and stimulates strife and disorder, which in their turn aggravate the economic difficulties. The numerical preponderance of the young also encourages violence, because nothing makes a situation so explosive as a large number of unemployed or impoverished young men.

Only in Argentina and Uruguay is the population growth such that it does not cause major difficulties. True, Argentina's growth is considerable by western European standards but the country has enormous and easily accessible resources, and its present economic troubles are due solely to political disorders. The birth rate in Argentina which has fluctuated during the last 25 years between 23 and 25 per thousand, has declined from its previously high level because of urbanization. In Uruguay, where the birth rate is now only 18 per thousand, the influence of urbanization has been accentuated by an educational effort without parallel in Latin America, conducted in the spirit of rationalism, libertarian socialism and anticlericalism.

Argentina and Uruguay differ from other countries of Latin America in important respects: they are unique in having populations descending mostly from recent European immigrants. Partly for this reason, the lower classes in these countries have never known the depths of misery and degradation which are still the lot of their counterparts in other Latin American countries, where serfdom of the Indians or slavery of the Africans has shaped the structure of society. As the process of urbanization in the other countries is taking place in an environment of greater misery, it cannot be assumed that it will have the same beneficial effect on the birth rate, particularly as the cultural traditions differ greatly. Actually, Mexico is not so far behind

Argentina in respect of urbanization as the difference in birth rates might suggest: in Mexico 50% of the population is urban compared with 68% in Argentina, but the Mexican birth rate is 64·4 per thousand while the Argentinian is 24 per thousand. So long as the birth rates remain so high, every economic improvement will be nullified by the population growth, and there is no way of diminishing, let alone eliminating, the misery. And as there are no grounds for hoping that in these circumstances the birth rate will decline spontaneously, we must conclude that all reforms are doomed to failure without a vigorous policy of encouraging and facilitating the practice of birth control. Naturally, there are many obstacles to such a policy. Some are technical: the present means (or at least those which do not greatly diminish satisfaction) can hardly be used by the homeless or those who live in abodes which do not even deserve the name of a slum. The technical difficulties can be fully overcome only when cheap, dependable and harmless contraceptive appliances become available.* However, the example of Japan shows that even with the present methods a determined effort by a government can bring the birth rate down very quickly. Secondly, there are economic difficulties: in the underdeveloped countries of the world the poor cannot afford to buy soap, let alone the more expensive products of the chemical industry, so that the only solution would be free distribution. Even the governments of very poor countries could afford this if they were prepared to spend a fraction of the sums spent on useless armaments and ostentation; if they were unwilling to do so, contraceptive devices could be provided as a part of international aid without greatly increasing the sums already spent. The real obstacles stem from traditions and attitudes.

The desire for the numerical increase of one's group is a common ingredient of nationalism and other kinds of ethnocentrism. Its roots stretch right back to the primeval horde, where victory in battle usually depended on numerical strength. This attitude, outdated in the era of nuclear weapons and automation, remains to impede the adoption of a rational approach to demographic problems. Moreover, attention to the problem of overpopulation requires foresight and concern for the public

---

* These requirements are satisfied by the contraceptive devices which have become available since this was written.

good, qualities which are nowhere overabundant – least of all in Latin America. The elimination of demographic imbalance does not put money into the pockets of any pressure group, and the advocacy of such a programme will never have such popular appeal as the promise of a redistribution of the existing wealth. The most formidable obstacle to a rational population policy in Latin America is the alliance on this point of two most powerful pressure groups: the Catholic Church and the Communist party.

The communists act with perfect rationality in this case. Unless the economic situation in Latin America radically and quickly improves, they have a very good chance of subjugating it, and therefore, by combating a measure which is absolutely indispensable to economic improvement, they are trying to ensure their victory. The fact that in Poland the communists propagate birth control in the teeth of a bitter opposition from the Catholic Church proves that they are not impervious to reason in this matter, and are quite capable of deviating from the dogma. The policy of the Church is less rational because the times when poverty drove people to religion have passed, except where the communists rule. The Church's opposition to birth control in Poland is as rational as the communists' opposition in Latin America because under communist rule poverty breeds anti-communism and devotionalism. In the countries where the Church is intimately linked with the upper classes, however, poverty breeds anticlericalism and, nowadays, communism. If the Church wishes to prevent the spread of communism and to maintain its influence in Latin America, it would be logical for them to abandon their opposition to birth control.

A curious feature of the situation is that the attitude of the Church does not dissuade people who are inclined, in virtue of their culture and economic level to limit their families, from doing so. An investigation conducted in Chile has shown a correlation between answers asserting regular religious practice and statements that a large number of children is desirable, but not between such answers and the actual number of children. However, the poor need organized guidance and help if they are to limit their progeny, and the Church has enough influence in most Latin American countries to induce the governments to shun the issue.

A population policy can never be an alternative to institutional reforms because without such reforms the policy is doomed to failure. Japan was fortunate in having a high rate of literacy and an efficient administration, without which such a profound change in popular attitudes could not have been effected. It is difficult to imagine that such a change could be achieved by an administrative machine ridden with graft, nepotism and evasion of responsibilities, operating in the midst of illiterate, apathetic, and fatalistic peasants, drugged with cola and alcohol. Furthermore the peasants' distrust of the intentions of the rulers, combined with little respect for their wisdom, is the result of centuries of wanton oppression and constitutes a formidable obstacle to all reforms, even if these are carried out by a government which deserves a better reputation. In Latin America, even more than in many other parts of the world, the poor automatically assume that whatever the government wants cannot be for their good, which gives to hostile agitators the opportunity to stir up opposition to even most beneficial reforms. To be effective, a population policy must be a part of a general and radical reform.

A vicious circle is more difficult to break if it is enmeshed with other vicious circles. I mentioned earlier how poverty, parasitism and violence are all interlinked by circular causality, but there is another vicious circle connected with this network. The objective situation fully justifies the worst forebodings among the privileged classes, but their fear is conducive to a flight into unreason and bigotry which incapacitates them from dealing with the situation. In particular, the flight from reality makes them oppose all rational demographic policies without which the threat of a murderous revolution cannot be removed.

CHAPTER TWO

GENEALOGY OF PUBLIC VICES

The Original Sin

UNDER the mistaken impression that it contained no gold, the Spaniards left Northern America to the French, the English and the Dutch. But no obstacles, however formidable, could deter them from reaching places where they thought that the fabulous city of gold – El Dorado – might be found. The English settlements in North America were confined to the relatively narrow area along the Atlantic coast during the first two centuries of their existence. Only in the middle of the nineteenth century did they complete their advance towards the west. In contrast the Spaniards got as far as Chile in less than half a century after the discovery of America: Santiago was founded by Pedro de Valdivia in 1541. The cities of the Northamerican Middle West are very young in comparison. For a long time even the cities of the north Atlantic coast were small compared with those of the Spanish empire. During the seventeenth century the chief Andean mining town, Potosi, was many times larger than any town in Northern America. Even when the USA proclaimed its independence, New York and Philadelphia were much smaller than Lima. But in spite of its earlier start Spanish America, as well as Brazil, belong to the category of so-called underdeveloped areas whilst the USA is the richest country in the world. Why is there such a difference?

Part of the answer lies in the countries' natural resources. Notwithstanding the romantic accounts, Latin America as a whole is not particularly favoured by nature. Outside Argentina there is nothing comparable to the Northamerican plains. The climate in most parts is much less conducive to human activity or to the growth of useful crops. Transportation is much more difficult.

The Atlantic coast of Northern America abounds in good natural harbours, from which there is easy access to the interior. In contrast the coast of Brazil is isolated from the interior by a contorted slope, except around the estuary of the Amazon where the interior consists of swamps. Chile's enormously long and indented coast seems as if it were designed to spite man: where there are natural harbours there is almost no interior of value, whilst where there is an interior there are no natural harbours. Peru is divided by chains of mountains into sectors in which all the roads run to the coast because of the difficulty of constructing roads parallel to it. Throughout Mexico communications in almost any direction are difficult. The Amazon, though the best inland waterway in the world, is hardly worth using because it leads into the swamps. Only the region around La Plata combines high economic value with easy accessibility.

As information on the natural environment and resources of Latin America can be found in any good book on geography, I shall not dwell on this matter, though I shall touch upon it again when the economic problems are discussed. The foregoing comments are designed only to illustrate the well-established fact that the territory of the USA is more favoured by nature than the rest of the continent. Nevertheless, we may doubt whether this natural inequality can account for the striking contrast between opulence and misery. After all, there are countries, such as Norway or Switzerland, which are less favoured by nature than a number of regions of Latin America, but whose populations have attained a high level of affluence. The causation, then, must be sociological in character.

The plight of Latin America is often regarded as the consequence of the character of its inhabitants, who are said to be lazy, improvident and dishonest. Such opinions usually reflect the prejudices of foreign observers, and are often greatly exaggerated. Nevertheless, if we judge by the standards prevalent in countries which score highest in respect of industriousness, providence and economic honesty – say, Holland or Switzerland – we must conclude that there is some truth in this opinion. However, this explanation does not take us very far, because it raises the question of why the inhabitants of Latin America are like that.

It used to be fashionable among the writers of fifty years ago, and still is among some, to blame the relative backwardness of

Latin America on the racial composition of its population: to be precise on the innate characteristics of the Amerindian and African races. The distinguished Peruvian writer Francisco Garcia Calderon, to give one of many possible examples, advocated encouraging immigration from Europe in order to improve the composition of the alloy. People who held such views were not necessarily criminal madmen like Hitler. Some had fairly good intentions, and their reasoning was based on a simple and plausible error: seeing the discrepancy in the level of civilization between their countries and Europe and the USA, they attributed it to the first thing that struck their eyes – the difference in racial composition. It is strange how this fallacy persisted and spread despite the conclusive arguments which were advanced by the writers of the eighteenth century. Blaming the plight of Latin America on the innate characteristics of the subject races is particularly absurd.

Latin Americans may be more inclined to laziness than the Germans, but we could infer that this difference has something to do with race only if among the population of the same country the individuals who exhibit Europoid racial characteristics were less prone to this vice than people of predominantly African or Amerindian descent; in other words, only if we could discern a correlation between racial features and the said character trait. In fact, the contrary is the case: the Negroes and the Indians do the hardest work, whilst the idlers are predominantly of European descent. Actually, there can be little doubt that if we compiled relevant statistics, we would find that in most countries of Latin America there is a negative correlation between whiteness of skin and the amount of work an individual does. However, it would be equally erroneous to conclude that such a correlation proves a congenital aversion to work on the part of the Europoid race. Only members of the richer classes can indulge in idleness; and, as the result of the conquest, those classes contain a larger proportion of Europoid elements.

Clemenceau once said that there are no bad soldiers but only bad officers. Like all such epigrammatic sayings, this is exaggerated, but it does contain a grain of truth: namely that, in view of people's tendency to imitate their social betters, the character and the fate of any human aggregate depend primarily on the qualities of its *elite*.

The pivotal contention of the present interpretation of the predicament of Latin America is that, speaking in broadest terms, it is the consequence of the original sin of the conquest, which bequeathed to the republics customs and institutions which constitute an enormous obstacle to political order and economic progress.

The passengers of the *Mayflower* came to America in search of a refuge from religious persecution – of a land which they could cultivate unmolested – whereas the Spaniards came in search of booty. Whereas the English settlers took lands hitherto scarcely populated by Indian hunters – fierce, unaccustomed to work, who preferred death to enslavement – the areas conquered by the Spaniards comprised centres of relatively dense agricultural population, thoroughly domesticated by their native rulers and inured to hard work. So, from the very start the Spaniards were able to lead a parasitic existence. The settlers of the northern-most English colonies refrained from importing slaves not only because they believed in the religious value of work, but also because they had no money with which to buy them: they neither had gold nor produced easily saleable crops. Furs constituted their most valuable export but this commodity could not be obtained with the aid of slaves. In contrast, south of the river Potomac slaves could be used for producing sugar, and later cotton, for which there were good markets in England. In consequence slaves were imported, and that river became the line which divided the area of industry and social equality from the area of parasitism and exploitation. The factor of initial selection accentuated the difference between the southern and northern English colonies: the emigrants used to hard work went to the north, whereas Virginia and other southern colonies attracted scions of the English gentry who often came with a capital sufficient to buy some slaves.

The backward state of the Northamerican South shows that parasitism inhibits economic progress regardless of race or language. If they were allowed to separate themselves from the union, the southern states would probably sink to the level of Iberic America. But the course of Northamerican history was determined by the hard-working descendants of the pioneers of the North.

The gravity of the handicaps with which the nations of Latin

26

America have to cope in their struggle for peace and bread depends on the degree to which the social life bears the marks of conquest or slavery. The situation is much graver in Colombia than in Argentina because the former suffers from racial divisions, whereas the latter was almost uninhabited during the colonial period, and its population consists of the descendants of immigrants who came as free men and had never been enslaved. The social ills are less acute in Chile, where the races have merged, than in Peru, where the gulf between the Peruvians and the Indians remains and where the traditions of exploitation are stronger.

Disdain for Work

In Europe and Northamerica the Latin Americans have a reputation for laziness; and usually this proclivity is attributed either to race or climate. When we examine how much truth there is in this stereotype, we must remember that Latin America is a very big place, that there are great differences between a typical Chilean and a typical Venezuelan, and that the idea of national type is only a vague approximation, and therefore in every country we find demons of work as well as embodiments of laziness. Nevertheless, certain broad differences in the attitudes to work of the Latin Americans and the 'nordics' or the Chinese are clearly perceptible.

As suggested earlier we must discard the idea, still widely held among less enlightened people, that disinclination to work is a genetically determined attribute of the African or the Amerindian race. Another common misconception is that the inhabitants of Latin America do not work much. This is true only of those who have the means of living without working, for the majority of the poor work much harder than the workers in richer countries. Owing to the lack of machines and even of the more rudimentary tools (such as wheelbarrows or carts) they have to walk very long distances and carry heavy objects. Even the peasant households of eastern Europe were better provided with equipment for lightening toil than are the huts of Latin America. In terms of mechanical efficiency – as measured by the relation of output of physical energy to the amount of food consumed – the Indians of Peru and Mexico have attained the limits of human possibilities, and have surprised even travellers who knew Chinese coolies by their endurance.

We must also remember that what is condemned as laziness by casual observers is in fact often exhaustion and apathy caused by under-nourishment (including pre-natal under-nourishment). We have here a vicious circle: starvation and disease make it difficult to raise the productivity of the workers, and without a rise in productivity these scourges cannot be eliminated.

Attempts to account for differences in national character date from Jean Bodin and Montesquieu, and most of the early writers who considered the attitudes to work regarded them as broadly determined by the climate. Adam Smith, for instance, suggested that the inhabitants of the cold countries had to work harder because their need for clothing, fuel and shelter were greater, and they could not survive without providing for the winter. Thomas Henry Buckle related the differences in this respect to the simple fact that movement is the natural reaction to being cold, and repose to being hot. These explanations are certainly not irrelevant, but their weakness is that they fail to account for changes in national character. More recently Ellsworth Huntington and some other writers have tried to show that changes of climate have been much more rapid than is usually believed, and that they determined the rise and decline of civilizations. In certain cases, such as the decline of the cities of Arabia, it is probable that changes in climate were important factors, but on the whole social changes are too fast to lend credence to this explanation. Aristotle regarded the inhabitants of what is now England, Germany and Holland as especially lazy, in contrast to the Egyptians, basing his judgment on observation of slaves brought from these regions.

Knowing Aristotle's powers of observation – well demonstrated in his works on biology – we can accept his opinion but we need not search for traces of climatic changes because the explanation is perfectly clear: when Egypt already had a complex civilization, northern Europe was populated by warlike tribes, obtaining food by hunting and fishing – a way of life which is not conducive to systematic work.

The foregoing arguments indicate the limitations of explanations in terms of climate, but by no means prove that we can disregard this factor. Durkheim's dictum that we must explain social facts in terms of social facts was a badly needed corrective to the facile geographical and biological determinism current in sociology at the end of the last century, but dogmatic adherence to this dictum amounts to sheer prejudice. We now have innumerable studies in physiological psychology which state the temperatures most conducive to various types of work; and it is common knowledge that tropical heat makes work less pleasant, or more unpleasant, than it would be in a more congenial temperature. The wise approach is neither to fall into geographical determinism nor to ignore the influence of geographical environment, but to regard climate as one of the factors which mould the pattern of social life – a factor which can be counterbalanced, or even overlaid, by other factors. Putting it into the terminology of economics, we can say that heat increases the disutility of work, and diminishes the responsiveness to the incentives.

The direct influence of the tropical climate upon the habits of industry is less important than its indirect influence, exercised through social parasitism; an initial slight disinclination to work stimulates the growth of parasitic institutions which then greatly strengthen this disinclination. Owing to the greater effort necessary for the accomplishment of a given task in the tropics, a parasitic mode of existence is more attractive than in colder countries, where the enjoyment of idleness is spoilt by cold weather. And once parasitism becomes widespread, it casts upon work the stigma of servitude which acts as a deterrent from work.

In the colonization of America the element of choice accentuated the impact of environmental contrasts: those who sailed to America with the intention of working with their own hands chose the temperate regions, whereas the colonizers of the tropics searched for gold or an idle existence based on exploitation of servile labour. Actually, slaves constituted the great majority of the immigrants into the tropics.

Disinclination to work does not always indicate aversion to effort: often people who work perfunctorily will expend enormous amounts of energy in amusements and sports. Moreover, people are sometimes blamed for laziness although they are quite willing to work to satisfy their needs, but these needs are very limited. There are examples of how financial incentives, proved effective in Europe, failed to bring result in indigenous America where the villagers were not interested in money once they had enough to satisfy their customary needs; so that an increase in rates of pay merely reduced the labour supply, because the men, being able to obtain the desired sum sooner, returned to the villages earlier. Family and clan solidarity, which involves an obligation to share the incomes with a large number of relatives, may also diminish the response to financial incentives. Such factors, however, affect only the more isolated rural population; the rest of the inhabitants of Latin America have as strong an appetite for material goods as anybody. If on the whole they work less keenly than the Northamericans and the Europeans, this is mainly due to disdain for labour and the lack of relationship between effort and reward.

The disdain for labour is a very common phenomenon in the history of mankind and it has deep roots in Latin America. The Spanish adventurers went there in order to avoid having to take up peaceful work when the wars against the Moors came to an end. They were all of humble social origins, and when they were compelled on occasion to build ships and fortifications they showed themselves to be expert craftsmen, but they soon surrounded themselves by crowds of serfs and slaves. Among their descendants the association of work with servile status and despised race deepened the contempt in which it was held. Though modified by the conditions of modern civilization, this sentiment persists among the inhabitants of the big cities of today.

In Latin America, as in continental Europe, the most rudimentary manifestation of social acceptance is a handshake. As judged by eligibility for handshaking the most profound chasm in Latin American societies lies between those who do not and those who do work with their hands. The self-evident, though unformulated, principle is: soft hands never shake rough hands. The fear of being taken for a manual worker accounts for the extreme concern for propriety of dress, from which even the most rabid leftists cannot free themselves: unlike the old-fashioned capitalists of Northamerica, they never dare to take off their neckties or roll up their sleeves.

It may be ventured as a general hypothesis that insistence on propriety of dress depends on the scarcity of clothing: when everybody can afford a jacket and a shirt with collar and tie, one cannot distinguish oneself by wearing them, and one incurs no risk of being taken for a member of a lower class by appearing without them. This factor accounts at least partially for the greater informality of dress in Northamerica than in Europe, In Latin America where the majority of the lower white-collar employees have great difficulties in dressing respectably, and are surrounded by people who cannot afford to do so at all, they would feel defiled by taking off their jackets in public.

The insistence on wearing dress adapted to northern climes causes severe discomfort and even illness, greatly lowers the efficiency of non-manual work, and in consequence enhances the attraction of parasitic existence. The situation in this respect was even worse in the previous century when dress was much heavier. During his brief presidency Janio Quadros tried to implant among Brazilians the sensible habit of working in open-necked short-sleeve shirts, but he was forced out of office too soon to put through this reform, which could have been of great symbolic as well as practical value. Whatever one might think of other aspects of the Cuban régime, it is difficult to deny the value of Fidel Castro's disregard of the taboo on workman-like dress, and of his willingness to take part publicly in manual work.

Disdain for work is by no means something uniquely Latin American: on the contrary, it is the rule rather than the exception. Even among the primitive tribes without class inequalities, steady work usually bears the stigma of being a woman's occupation, unworthy of a warrior or a hunter. On a higher level of civilization, societies are normally divided into lords, warriors and priests on one side and the toilers on the other. Adam Smith's dictum, 'the state exists for protection of the rich against the poor', applied perfectly to all states of the past. As Veblen has shown in his *Theory of Leisure Class*, many customs and fashions serve the unavowed purpose of proving the exemption from the necessity to soil one's hands: the long nails of the mandarin and the bound feet of his womenfolk; the white gloves of the gentleman; neatly pressed suits, stiff collars, corsets and many other things of this kind make manual work impossible.

The communities of New England constituted a new species of polity: abundance of land prevented a thoroughgoing subjugation of the workers by the owners of capital, and the democratic character of the political institutions did not permit the rise of powerful officialdom. In consequence there was no ruling class on the European pattern, and manual work was held in high esteem. In Europe this was not so, but in its north-western countries the regard for work, though a great deal lower than in New England, was considerably higher than in the rest of the world. The peculiarity of the Western civilization was the emergence of autonomous cities in which craftsmen, organized in guilds, could enjoy the fruits of their labours and preserve their dignity instead of being mercilessly exploited and ill-treated by lords and officials, as was the rule in Asia.* The positive valuation of work was finally sanctioned by protestantism, particularly in its puritanical forms which drew their converts chiefly from among the artisans.

In Spanish and Portuguese America the artisans were mostly slaves, serfs or freedmen – Indians, Negroes, *mestizos* and mulattos – and even those artisans who were nominally free and of Spanish origin lived in degradation. Their associations which existed only in a few cities, were miserable affairs of mutual help at funerals, not even remotely resembling the proud guilds of Rhenian or north Italian cities. The organs of municipal self-government – called *los cabildos* – led a moribund existence in the shadow of powerful lords and officials.

Outside Scandinavia, the European peasants had a status distinctly inferior to that of the city artisans, but nevertheless their condition was better than that of the land labourers in Latin America today, many of whom live worse and have fewer real rights than the serfs of medieval Europe. It must be remembered that only after a long debate did the Church decide that the Indians have souls, and that the Negroes were denied this privilege until later times.

One of the consequences of disdain for work generated by these circumstances is the tendency of people whose economic equivalents in Europe or Northamerica would exert themselves hard to increase their income to choose leisure in preference to activity. In consequence large numbers of able-bodied men and women contribute nothing to production and constitute a heavy burden on the producers. Most of the big land-owners do not attend to their estates, which are badly run or even ruined by

* This point is treated in Chapters 15 and 16 of my *Elements of Comparative Sociology*.

overseers. They are very different from the industrious Junkers or economy-minded English squires who used to look after their estates very carefully. A lack of interest in work accounts for the small fractions of large incomes which are saved and usefully invested.

Amongst those who are compelled to work the disdain for work manifests itself chiefly in negligence. Owing to the fact that even the brightest children of the poor have little chance of rising on the social ladder, many workers in Latin America are very ingenious and quick to learn – perhaps more so than their counterparts in Britain – but negligence seems to be very common. This procilivity has serious results on the higher level of the social hierarchy: dedicated managers and technicians are too few for the smooth functioning of the economy.

Disdain for work may also be responsible for the paucity of contributions to science and philosophy. The inferiority of the countries of Latin America in this field in comparison with the United States or Britain could be attributed to the lack of provision for academic work and to the general poverty, but these factors do not explain the fact that Latin Americans have been less productive than Hungarians or Poles who suffered from similar handicaps. Hungarians and Poles were, of course, spurred by the threat to the survival of their national cultures, which has never been the case in Latin America. Moreover, in Latin America the national cultures were of more recent origin and less distinct from one another.

Combined with the low respect for work there is an unwillingness to pay for it. Not that employers elsewhere enjoy paying – wages everywhere depend chiefly on bargaining power – but this prejudice often leads employers to act myopically to their own disadvantage. To give an example: in Chile every worker has a right to two weeks' holiday with pay after a year's service, but the common practice is to dismiss the workers a few days before they complete a year, and to re-engage them later, despite the indirect losses caused by the lowering of the morale, dislocation of the teams and deterioration of labour relations.

Matters of everyday life in Latin America (as in Spain and Portugal) are adapted to the convenience of gentlemen and ladies of leisure. The hours of work – from 8 or 9 till 12 or 1 and from 3 or 4 till 7, 8, or 9 – may be bearable in small country towns but in big cities they can suit only those who do not work. The factory, office and shop workers either exhaust themselves in unnecessary and extremely uncomfortable journeys home or have nowhere to go during lunch breaks, wasting their time on loitering in hot and dusty streets. Having little really free time, they never sleep enough and keep themselves awake with large quantities of coffee, which cannot fail to lower their physical and mental energy, and stimulate their tendency to shun work or do it badly.

Mañana

Visitors from western Europe and Northamerica – especially those who come on business – usually complain about the Latin Americans' unpunctuality and disregard for even the most specific arrangements. Like all other images of national characters, this view is exaggerated and over-simplified but not without foundation. The popular images of national character are indeed caricatures; but, like caricatures, they usually contain a good deal of truth, though in an exaggerated, stereotyped and often out-of-date form; so we shall not be far wrong if we assume that by and large the Latin Americans are less punctual and less reliable than the inhabitants of the regions bordering the northern Atlantic.

In attempting to explain this difference we must bear in mind that punctuality is the product of machine civilization: there can be no punctuality if people have no watches; and, in view of the slowness with which modes of behaviour acquire the normative force of a custom, there is nothing surprising in the unconcern for punctuality among peoples who have only recently been drawn into the orbit of mechanical civilization, and many of whom still live outside it. Even today, wandering around the cities of Latin America, one notices that most of the clocks stand still or are inaccurate. This curious detail indicates either carelessness in tending mechanical objects or a lack of regard for time. Obviously, nowhere where the adage 'time is money' is taken seriously, would clocks be neglected.

Machines not only make punctuality possible but they make it imperative because a civilization based on machines requires elaborate dovetailing of the activities of large numbers of individuals. Furthermore, competition in business produces a striving towards maximal utilization of time, which stands in marked contrast to the slow rhythm of agricultural life. Thus, one may regard the unpunctuality of the Latin Americans as a natural consequence of the recent incomplete and rapid industrialization, which may eventually be overcome. It must be noted that in the countries of Europe which are more advanced in this respect, industry grew sufficiently slowly to permit a gradual adaptation of customs to new conditions, whereas in Latin America many people have moved within their own lifetime from conditions resembling those of a medieval village into the hustle of a megalopolis where their ingrained habits cause a great deal of trouble.

Much of what has been said about unpunctuality applies to other forms of unreliability: a failure to adhere to an arrangement usually causes less trouble in a loosely integrated economy than in one based on an intricate division of labour, where there is likely to be less tolerance of this kind of behaviour. Industrialization, however, is not the only factor which fosters habits of reliability. During the centuries which separate the rise of organized states from the appearance of industrial civilization warfare was the activity which required the highest degree of co-ordination, and in which the reliability of the participants was of greatest importance. For this reason, the agricultural nations which had outstandingly good armies, such as the Romans or the Prussians, were known for their habits of punctilious fulfilment of undertakings. The nations of Latin America have never undergone a thorough indoctrination in this type of military virtue, as their armies were always turbulent and badly organized; and warfare, though endemic, has seldom been intensive or conducted in a systematic manner. Owing to the weakness of the Amerindian polities, the initial conquests were carried out without elaborate organization, and under the Pax Hispanica there was little opportunity for large-scale warfare. After independence the enormous distances and the sparseness of the population prevented the states from coming really to grips with each other, and later when serious wars became technically possible the overwhelming might of the United States made them impracticable. So, the armies of Latin America could lead the effortless lives of internal parasites, free from the need to cultivate the virtues necessary for the efficient action of large organizations.

In trying to understand the characteristic attitudes of Latin Americans, we must take into account the fact that no other region of the world has been dominated for so long and with so little interruption by the idle classes. The French nobles were soldiers until the end of the seventeenth century, and lost their dominating position a century later; so that they were both parasitic and dominant for only one century. In Prussia the nobles were always thoroughly disciplined and their lives centred around military service. In Russia after Peter I, a patent of nobility was equivalent to a rank in the military and administrative machine, and it was not until the nineteenth century that the Russian aristocracy ceased to be a service nobility and acquired the characteristics of a leisured class. In England, in virtue of entailment of estates and exclusion of younger sons from the inheritance of titles, as well as the practice of knighting everybody who made a fortune, there was always a penetration of the business class into the nobility. The Polish and the Hungarian nobles had been idle enough but at the end of the eighteenth century they came under the domination of foreign bureaucrats. Nevertheless, the Hungarians and Poles resemble the peoples of the Iberic civilization (or at least did resemble them until the recent upheavals) in their lack of bureaucratic virtues, and in their inclination to look at life from the standpoint of the idle nobleman who need not worry about time or keeping appointments; although in Latin America these attitudes are more prevalent and more extreme.

Unruliness

A peaceful and orderly polity is a delicate plant which can be easily destroyed and which grows slowly and under specially favourable conditions. Taking the broad view of history, it is clear that political stability of the kind known in Britain, Switzerland or the United States is something exceptional, and violent strife is the rule.

The Spanish empire in America was an imposing edifice in spite of its faults. It succeeded in maintaining relative order over vast areas with a very small outlay of energy, and it did not disintegrate when Spain lost its power. When it was destroyed it left behind a vacuum.

The American colonies did not rebel against the Spain of absolutism and the Inquisition but against the Spain dominated by Napoleon and undergoing reforms inspired by the ideals of the French Enlightenment. These ideals were used to justify the rebellion but they hardly affected the tenor of social life in the colonies. The king lost his nimbus when he became Napoleon's puppet, but the spread of liberal ideas was only of secondary importance. The rebels, though traditionalist in sentiment, justified their actions by invoking liberal ideals and promulgated constitutions modelled on that of the United States, which had no roots in any feelings of moral obligation. This initial ambivalence had far-reaching consequences.

The wars of independence were not popular movements. Naturally, most of the soldiers were lower-class *mestizos* and Indians but the leadership remained in the hands of the landowning class. The American-born aristocracy had two main aims: to obtain access to the administrative posts hitherto reserved for Spaniards and to abolish their monopoly on external trade.

In order to keep control over their distant colonies, the kings pursued a policy of ruling through officials sent out from Spain and withdrawn after a few years before they could strike roots in the local society. Many of the lower officials never returned to Spain upon the expiry of their office, but by settling in the colonies they and their sons ceased to be eligible for high office. Thus the upper class of the colonies was divided into two sections: the officials from Spain and the American born (*criollos*) landowners, who maintained close social contacts with each other but were nevertheless separate. The exclusion of the American-born from office had grave consequences because when independence was won the ruling classes of the new states had no experience in administration. This was one of the chief causes of the disorder which ensued, and also accounts for the establishment of constitutions which in no way corresponded to real possibilities.

What happens when an unrealistic constitution is adopted? There are only two possibilities: it is either replaced or disregarded. In Spanish America no convincing substitute could be found for the deeply rooted reverence for the monarch, with the result that the republican régimes came to be based on naked force and contempt for the law.

Contempt for the law has other roots too: the kings issued a large number of decrees which could not be enforced – in particular those intended to promote the welfare of the Indians remained a dead letter – and in this way accustomed the settlers to lawlessness. The decrees could not be enforced primarily because of the immensity of the empire. By outgrowing its administrative capacity the Spanish empire left a burdensome legacy to its successors.*

The administrative machinery of the empire embraced a vast area but it did not penetrate deeply. Even apart from the regions occupied by independent tribes, the activities of the royal official had little effect on the lives of the peasants, who had only one real master: the owner of the estate on which they lived. The officials concerned themselves with ports and the mines, from which income accrued, leaving the rest of the empire to fend for itself, so long as there were no rebellions.

The initial conquests were really private ventures. An adventurer would obtain a royal charter permitting him to conquer lands lying in a certain direction, to use them for his profit and to distribute them among his followers. The tenure was essentially feudal: the lands were granted on condition of rendering various services such as fighting under the orders of royal officers, administering the territory, converting the Indians to Christianity and so on. During subsequent centuries, when the bureaucratic machine had evolved sufficiently to ensure the continuity of the empire, land tenure lost its feudal character and turned into simple ownership. These changes, however, concerned only the relationship between the lords and the government, the internal structure of the estates remaining essentially the same: whether as a semi-feudal *encomienda* (or *repartimiento*) or as a privately owned *hacienda*, the large estate was always in practice an autonomous unit, and its inhabitants were under the absolute and exclusive authority of its holder. No matter what decrees the king might issue about how the Indians were to be treated, the effective control of his officials stopped at the gates of the *hacienda*.

The Northamerican insurrection was essentially conservative: it was an uprising of the colonists in defence of their traditional self-government against the centralizing encroachments of the

* According to one estimate 400,000 decrees have been promulgated.

British Crown. So the severance of the link with the Crown amounted only to a removal of the highest rung of the administrative machine, which was quickly replaced by an elected president and Congress. In contrast the rebellion of the Spanish colonies destroyed the entire apparatus of the state. As there were no self-governing assemblies in the Spanish empire apart from the shadowy *cabildos*, the collapse of the imperial administration left the continent not only without any organs of government but even without trained personnel, for most of the Spaniards who occupied the key posts either fled or perished, whilst those who remained were distrusted. The ex-colonies could not escape anarchy because they had neither networks of self-government nor efficient bureaucratic machines.

The extension of the territories of the new states also impeded their stability. The Northamerican colonists advanced slowly towards the interior: as the motive was the search for land for cultivation, the speed of the expansion was governed by the growth of the population. In consequence, the English colonies on the eve of independence covered only a narrow strip along the Atlantic, and it was not until the middle of the last century that the westward march reached the Pacific. The incorporated areas were contiguous, inhabited and well connected by navigable rivers and roads. In contrast, the Spaniards, searching for gold and slaves, rampaged throughout the length and breadth of the continent, and within a few decades subjugated most of what became Spanish America. The Portuguese proceeded more slowly, but nevertheless they attained more or less the present frontiers of Brazil at the end of the eighteenth century; that is to say, some time before the union of the thirteen English ex-colonies. At the beginning of the last century Mexico was much larger than the United States. The extension of the territories, which outgrew the means of maintaining order, helped to implant the patterns of unruliness.

When the empire collapsed, disintegration threatened even the successor states. Many of the struggles which are listed as civil wars or revolutions were in fact territorial wars between nuclei of power which accidentally became parts of the same embryonic states, as there were no well-defined nations at the dawn of independence. The absence of linguistic and religious differences retarded the growth of national consciousness. Therefore no moral forces restrained the tendencies towards faction and strife. In these circumstances the process of political socialization – the inculcation of obedience to law and voluntary self-discipline – could not proceed very far, and the tradition of unruliness perpetuated itself.

The Habits of Violence

The long struggle against the Moors, which ended with the elimination of their rule from the Iberian peninsula immediately before the discovery of America, produced among the Spaniards a type of warrior extraordinarily intrepid even by the standards of that warlike age: and those who went to America were among the most adventurous and eager for bloodshed. Prompted by the desire for gold, Cortes, Pizarro and their companions slew, tortured, maimed and burned without the slightest compunction and often with pleasure. In a recent book, *Los Viajeros de Indias*, a Venezuelan physician, Felipe Herrera Luque, maintains that the murderous proclivities of the conquerors were genetically determined (as they were a self-selected collection). Owing to their extraordinary prolificity, he claims, the genes of these men account for the contemporary Venezuelan's addiction to violence which manifests itself in (among other things) an extremely high number of murders. Even if we reject this genetic interpretation, the fact remains that the conquest, besides being a traumatic lesson in butchery, fused together peoples with strong cults of violence. To the Spanish traditions of duelling and bullfights were added the legacies of human sacrifice and cannibalism.

Spanish historians have on many occasions tried to demolish what they call 'the black legend', and to show that the Spanish conquest and rule were not so cruel as is generally believed. Their arguments, however, are far from convincing except in a relative sense: it is perfectly true that other conquerors have committed deeds just as atrocious as those of the Spaniards. The annals of human cruelty are inexhaustible and one can find thousands of examples of massive butchery. This, however, does not alter the fact that the Spanish conquest of America belongs to the category of the greatest butcheries. Other European settlers treated the natives no better but the numbers involved were much smaller. According to fairly credible estimates, Mexico had between seven and nine million inhabitants in 1521 and only four and a half million at the end of the eighteenth century. Not until 1870 did the population of Mexico reach the number which the Spaniards had encountered. Within the fifty years which followed the conquest the population of Peru was reduced by two thirds. It must be remembered, however, that outright killings were responsible for only a small proportion of these numerical declines; far more lethal were the diseases brought from Europe, and starvation occasioned by the destruction of native economies.

The conquest of America caused a greater loss of life than the British conquest of India, or the British and French conquests in Africa. The reason was not, of course, any innate blood thirstiness on the part of the Spaniards but the very fact that the Spanish conquests took place at the end of the Middle Ages when the customs were more barbarous – when torturing to death in public (preferably on Sundays) constituted the most popular spectacle. Another cause of the barbarity of the Spanish conquest was the relatively small superiority of the Spanish arms over those of the natives. The Spaniards had horses, steel swords and body armour, and muskets, whilst the natives had only stone spears, axes and knives, but in view of the small numbers of Spaniards (whose expeditionary forces were counted only in hundreds), the natives could have easily overwhelmed them had they not been dumbfounded by the strangeness of the appearances and the tactics of the Spaniards. In order to conquer, the Spaniards had to sow panic among the natives, which they did by exemplary slaughtering. This was particularly true of later expeditions which were much bloodier than the initial conquests of Cortes and Pizarro. In contrast, the European troops who conquered Africa had fast-firing rifles of long range which ensured almost effortless victories over spear-wielding natives.

The British conquest of India was much more superficial than the Spanish conquest of America: the East India Company did not supplant the native ruling classes, but merely superimposed itself as the overlord upon the pre-existing feudal hierarchy; and by playing the native peoples and princes off against each other it succeeded in subjugating this immense land without much fighting. Moreover, most of the European conquests in Asia and Africa were carried out under the direction of the merchants (or at least with their participation in control), who knew that straight robbery and wanton destruction are seldom good business: they had some notion of husbanding resources, including manpower, whereas the Spanish and Portuguese adventurers were ready to depopulate whole areas for the sake of a few grains of gold.

The extension of the colonies precluded effective administration and, therefore, armed force was the most common arbiter in relations between the semi-feudal lords. Internecine strife broke out even before the conquest was completed, and it was at the cost of great efforts that the administrators in Madrid prevented a break up of the newly acquired empire. Even when the improvements in the administration relegated armed strife among the Spaniards to the background, the tradition of violence was retained by continuous expeditions into the interior and forcible incorporation of village communities into large estates. In Brazil the eighteenth century was the great age of the *bandeirantes* – a mixture of robbers, slave-traders, gold diggers, pastoralists and nomad soldiers – who conquered the interior of that enormous country. Violent spoliation of the Indian still goes on in Brazil, Colombia, Ecuador, Guatemala.

The collapse of the Spanish empire led to turmoil and strife which lasted for generations (and in some countries have not yet ended) and in which the process of violence breeding violence operated in full force.

As illustrated below, living among slaves diminishes the necessity of self-control on the part of the masters, and stimulates sadism and irascibility. Nowadays, of course, fewer individuals find themselves among beings over whom they have absolute power, but the patterns of behaviour generated by centuries of slavery do not disappear overnight.

There are several examples of how very warlike and turbulent nations became peaceful: not so long ago the Swedes and the Swiss, now paragons of peacefulness, had the reputation of bloodthirsty savages. Why then should the Latin Americans be unable to shake off the burden of evil traditions? The answer is that, although the tradition of ready recourse to violence does not constitute an insuperable obstacle to the establishment of a stable political order, it aggravates a situation in which there are other obstacles. The relationship between traditions of violence and political strife is one of mutual stimulation: the habits of violence make the elimination of strife difficult, whilst political instability and strife perpetuate the habits of violence.

The Lack of Public Spirit

The psychologists concerned with traffic accidents have come to the conclusion (plausible in the light of common sense) that the manner of driving depends on and reveals the entire personality of the driver. If one applies this principle to the Latin Americans, one must conclude that their chief characteristic is brutal and blind pursuit of momentary advantage: they drive with utter disregard for the safety of others and with very little concern for their own or for the condition of their vehicles, which are very rarely insured. In a large city like Santiago de Chile only about 5% of the vehicles are insured. It is a common sight to see cars of the latest model without mudguards, windows, bonnets or boots. Courtesy on the road is entirely unknown: nobody ever stops or slows down to let somebody else turn or get in or out, and the biggest vehicle, which can do most damage, always has the right of way regardless of the rules of the road. The selfishness of the opulent classes shows itself in the utter disregard for the safety and comfort of the pedestrians on the country roads. As there are no lanes for pedestrians, despite the fact that they are much more numerous than the travellers in motor vehicles, they must wade through stones and sand, and on occasion jump into a ditch, to avoid being killed. These habits cannot be simply due to the embryonic stage of industrialization because the country which is most developed economically – Argentina – has the worst reputation for brutal driving. *A comparison of Argentina with Britain or Holland thirty years ago shows that reckless driving cannot be a mere consequence of novelty or the smaller number of cars.

The lack of concern for the common good manifests itself in innumerable other ways. To mention one example: in Santiago de Chile there was an open drainage canal running through a fairly high-class part of the town. Every few months a child was

---

* Latin America, of course, is not the only area in the world where ruthless driving can be taken as a symptom of the deficiency of public spirit.

drowned in it but nothing was done, even though some of the victims came from 'good' families. In other places there are widely paved roads which abruptly come to an end without a warning sign, unmarked gaping precipices, protruding rocks and various other traps. Every few days accidents take place at these spots but nothing is done, although the cost of putting up adequate signs would be a fraction of the cost of the damage caused by one of these accidents. The scarcity of public conveniences and parks, the frightful pollution of the air and erosion of the soil are also symptomatic of this state of mind. However, to see the matter in correct perspective, one must remember that, although all countries of Latin America suffer a deficiency of public spirit in comparison with Holland or Switzerland, there are other countries in the world which are no better in this respect, and that no where has there been too much or even enough public spirit: its deficiency is ubiquitous, and is a matter of degree.

One of the gravest ills of Latin American public life is tax evasion among the rich. Not that the poor are more scrupulous, but they have fewer chances of escaping the fiscal burden which consists mainly of taxes upon articles of mass consumption. Here again, one must keep one's sense of proportion and remember that even in Britain and Scandinavia tax evasion is by no means unknown, whereas it is rampant in France and Italy. However, in Latin America it is universal: a businessman or an estate owner who paid the taxes for which he is liable according to the letter of the law would be regarded as mentally ill. In many ways the governments themselves are to blame because their conduct of the finances strikes the citizens as wasteful and absurd, or even fraudulent. Tax evasion is made possible by the venality of the officials, and here again we find a vicious circle: the miserable salaries of the officials drive them to collusion in tax evasion, as a result of which the state has no funds to pay them more. Moreover, the knowledge that so many people, including the most highly-placed members of the community, evade taxes, deters even those who have particularly strong feelings of civic obligation from paying them, because it makes them feel that by doing so they would subsidize the tax evaders. With the poor this attitude is perfectly excusable because they have very good reasons for regarding the state as a machine of oppression.

From the very beginning of the Spanish empire the state set an example of short-sighted avarice in matters of the public good. For the sake of a meagre income from trading monopolies, the imperial government inhibited the development of most of the continent. They countenanced the destruction of the Indian population and of the irrigation works of the Incas. Like other monarchs, the Spanish kings practised the sale of offices, but they persisted in this practice longer than others: offices remained saleable until the end of the empire. The buyers of office naturally tried to make a profit on these transactions. The offices which were not formally bought were usually obtained by means of gifts to influential courtiers, and these could be even more costly than a direct purchase.

By making their tenures brief, the government in Madrid prevented viceroys and other officials from building up private power in the colonies, but it also prevented them from becoming personally involved in the fate of their subjects, so that most of them regarded their missions as an opportunity for amassing a fortune. Actually even the more conscientious officials had to engage in peculation because unless they made costly gifts to influential courtiers, they would be falsely accused of dereliction of duty. The example given by the highest dignitaries inevitably moulded the political tradition of regarding office as a commercial proposition, and this the Spanish empire bequeathed to the republics.

Virtue flourishes where it is rewarded and vice castigated. The Hohenzollern dynasty forged the formidable military and administrative machine of the German state, and instilled into all grades of public servants their proverbial devotion to duty and order by their own meticulous observance of the rules which they laid down, and by the example of austere devotion to the impersonal idea of the state. The reality did not, of course, correspond exactly to the ideal but by and large, and in comparison with other monarchs, the Hohenzollerns did behave as the 'first servants of the state', which was the name by which Frederick II liked to refer to himself. In contrast, the heirs of Phillip II did not have the virtues of a competent manager, and almost invariably preferred deft courtiers to hard-working administrators. Moreover, the flow of gold corrupted the Spanish aristocracy and fortified its inclination towards parasitism, whereas the

Prussians had to work hard and live frugally. Finally, as mentioned before, the Spanish empire in America was too big to be efficiently administered: even such an industrious monarch as Phillip II could not properly control his officials. The American estate of the Spanish monarchs lay prey to the selfish interests of its administrators because it belonged to absentee owners.

This privateering approach to public office continued in the republics. Authority, normally attained by illegal use of force and never secure from attempts to overthrow it, was seldom held long enough to encourage its wielders to identify themselves with the long-term interests of their domains, and its constant use for predation ensured the perpetuation of disorder.

The negative attitude of the ordinary people to all actions of the government would be less pernicious if it were coupled by an eagerness and aptitude for spontaneous organization, but this is not the case. The chief cause of this state of affairs has been the persistent hostility of the state, the Church and the semi-feudal lords to all independent associations.

The agricultural tribes of America lived in village communities. The Inca empire, which was the best organized state that ever existed in South America, incorporated them into its structure, superimposed upon them its administrative and military machine, controlled them minutely, extracted tribute and conscripted men, but did not break up the communities. Their annihilation came with the Spanish conquest which amounted to the carving up of Indian lands into manorial estates and slave compounds. Although in the most inaccessible or insalubrious regions village communities have survived till the present day, the great mass of the Indians and *mestizos* were forced into passive obedience. Apathy, fear and mendacity, punctuated by outbreaks of murderous rage, characterized the personality formed by age-long oppression. Living under the lash, the peasants of Latin America could hardly have developed initiative and public spirit; nor have these virtues had time or opportunity to grow in the souls of their descendants who have migrated to towns.

In order to forestall separatist movements the Spanish Government suppressed the seeds of local autonomy and prohibited voluntary associations. The Church, fearing heresy, concurred in this endeavour, and with even greater insistence inculcated

46

passive obedience. Together, they have succeeded in extirpating from the minds of the upper classes any concern for public good, as well as any eagerness or aptitude for forming voluntary associations.

Sexual Roots of Anti-social Attitudes

It would be surprising if the conduct in public matters did not reflect habits formed in personal relations, and if it in turn did not influence them. A person whose behaviour towards his family and friends is guided solely by promptings of unbridled egoism is not likely to act altruistically and responsibly in politics or business, or to treat his subordinates better than his wife and children. (It must be noted, however, that the obverse is not true: family loyalty and devotion to friends are perfectly compatible with sharp business practice.) The stern but law-abiding authoritarianism of the Prussian army and the administrative machine moulded and was moulded by the disciplinarian customs of the family. Northamerican egalitarian informality manifests itself in politics as well as in relations between parents and children. Similarly, anti-social inclinations, which are so conspicuous in the conduct of political and economic affairs in Latin America, have their domestic equivalents.

To repeat once again, Latin America is a very big place, circumstances differ widely from country to country and, therefore, all generalizations must be qualified. In the following analysis we shall concentrate in the first place on Mexico which is the most extreme case. Broadly speaking, deviations from the Mexican pattern roughly correspond to the distance: customs are very similar in other Spanish-speaking countries situated in the tropics; they are less similar in Brazil (where there are wide regional differences); whereas in Argentina, Uruguay and Chile the situation resembles the southern European more closely than the central American pattern. Mexican attitudes are depicted in the following translated extracts from *La Vida Familiar del Mexicano* by Maria Elvira Bermudez (pp. 51 ff.; 103).

A boy . . . learns that everything connected with affection, harmony, care or beauty is unworthy of a man . . . who ought to be aggressive, pitiless, unthinking, careless and ugly . . . With the arrival of adolescence an additional quality is expected of him: that of a Don Juan. An average Mexican lusts after every woman he sees, and in this indiscriminate pursuit finds his greatest source of pride.

Parallel to the attitude of a Don Juan is that of an Othello. To the Mexican his own fidelity is ridiculous and insulting. The feminine fidelity, in contrast, is a dogma. A Mexican easily tires of a woman who accepts him, but a woman who rejects him gets a warning: 'God will punish you.' After he has ceased to be interested in a woman he still demands eternal fidelity, and objects to anybody taking the place which he has voluntarily abandoned. Any woman on whom he ever deigned to cast his eyes must cherish his memory unsullied or take the risk of injury or even death.

The Mexican woman regards the man as her enemy; and her mother, aunts and teachers are continuously admonishing her to live in constant vigilance against his unworthy tricks: if she gives him a slightest opportunity he will deceive and humiliate her. To this predicament is added the conviction that the woman's situation is hopeless.

The wife rarely remains the object of the husband's deeper sentiments . . . the solidarity, which is an indispensable ingredient of affection, does not exist in the marital relations of ordinary Mexicans. The man displays respect for his mother but ridicules his mother-in-law. He takes no trouble to guide or educate his children, and only beats them when they disturb him.

To the average Mexican woman friendship appears incomprehensible. She sees other women only as concealed rivals in the terrible struggle for subsistence or a secure social position . . . A slightest transgression of the accepted norms, a slightest move towards independence, is at once seized by the majority of women as a pretext for excluding a competitor from the arena.

In many middle-class Mexican families barbarous beating of children is perfectly normal . . . Hysterical screams and savage beating inflicted upon the children by their mothers can be regarded as outbursts of resentment of the female humiliated and ill-treated by the male.

The Mexican suffers from the loneliness which is an inevitable consequence of his conduct: he cannot rely on his wife who fears or hates him . . . The other women do not provide him with a true companionship either; partly because he takes care to substitute them quickly, and partly because, far from being admired and loved as he imagines, he is regarded as worthless and easily replaced by another who promises more . . . A man is valued in accordance with his earning capacity . . . and this criterion is the one which is most frequently applied even to the relations within the family.

The family is most often a battlefield of egoisms . . . Among the peasants it does not exist at all ... the cult of masculinity pervades relationships between the sexes, and produces an atrophy of paternal feelings ... to the extent that a peasant who feels that he has been wronged by a woman kills his children by her ... The Mexican feels hostility and distrust towards everybody and everything.

Obviously, not every Mexican acts in the ways described in these passages, but those who do so seem to constitute the majority; and even if they were only a substantial majority, their conduct would affect the entire social order. As everybody knows, this kind of behaviour is quite common everwhere, but what happened in the Spanish-speaking countries – especially in tropical America – was that these commonplace proclivities have been elevated to the status of a social obligation and a point of honour. And how can one expect honesty and decency in politics if the relations between men and women are determined chiefly by force and fraud?

The behaviour depicted above amounts to trying to get everything while giving nothing in return, and inevitably leads to a war of all against all. It is a great deal worse than the behaviour of West Indian proletarians who often shirk the responsibility of maintaining their women and children, but who at least do not demand fidelity in exchange, and who do not persecute the women when they take steps to obtain sustenance from other sources. The Hispano-American pattern produces much more misery and strife than the subjection of women practised in Islamic lands. The Moslems lock up their women and treat them badly, but at least they normally maintain them, do not disclaim the responsibility for the children, and do not persecute wives or concubines whom they have discarded. And what is very important from the point of view of the effects upon the general tenor of social life, the Moslems obtain their women by honest though somewhat callous transactions – not by deceit or force. The Moslems, moreover, refrain from interfering with other men's women, whereas a compulsive Don Juan not only treats women as mere objects for satisfying his lust or vanity, but also continuously commits, or at least attempts to commit, acts of trespass backed by force or fraud. The lack of compunction in venting these proclivities also embitters the relations between the classes, as nearly every boss feels entitled to the sexual services of women working under him, and does not hesitate to use economic pressure (irresistible in a poverty striken country) to ensure compliance, thus inspiring hatred in the hearts of his victims, their relatives and friends. The effects of these habits on the efficiency of establishments employing women do not need to be emphasized.

Disregard for other people's interests, the aversion to the precept of 'live and let live', the unbridled wilfulness and the lack of sympathy for the weak also stem from the effects of the extreme class inequality upon the upbringing of the children who, in virtue of the positions which are their birthright, set the example which their less fortunate brethren tend to follow. A child acquires a conscience (or, as psychologists prefer to call it, a super-ego) according to the standards by which he is rewarded and punished – using the terms reward and punishment in the wide sense which includes bestowal and withdrawal of approval, admiration and love. As a general rule, he can develop a conscience only if he is treated consistently in accordance with well-defined and permanent standards, and brought up by persons whom he respects. For this reason, the custom of leaving children in the care of servants causes them to grow up with scant respect for law and morality. In all probability this practice is responsible for the universal phenomenon of the deterioration of wealthy families. In England it has been customary in the upper class to send their sons to expensive private boarding schools (perversely called 'public schools') which, despite their contribution to the spread of snobbery and homosexuality, do instil into their pupils a sense of responsibility and solidarity. Among the Prussian Junkers military schools prevented any loosening in the code of behaviour. Moreover, the wider opportunities for social ascent in western Europe ensured that individuals who had been brought up by their parents personally played a prominent part in setting the tone of social life. The same was true to an even greater extent among the Northamericans, except of course in the southern states. In Latin America, as in the Islamic lands, the men who occupied the leading roles in society had been with very few exceptions brought up by servants who had had to comply with their slightest whim.

In *The Masters and the Slaves* (*Casa Grande e Senzala*) Gilberto Freyre gives poignant illustrations of the way in which slavery affected the character of the children of the plantation owners.

'And what', inquires Father Loes Gomes, 'are the sons of these sluggards like? Many of them do not even learn to read and write ... The inhumanities and the cruelties that they practise from early years upon the wretched slaves render them all but insensible to the sufferings of their neighbours ... And how, in truth, are the hearts of us Brazilians to acquire the social virtues if from the moment we open our eyes we see about us the cruel distinction between master and slave, and behold the former, at the slightest provocation or sometimes out of mere whim, mercilessly rending the flesh of our own kind with lashes? ... No sooner do we acquire intelligence than we observe, on the one hand, the lack of delicacy, shamelessness, dissoluteness, and disorderly conduct of the slaves, and on the other hand the harsh treatment, the thrashings, the blows that these unfortunates receive almost every day from our elders ... And what is the inevitable result of all this, if not to render us coarse, headstrong and full of pride?' In his recollections of his infancy, the Viscount Taunay, a man almost as gentle and mild-mannered as a girl, confesses that he took pleasure in tormenting the Negro lads. And there is a passage in one of Machado de Assis's novels in which that fine observer of Brazilian society in the time of the Empire portrays for us the type of sadistic child, the child who has been perverted by the social conditions of his upbringing, in the midst of passive slaves who were docilely responsive to his whims. There is not a Brazilian of the upper classes, even one born and brought up after slavery had been officially abolished, who does not feel a kinship with the young Braz Cubas in the latter's maliciousness and fondness for teasing Negroes. The morbid pleasure of treating inferiors and animals rudely is one that is characteristic of us.

The method of bringing up children is only one of the factors which determine the prevalence of certain personality traits in a nation, but its influence is deep; and once a pattern of behaviour becomes widespread, it may persist through cultural inertia long after the conditions which brought it into existence have disappeared. When the pattern is set by the upper class, individuals whose backgrounds might predispose them to a different mode of behaviour will imitate it.

Another aspect of family life among the lords of the land had a deep and deleterious influence upon the formation of the character of the nations of Latin America. Amongst the urban middle class in Argentina or Chile the patterns of family life do not differ radically from those of comparable classes in Europe before servants became scarce. But in rural districts illicit polygamy is common; and the traditional patterns of behaviour were formed when polygamy was absolutely universal among the wealthy. Its illegal character and the opprobrium cast upon it by the teachings of the Church produced psychological difficulties among most children of the upper classes. The Church could never prevent the procreation of a large number of illegitimate children but was influential enough to prevent the regularization of their social position, even though it never damned them so thoroughly as the Protestant faiths. The proverbial touchiness of the tropical Ibero-americans – their quickness to sense a veiled or imaginary insult and to answer it with violence – seems to be a legacy of the ambiguous social positions of so many of their ancestors or even of themselves, as to this day there are few places in tropical America where legitimate births outnumber the illegitimate. In Venezuela more than 60% of the births are illegitimate and the situation is the same in other countries of that region: in San Salvador, for instance, the equivalent percentage is 59% and in the Dominican Republic 54·9; in Haiti the ratio is over 80%. Even in Chile only in the present century did legitimate births rise from 40% to 60%

In Uruguay the illegitimacy rate was still 28·2 in 1948. For the sake of comparison it is worth recalling that the corresponding figures were 4% in Switzerland, 4·8% in Italy and 6% in Spain.

In his book *Bandeirantes e Pioneiros*, a distinguished Brazilian writer, Vianna Moog, says (the translation is mine):

> What could we expect the *mestizos*, conceived and brought up outside the conjugal group, to be? Adjusted and well-integrated individuals? Clearly, that could happen only in exceptional cases . . . For three centuries the rule had to be: emotional disequilibrium, inner disharmony, insecurity, instability, resentment, marginalism, prejudice, depression; vague desires for a return to infancy and for an ideal father, combined with the hatred for the real father; maternal fixations, and all the peculiarities common to neurotic conditions, which de Gobineau and Chamberlain attributed to hereditary taint.
>
> Abandoned or repudiated by the father, brought up in his mother's miserable hut, the mulatto had a good basis for developing a neurosis.

But what about a mulatto whom his father took into the mansion and treated on equal footing with his legitimate sons? His fate was perhaps even more tragic. Torn from the arms of his black mother and handed over to the slave-owning stepmother ... Ah, if he could only kill the stepmother and blast the whole house ... what a wonderful basis for learning social duties ... We find in him, simultaneously or successively, all the states, all the symptoms of the most varied neurotic conditions: indolence, depression; indiscriminate chasing after women, motivated by yearnings for the perfect woman of his infantile dreams and a compulsive need to prove his manhood; excessive susceptibility, exhibitionism, masochistic pleasure in self-degradation combined with violent reactions to any kind of criticism or advice; morbid concern for other people's opinions concealed under a mask of indifference; persecution mania, boastfulness, sudden flights of enthusiasm followed by quick discouragement; the habit of relying on those in authority for everything, lack of initiative combined with atrocious resentment against those who show it ...

Needless to say, anybody who exhibited all the traits enumerated by Vianna Moog would be an extreme case. But there can be no doubt that slavery and serfdom have left a terrible psychological legacy, which the continuing inequality and exploitation maintain at least partially alive.

A Mexican psychoanalyst, Santiago Ramirez, regards the average Mexican family as a school of brutal and perverse selfishness for men, and of masochism for women – qualities which are later applied to social life. Like Vianna Moog, he traces the roots of these attitudes to the social structure originating in conquest and based on slavery and serfdom. The following (freely translated and arranged) extracts from his book, *El Mexicano : psicologia de sus Motivaciones*, present the essential points of his thesis.

Woman is devalued to the extent to which she is identified with the native; man is elevated in virtue of his identification with the conqueror and the master. Though also known elsewhere, this equiparation of masculinity with aggression, and of femininity with passivity, assumes in our civilization its most striking and dramatic forms ... The seigniorial sentiment of superiority over women bound to unconditional service has coloured all aspects of family relations.

The habit of leaving their children to the care of native nurses, prevalent among the Spanish-born legitimate wives, who were busy with

53

ceremonial and religious activities, has produced a split in the personality of the Mexican. As Santiago Ramirez puts it: 'A woman who satisfies a man's needs is regarded as an inferior being, and only a woman who is cold and distant is esteemed.'

The *mestizos* [from whom the majority of the urban Mexicans descend] were usually born under the stigma of disdain and abandonment by the father . . . [and even today, particularly among the lower classes] a man lives a short time with a woman, makes her pregnant and then leaves her. Then comes another man who proceeds likewise. If a father settles down it is out of a sense of guilt rather than love; and the home consists of an absentee father, whose occasional appearances are accompanied by violence, and a mother sunk in passivity and abnegation. A Mexican child very early learns to hate and deceive his violent and capricious father or successive stepfathers . . . Soon he joins a gang which tries to waylay men of that generation . . .

Deprived of the possibility of identifying himself with a strong, constant and protective masculine figure, he develops an obsession with virility [*machismo*] . . . He enters life with the constant need to prove that he is a very masculine and virile man [*muy macho*] and will regard the slightest doubt on this score as a deadly insult.

As Santiago Ramirez points out, a measure of the hostility commonly existing between fathers and sons is shown by the fact that the expression, 'I am your father' [*yo soy tu padre*] is used in Mexico as one of the gravest insults often leading to deadly fights. This largely explains why in Mexico authority was always brutally abused and viciously attacked.

CHAPTER THREE

VARIETIES OF PARASITISM

Latifundia

LATIN America is a continent of large estates. There are some smallholders in southern Chile and southern Brazil, and since 1952 in Bolivia, as well as some village communes in Mexico, but Costa Rica is the only republic where the greater part of the land is in the hands of small and medium proprietors. Elsewhere smallholdings may be numerous but occupy only a small part of the land, and account for an even smaller part of total agricultural production. Thus with the exceptions of Bolivia, Cuba, and to a lesser extent Costa Rica, the latifundia dominate the Latin American rural society; and in less urbanized countries they dominate the entire society.

In Argentina 85% of the land belongs to owners of estates larger than 500 hectares; 500 owners possess 18% of the land, and only 1·5% belongs to owners of farms smaller than 50 hectares. In the province of Buenos Aires there are 50 estates larger than 75,000 acres which jointly comprise 15% of the land. Fifteen of them exceed 25,000 acres, and one exceeds 1,000,000 acres. In Chile 70% of the land belongs to 1·5% of the owners; 64% of the land is in the hands of proprietors of estates larger than 5,000 hectares, who number 570, while only 1·8% of the land belongs to the owners of farms smaller than 50 hectares. In Brazil 8% of the owners hold 73% of the land. Taking Latin America as a whole, about two-thirds of the land is in the hands of big landowners but the inequality is even greater than this proportion indicates because the majority of the small holdings are situated on the poorest soils. About three-quarters of those who till the land are either labourers or tenant farmers, and of the remaining quarter only a small minority consists of prosperous farmers of medium-sized holdings; the rest eke out a miserable existence from minute bits of infertile land. Equally wretched is the life of hired labourers, tenant farmers and share-croppers.

In the colonial era a lord of the land had legal authority over the serfs and the slaves who lived on it. The successor states abolished slavery and serfdom, though some did it several decades after attaining independence. Slavery was declared illegal in Chile in 1811, in Argentina in 1813, in Bolivia in 1825, in Mexico in 1828, in Uruguay in 1842, in Paraguay in 1844, in Colombia in 1851, in Ecuador in 1852, in Peru in 1856, in Venezuela in 1858, in Cuba and Puerto Rico (which remained Spanish colonies until 1898) in 1886 and 1873 respectively. In Haiti, where the slaves rebelled and wiped out their masters, slavery was abolished as early as 1794. Unfortunately these legal acts in no way eliminated exploitation, and *de facto* serfdom continued to exist under the form of debt bondage. In most of the republics even today a labourer is not allowed to leave an employer if he owes him anything. By giving small loans in money or kind a landlord can easily obtain control over his labourers permanently living on the verge of starvation. The lower their wages, the more prone they are to contract debts, and the smaller is their ability to repay them; and the bondage into which they are thus driven prevents them from obtaining higher wages.

The debts to the landlord are hereditary and the bondage is passed from father to son. What is worse is that as the landlord or his agent keeps the books, a fictitious debt can be easily entered. An illiterate peasant is incapable of recognizing or keeping receipts, or of defending himself in a court of law, which in any case would accept a statement from the landlord as true. The net of bondage is made tighter by the practice of keeping on the estate only the shops owned or licensed by the landowner and these, being monopolies, charge exorbitant prices. On some estates, particularly on those owned by companies, workers are paid partly or wholly in tokens exchangeable only at the proprietors' shops. The same practice used to be followed in mining camps and on oil fields.

In many areas, particularly where no crops are produced for export, no wages are paid, and the structure of the estate is almost exactly analogous to that of the medieval manor: the peasants cultivate for their use pieces of land which are assigned to them on condition that they till the soil which the landlord retains for his own use, and render him other labour dues. The extent of their obligations varies according to the circumstances and the inclination of the lord but unlike the serfs of medieval Europe, the *peons* of Latin America are not protected by formal contracts or customs which limit the landlord's exactions. The only limit is that the *peons* must have enough to stay alive. Even more miserable than the hired hands are the share-croppers who, although they usually receive neither equipment, animals nor seeds from the owner, must surrender to him more than half of the crop, normally 60%.

The obligations of the *peons* are not limited to tilling the soil. In addition they are obliged to work for limited periods (usually two or three weeks of the year) in the landlord's town house. They are obliged to transport themselves (which may mean that they have to walk a hundred miles or more) and bring with them a supply of food sufficient for their stay in town. The landlord is under no obligation to feed or house them, and they often have to sleep in the yard or on the porch even in cold weather.

The wealth of the landlord and his connections in the capital, combined with the indigence and venality of the local representatives of authority, enable the landlord to play the role of an absolute ruler. Although the laws forbid it, the police turn a blind eye when a landlord imprisons or flogs a recalcitrant servant or even kills him. A qualification must be made : such abuses are rare in Chile, Argentina and Uruguay, but they are quite common in Peru, Ecuador, Colombia and Paraguay. There are reports that in the backlands of Peru *ius primae noctis* still finds favour with some landlords.

That the landlords can live in luxury and idleness, while those who do the work starve, offends the most rudimentary sentiments of justice, and would in itself justify agrarian reform. But great as is the harm wrought by iniquitous consumption, the discouragement of production constitutes an even greater evil. The spectacle of absentee landowners, squandering in Lima or Paris large sums wrung from miserable peasants, must not lead us to imagine that by confiscating this wealth and distributing it among the poor, we could radically improve their fate : the very wealthy are few whilst the poor are many. The chief argument for agrarian reform is that the present distribution of land prevents its full utilization and the consequent increase in food production. There is a vicious circle here: the weakness of the farm labourers' position prevents them from obtaining higher wages and helps to keep down the urban wages too; and the low income of the working classes restricts the effective demand for food, so that the landowners have less incentive to expand its production. The second argument is that the traditions of the landowning classes are such that they prefer leisure to additional income, shun the arduous task of making their estates more productive, and prefer to squander their large incomes; and if they save, they put the capital into ventures which do not require much managing, which usually means that they are not very productive.

With few exceptions the methods of cultivation are antiquated and little is invested in the land. The big estates are so big that their owners can live in luxury no matter how they manage them, so long as the wages of the workers are kept down – a much easier task than organizing efficient production, and one that can be entrusted to ignorant overseers. If the size of the estates were to be reduced so that their owners could live in opulence only if they managed them efficiently, they might quickly abandon their present attitudes. On the other hand, the owners of diminutive holdings, who at present are so near starvation level that they have nothing to invest into improvements, might make the land more productive if they were allowed to own more.

Better conditions for labourers and tenants should raise their productivity because in the present circumstances they know that any increased production would be at once appropriated by their employers without any benefit to them, so that they have no incentive to produce more.

The atmosphere of improvidence exuded by the traditional structure of rural society generates unconcern even for the conservation of the land: the peasants are too ignorant and miserable to care, and the landlords are too lazy and improvident to do anything about the erosion of the soil which advances at a terrifying pace.

Another evil connected with concentration of ownership of land is monoculture. It appeared first in the Antilles and northeastern Brazil where the planters produced large quantities of sugar but not enough food to feed the workers: they preferred to produce sugar, exportation of which enabled them to buy luxury goods from overseas, rather than food for the slaves who could be kept on subsistence rations. The same logic operates to this day, and leads to the diversion of land to the production of coffee or other exportable commodities while the poor starve: to grow food for local consumption does not pay because those who need them most cannot pay, whereas the dollars obtained for coffee bring in motor cars, radiograms and other similar articles. The ample supply of such goods from abroad, and the demand for them created by advertisements, makes a more socially useful orientation of production even more difficult to achieve, and diminishes the supply of funds available for investment in agriculture.

The most modern plantations, with the largest capital and the best equipment, belong as a rule to Northamerican companies. The drawbacks of these units of agriculture lie neither in managerial inefficiency nor in unwillingness to invest, but in the disregard for the long-term interests of the local inhabitants. In many cases these companies have not hesitated to ruin the soil for ever for the sake of making big profits quickly. For a few years the local labourers were earning much more than they had before, only to be thrown in the end into misery worse than ever. True, ignorant peasants and improvident native landlords are no less guilty of eroding the soil, but big firms which pride themselves on scientific management ought to show a greater sense of social responsibility.

In many areas the existing patterns of landholding preclude the development of communal life and even disrupt families. For example, the *sereingueros* – men who tap rubber-bearing trees in the forests of the Amazon basin – lead a wandering and solitary existence for months or even years at a stretch. The fate of the shepherds of Patagonia is fairly similar. Even in the model republic of Uruguay such evils are by no means unknown, as can be seen from the following passages from R. H. Fitzgibbon's *Uruguay* (London 1956), p. 114.

The tradition that the colonial *gaucho* was a single man carries down to the contemporary *estancia* in the almost universal practice that rural workers (except foremen and the office staff) may not have their wives and children with them on the *estancia*. This practice is not solely a matter of tradition and prejudice. In the mixed-farming areas in the south, where the labour needs are more varied, there is much more economic use for the wife and even the minor children. On the *estancia* however, those persons are largely economic dead weight.

The resulting unnatural situation means that, especially in the northern departments, the families of the rural workers must often live in a shack town thrown together along some stream bank, in an *arroyo*, or at some other undesirable location. This is the infamous *rancherio* or rural slum. It is inhabited by squatters who exist, rather than live, in squalor, idleness and hopelessness. Many of the personal unions which are established are on an irregular and sometimes temporary basis; a single *rancherio* may be composed of the descendants of but one family, though most such settlements will have from 20 to 200 families. The customary absence of many resident men (except boys and old men) makes for a sort of *de facto* matriarchy.

Promiscuity, concubinage, prostitution, illegitimacy and venereal disease are common in the *rancherios*. The simplicity, monotony and irregularity of social life make chronic and long-standing problems of drinking and gambling in many such places.

It seems that the lack of family roots among large sections of the population is one of the chief causes of disorder and violence which percolate into the affairs of state.

The existing agrarian structures are indubitably the source of many evils, but it does not follow that a breaking up of large estates necessarily brings about a happier state of affairs. That a wide diffusion of ownership of the soil does not suffice to ensure prosperity can be seen from the example of Haiti, which remains the poorest of Latin American republics although it has few large estates. The prevalence of peasant proprietorship in Haiti, is the fruit of the first social revolution in Latin America: the rebellion of the African slaves who, hearing the rumours about the revolution in France, killed their masters and broke up the estates, with the exception of the few seized in their entirety by the leaders of the revolution. The liberation of the slaves eliminated a great deal of degradation but it could not remove the poverty which remained as the chief source of suffering. Something analogous can be said about Latin America's next but one social revolution which took place a century and a half later in Bolivia; the breaking up of large estates more or less put an end to personal ill-treatment of the peasants, but the poverty remained. And indeed it would be a miracle if a transfer of the titles of ownership were to boost production immediately.

Disparity of possession is seldom directly proportionate to disparity of consumption: the owner of an estate may own practically everything within its boundaries while the labourers may own practically nothing, but this does not mean that he consumes all its produce while they consume nothing. When he is removed, his servants will no longer need to minister to his wishes but they will still need the same amount of food as hitherto. Without an increase in production the peasants can augment their consumption only by that amount which the landlord used to sell in order to acquire luxury goods, but such diversion of ouput to self-consumption may not be entirely beneficial to them in the long run because it may arrest general economic development by depriving the towns of their supply of food. This happened in Russia in the early stages of the revolution and more recently in Cuba.

As several examples show, an agrarian reform may not only fail to raise production but may very well bring it down if it is unwisely carried out. Primitive though it may be, even a typical Latin American *estancia* cannot be suddenly cut up without dislocating production. It may have large stables and granaries or a mill which cannot be apportioned out in small pieces. Nor can all the peasants move into the mansion (even if it could contain them all) because they would have too far to travel to their plots. The more modern plantations are, of course, more highly integrated and a sudden breaking up would bring their production to a standstill. Only the estates which do not at all function as units of production, and consist entirely of parcels cultivated separately by tenant farmers and share-croppers can be quickly divided without detriment to production. In all other cases a considerable capital outlay and a great deal of reorganization would be necessary for agrarian reform to bring its benefits.

The agrarian reforms which belatedly followed the revolution in Mexico included a highly original attempt to restore or rather re-create the traditional village communes in a modernized form. It has met with only a limited success in the economic field although it has, no doubt, raised the self-respect of the peasants. Rural poverty has not, however, been alleviated. The reforms have been severely hampered by inefficiency, venality and massive embezzlements of funds assigned to this purpose, with the consequence that the lands allocated to the peasants were frequently unusable. During the last decades agricultural production made great strides but this was due firstly to the bringing under cultivation of additional large areas with the aid of large-scale systems of irrigation, and secondly to commercialization of large estates, many of which have been taken over by joint stock companies. Since 1939 Mexico's cultivated area has increased by more than 40%, production has doubled, and productivity has risen. New lands, new crops, new techniques and important investments were jointly instrumental in bringing about this result. The chief lesson which emerges from the Mexican example seems to be that great advances can be made in agriculture even without the elimination of large estates.

*Kleptocracy**

We obviously have no statistics to indicate the extent of graft but there can be no doubt that in all countries of Latin America the wealth acquired through illegal use of public office is enormous. Naturally there are variations from country to country as well as over time: there is more graft in Mexico or Colombia than in Uruguay or Chile; and in Mexico there was less of it during the presidency of Cardenas than during those of Calles or Aleman. The Chilean *carabineros* have a high reputation for not taking bribes, but everywhere else (except Uruguay and Costa Rica) people fear the police and their extortions, of which the most common form is the imposition of fines for fictitious offences, the money naturally going into the pockets of the policemen. Mexican and the Argentinian police have very bad reputations, and are regarded as extortioners or even uniformed bandits by the ordinary people. In most countries the clerks who deal with innumerable small formalities expect to be paid for them, and if they are not they attend to the matter with deliberate delay or invent a pretext for not doing it at all. In Brazil it is quite impossible to get through any official business without the services of special contact men who know how and to whom to pass a bribe, part of which they keep for themselves.

* The type of ascendancy, which is designated by this self-explanatory neologism, is sufficiently widespread (and by no means only in Latin America) to deserve a special name.

Customs inspectors derive most of their incomes from bribes taken for conniving at evasion. Porters, who may be able to charge an arriving passenger more than a factory worker earns in a week or even two, have to pay big bribes to officials who issue permits to work within the harbour. In Chile, where other branches of administration are less ridden with graft than in other countries of Latin America, customs officials are conspicuous for their dishonesty: in addition to taking bribes, they help themselves to the goods which they are inspecting or enter into collusion with bands of thieves organized among the porters and shunters. In order to squeeze out bribes, they deliberately damage the articles of those who have paid nothing and delay the delivery. Moreover, nobody can attend personally to the formality of getting through the customs the goods which he has imported. This is the function of special firms, recourse to whom is obligatory, and who charge very high fees for these services, part of which goes to ensure the good will of the appropriate officials. These agents compete with each other by trying to obtain preference for their customers, and here the biggest firms have the advantage of being able to offer bribes acceptable to the highest officials.

The reason why no government has been able to reform the custom houses is that the circle of beneficiaries includes influential politicians and wealthy businessmen and landowners who make big profits on illicit exemptions from tariffs. As the tariffs are 400% on some goods and the exchange rate of Chilean currency is out of all proportion to its purchasing power, the rewards of fraud are enormous in this field. It is even possible that the rate of exchange is maintained at such an absurd level partly in order to make these gains possible.*

Valparaiso is in no way exceptional. In Vera Cruz (Mexico) operators are known to have amassed fabulous fortunes. It is said that the loot from its customs house enabled two individuals to buy enough support to get themselves elected to the presidency. The rapacity of the Argentinian customs officials is proverbial, and one constantly hears about illegal seizures not only of small things but of motor-cars and even bigger consignments. Such goods disappear mysteriously and no amount of appeals to the ministry can bring them back. It must be noted,

* Written in 1961.

however, that such acts are not perpetrated upon persons of influence. The habits in other ports of Latin America are more or less similar, which is one of the reasons why many insurance companies who are ready to insure motor vehicles going to Russia and other countries behind the Iron Curtain refuse to give cover for Latin America.

Although tax evasion is universal throughout Latin America, it seems probable that the proportion of income lost by the state is no larger than in France or Italy because the income taxes are lower in Latin America. Owing to their political power, the wealthy have been able to keep direct taxation low and to shift the burden on to the poor by making the state rely on taxes on sale of articles of popular consumption.

Latin American dictators can justifiably claim to be the biggest kleptocrats in the world. Not that they appropriate a larger share of their countries' wealth than the sheikhs of the oil-bearing lands of Arabia, but the latter claim to be the rightful owners of their kingdoms, whereas the dictators of Latin America are supposed to be only the highest officials. Despite the normal wasteful splendour of the court, absolute monarchy has certain advantages over a kleptocratic dictatorship: a monarch who regards the state as his property need not feel any desire to rob it, whereas a ruler with uncertain prospects more often than not feels that he must amass a fortune quickly. In consequence, a succession of dictators costs a country much more than would an absolute king.

The obsession with gold distinguished the dictators of Latin America from those of Europe, who on the whole cared more for power than for money. This may have been to the advantage of Latin America because an austere fanatic obsessed with the lust for power can do more damage than a sybaritic bandit.

A Latin American president, even if he comes into office legally, usually makes a fortune during his tenure, although there have been examples of men of outstanding probity who have not abused their opportunities. One very common method is to give government contracts to firms which pass on some of their gains to the president or his relatives in the form of cash payments or shares or gifts of real property or something similar. The same method is employed by the ministers and other high officials concerned with government contracts. Usually the profits from granting a big contract have to be distributed among a fairly wide circle of senior officials and politicians to keep everybody happy and quiet. The general rule is that anybody who has direct access to such secrets must be implicated himself. The extension of governmental control over economic life multiplied the opportunities for graft. It appears to involve the biggest sums in Mexico, where the state participates in industry most extensively.

All sales and purchases effected by the government are liable to be decided by graft. There are many examples of lands belonging to the state having been sold to plenipotentiaries or the favourites of men in power, or to buyers who gave bribes, at prices many times lower than the market value. Obversely, land required for government installations or roads has often been bought from similar persons at grossly exaggerated prices; and decisions about locating roads, railways and other installations have often been guided solely by the aim of enlarging the profits of such individuals. From Peru comes one of the most extraordinary examples of legalized appropriation of public funds: namely, tax-farming reminiscent of the practices of the *publicani* of ancient Rome. A private company called Caja de Recaudacion has the right to collect taxes in exchange for lump sums paid in advance to the treasury. Mystery shrouds the details of the agreement and the profits, but it is known that the governing politicians and their relatives hold most of the shares of this company.

Whilst the private banks make big profits through direct or indirect usury, the banks owned by public authorities sustain heavy losses on loans which they made to influential politicians, and which are either never repaid or repaid in depreciated currency at unrealistically low rates of interest. The most famous case is that of the Mexican Banco Agricola, set up as a part of post-revolutionary agrarian reform with the ostensible purpose of providing credit for small farmers, whose coffers soon became empty in consequence of the depredations of politicians. The presidents Calles and Obregon are said to have 'borrowed' about a hundred million dollars, and there were many other 'borrowers'.

The simplest form of graft is the straightforward transfer of funds from the state treasury to the private accounts of the principal members of the ruling clique. This method prevails only under dictatorships because even an imperfectly functioning parliamentary régime makes it difficult. In Chile, all the recent presidents have quitted office much richer than they were before but none of them is suspected of straightforward embezzlement. On the other hand, Peron and Perez Jimenez (to mention only two out of the many examples) had ample recourse to this method, and succeeded in accumulating in foreign banks sums which are estimated to amount to 700 million and 400 million dollars respectively. They were surpassed however by the late Rafael Leonidas Trujillo Molina, whose official title was The Benefactor of the Fatherland, and who paid most of the reserves of the foreign exchange of the Dominican Republic into his private accounts with foreign banks.

Though ruling one of the smallest and poorest states in the world, The Benefactor holds the world record in embezzlement: the fortune which he left behind has been estimated to exceed a thousand million dollars. He converted the Dominican economy into something that could be called patrimonial statism; the nearest analogy to which can be found in ancient Egypt where nearly everything belonged to the king. When The Benefactor died nearly all the bigger estates, factories, banks and commercial firms belonged to him personally or to the members of his extended family. As many of the former owners were killed, this property was taken over by the government when Trujillo's heirs were expelled, and in consequence the Dominican economy has become the most collectivist in Latin America after Castro's Cuba. Massive seizures of private property by a dictator and his henchmen have not been very frequent in recent times outside the Dominican Republic. More common has been the levying of tribute by the pretorians. The procedure is simple and exactly analogous to that used by the Mafia in Sicily or by Al Capone in Chicago, the only difference being that here the gangsters are recognized as the official government. The most notorious recent example comes from Haiti where the president Duvalier rules with support of a private gang of terrorists who because of their poor organization and armaments do not even deserve to be called a private army. As there is no money in the treasury to pay them for suppressing the opposition, these terrorists (operating at night, wearing hoods and some of them armed only with sticks) are allowed to live off the country, extorting what they can. They are not even afraid to attack foreign businessmen.

Licences of various kinds and exemptions from import duties

on articles which can be sold at great profit are frequently given to the favourites of the government or in exchange for bribes. Fabulous sums were obtained by the Venezuelan dictators for granting concessions to oil companies, and in other countries great fortunes were made from sales to mining or agricultural companies of lands belonging to the state. A relatively minor form of corruption is the misappropriation of movable objects. One of the most repulsive examples of such felonies was the theft of the blankets, foodstuffs and other materials which were sent to Peru for the victims of earthquakes and floods, but in fact found their way into the shops of Lima and elsewhere. Although it would have been easy to catch the perpetrators of a theft committed on such a scale, no prosecutions were instituted. During the year which followed the terrible earthquake in May 1960 Chile received 120 million dollars from the United States as an aid for the victims. Nevertheless, by October 1961 out of 40,000 homeless only 3,000 were rehoused, which would make it appear that it costs many thousand dollars to build a peasant's hut.

There are extenuating circumstances for the corruption of minor officials: most of them receive salaries on which they cannot feed their families, so it is not surprising that they take bribes whenever they can. Their salaries cannot be raised because there are too many of them for the work they do, and because the income of the government is reduced by tax evasion; so that we have a vicious circle. There is no excuse, however, for the big profiteers who already have much more than they need for living in luxury, but who nevertheless make use of every opportunity for criminal gain.

The losses caused by corruption far exceed the sum of individual profits derived from it, because graft distorts the whole economy. Important decisions are determined by ulterior and anti-social motives regardless of the consequences to the community. When a useless factory is built in an impossible place simply because the former owner of the site bribed the officials into buying it for an exorbitant price, then the cost to the community must far exceed the profits of the manipulators. An administrative machine permeated by graft does not respond to direction, so that even a most enlightened cabinet or president can achieve nothing, and his instructions are perverted in execution. The network of collusion is so thick that an honest president, even one as energetic as Cardenas, gropes as in a fog. Every bureaucratic machine suffers to some extent from an antipathy towards initiative and originality, from sycophancy and from the preferment of intriguers and yes-men. But when graft is added to these disorders, the machine ejects all the incurably honest men, selects for promotion the most ruthless and astute rogues, and compels the rest to follow their example.

In addition to corroding the administrative machine, graft makes its tasks much more difficult by destroying the good will of the people, and ensuring that every initiative of the government will be met with suspicion and hostility. Once the idea that all governments are merely bands of thieves strikes deep roots in the popular mind, then the task of governing becomes exceedingly difficult. It seems that in this respect the situation in a number of Latin American countries has worsened after the introduction of measures which were designed for the welfare of the poorer classes, but in practice have been disregarded. A form of graft which particularly excites the hatred of the poor is allocation of subsidized flats with uneconomic rents (ostensibly designed for housing the wage earners) to better situated persons in exchange for bribes.

A sudden influx of unearned money stimulates corruption. American gold contributed to Spain's ruin. The profits from the nitrate mines aggravated corruption in Peru. When the Chileans were preparing to rob Peru of its nitrate-bearing fields, some of their farsighted thinkers warned them that the ill-gotten gains might demoralize the nation and bring its public morals down to the level of the rest of Spanish America; and in fact the easy income from the nitrates helped to spread the taste for parasitical existence and eroded the sterner virtues for which the early Chileans were renowned. The fabulous income from oil contributed little towards the prosperity of Venezuela: it was squandered by its ruling cliques whose taste for spendthrift ostentation was whetted in the process, and whose evil example further stimulated the traditional improvidence of the lower classes. The financial aid which the countries of Latin America are receiving from the United States also has bad effects, for although only a small part of it can be simply embezzled, much of it is spent wastefully. No foreign aid can cure the plague of graft: the remedy must come from within.

The foregoing account should not give the impression that graft is something peculiarly Latin American. On the contrary, it is a very general disease which was rampant in ancient Rome, in the Turkish empire, in China under the emperors as well as more recently under Chiang Kai-shek, and in many other places. Indeed it still flourishes in most countries of Asia and Africa.* Nor is it absent in Northamerica or western Europe: it merely is less prevalent there. It must be remembered, however, that just as a body can tolerate a certain number of bacteria without suffering much harm, but succumbs to them once the white corpuscles can no longer keep them in check, so a society which can withstand sporadic graft suffers severe deformations once it becomes brazen and widespread.

Taxation

Throughout Latin America taxes fall less heavily upon the rich than upon the poor. As the bulk of the revenue is derived from indirect taxes, the burden is proportional not to income but to expenditure, and income which is saved or sent abroad escapes taxation. Such income, of course, always belongs to the rich. This inequity is perhaps less pronounced in Chile – whose government relies for its income chiefly on export duties (nearly all of which are paid by the Northamerican owned copper mining companies) and on import duties, which are particularly heavy on luxury articles – than in Brazil and Argentina where the excise on articles of popular consumption, such as alcohol, cigarettes, sugar, coffee and matches, constitutes the chief source of revenue. True, the excise on tyres and petrol affects commodities consumed in much greater quantities by the rich, but it also affects the costs of public transport and freight, and therefore raises their prices.

During the nineteenth century import duties provided the governments of Latin America with between a third and a half of their revenue, but, with the growth of the economies, the ratio of imports to internal trade diminished, and now import duties retain their former position only in the smallest states. Unlike Europe and Northamerica, Latin American governments

* A comparison between Latin America and the more complicated situation in the new African states can be found in my forthcoming book *Pathology of African Development*.

69

tax exports as well; and this is an important source of revenue in countries which export large quantities of raw materials. In Chile the export duty on nitrates supplied more than half the public revenue during the period of more than 50 years before 1920 when artificial fertilizers came on the market. Since then the tax on export of copper has become the most important, and together with import duties provides nearly half the revenue of the Chilean government. Venezuela obtains three-quarters of its public revenue from various kinds of taxes on extraction and exportation of oil. On the other hand, in Argentina less than a sixth, in Brazil less than an eighth, and in Mexico a little more than a fifth of the revenue of the government is obtained from import and export taxes. In contrast, the revenue from excise keeps pace with economic growth, and in Argentina and Brazil it now exceeds the proceeds of custom duties. In Argentina a general sales tax remained for several years as high as 8%.

An unusual feature of the Latin American revenue systems is the stamp duty, which in many cases amounts to as much as 10% of the total revenue. The stamps are used extensively, more than in the most stamp-ridden countries of Europe. The rate seldom exceeds 1% but the cumulative impact is important.

Concessions for the extraction of raw materials usually have to be paid for; thereafter an annual tax is levied on the area conceded, a severance tax on the volume of production and a duty on that part of it which is exported. These taxes are perfectly just: they are a legitimate means of protecting the national resources, and of preventing foreigners from despoiling the country, while still allowing them to make handsome profits. Nevertheless, the fact remains that the public revenue is obtained mainly from wealthy foreigners and the local poor, while the local rich pay very little.

Income taxes began to be levied only within the last thirty years and remain very small in comparison with those of Europe. In Argentina the tax starts at the rate of 3% and rises to 22%. In Peru the highest surtax is 30% and it is about the same in Colombia, Venezuela and Mexico; in Panama it is 16%; in Guatemala it is 12%, but in Brazil 50%. However, in view of the prevalence of evasion, the real burden is many times lighter. The very large foreign companies whose size makes proper accountancy indispensable, and therefore evasion more difficult, seem to pay the taxes honestly in countries like Chile, or Venezuela since Romulo Betencourt became the president, where they cannot manipulate the governments at will. What happens in Nicaragua or Guatemala is another matter.

The unfairness of taxation cannot directly damage peasants living in self-sufficient communities, who have few occasions to pay sales or stamp tax. The peasants suffer most from forced labour on public works and from extortion by the landlords. The people on whom the fiscal burden weighs most heavily are the urban poor and the urban lower middle class.

Little can be achieved by increasing the rates of income tax, but mere reduction in the extent of evasion would achieve a great deal. Perhaps more effective could be an increase in the hitherto insignificant inheritance taxes. This would have the advantage of helping to distribute a little more widely the ownership of real estate. However, probably the most desirable addition to the fiscal armoury would be a tax on property which, in addition to promoting more equitable distribution of wealth, would penalize idle resources, arrest the flow of capital into the ostentatious accumulation of landed property, and direct it into more profitable uses.

Militocracy

When there is neither political consensus nor institutions permitting orderly government, the only possible way of ruling a country is by force. Thus pretorianism was the inevitable consequence of the wars of liberation which destroyed the colonial administration together with its ideological basis, without putting in its place any institutions which could command general assent. And as arbiters of politics the military arrogated to themselves extravagant privileges and consumed a ruinously large share of the national wealth.

Latin American militocracy is radically different from the militarism which afflicted the European states and Japan. The Prussian militarism – to take the most developed example – entailed militocracy, that is to say, social and political predominance of the soldiers; but it exhibited few pretorianist proclivities, and its ideology was that of service for the sake of national pride. Although the Prussian officers insisted on occupying the places of honour in the society, and expected to live in a manner befitting their exalted position, they were not money grabbers. Even when they became ideologically disoriented after the fall of the monarchy, and began pretorian incursions into politics, their chief aim was to prepare a renaissance of German military power. All militarists shared the assumption that what was good for the officer corps was good for the nation, but on the whole European militarism – and the same is true of Japan – was extraverted: it was oriented primarily towards fighting foreigners, and only secondarily towards the task of protecting the social order from internal subversion. Naturally the relative emphasis varied according to the place and the time, but only in Spain was the protection of the privileged classes against internal dangers the chief function of the army.*

In Latin America there was only one example of militarism in the sense of regimentation of the entire population for the purpose of waging war: it was in Paraguay in the middle of the last century, where the dictators Francia and the two Lopez made it into one great military camp. Its militarization was so thorough that this sparsely populated country could wage war for several years against the combined armies of Argentina, Brazil and Uruguay; and by the time it was defeated it had lost three-quarters of its male population. However, the Paraguayan war was the biggest in Latin American history. The war of the Pacific (Chile against Peru and Bolivia) was decided by naval engagements and the land forces were small.

Militarism has become introverted in the Latin American republics: with few opportunities to fight for their countries, soldiers remained preoccupied with internal politics and the search for personal and collective advantage. One of their most striking characteristics is their unideological and mercenary outlook.

The armies of Latin America cannot fight each other because in virtue of a multilateral treaty the USA would come to the defence of the invaded country. The security of the hemisphere against invasion from outside is also guaranteed by the US, and should their forces prove inadequate for this purpose, the balance could not be redressed by the armies of the Latin

* These problems are treated from a widely comparative perspective in Military Organization and Society.

American republics, which lack modern equipment and training; particularly as officers accustomed to insubordination and intrigue would be of little value in war. The events in Colombia have shown that such an army cannot even cope with guerrillas

When viewed as props of the social order the Latin American armies are highly defective and unreliable instruments. The conscripts cannot be relied upon not to go over to the rebels, and even the loyalty to the present régimes of some of the officers is doubtful. For the purpose of suppressing internal subversion a smaller but well-trained police force, such as the Chilean *carabineros*, is much more reliable than a conscript army; and it seems that conscription is retained in so many republics chiefly in order to swell the numbers so as to provide jobs for officers. The armed forces behave as cancerous growths which, instead of performing any service to the social organism, only harm it.

According to UN sources the military establishments in Latin America in 1956 were as follows: (see overleaf)

This list shows that the armed forces of Latin America are too large for police duties but too small for waging war. Apart from Cuba since 1961, only Argentina and Chile could resist even a minor invasion.

In relation to their size and lack of equipment these forces are extremely expensive, owing to the disproportionately large numbers of high-ranking officers, retired or on active service, all of whom receive high emoluments. Argentina, for instance, has as many generals as the United States.

In *Arms and Politics in Latin America* New York, (1960), Edwin Lieuwen gives the following data (pp. 147–50):

Traditionally, since the turn of the century, the armed forces' reported share of the national budget has averaged about 20–25% annually in most Latin American countries. Official figures of war and navy departments, however, do not tell the whole story. Sizeable appropriations for the armed forces, amounting to perhaps 5% of the total budget, were often concealed in appropriations for the ministries of interior, public works and communications. In Paraguay, after the military coup of 1954, the share of the armed forces went up to 50%, and in Colombia and Cuba, owing to the civil wars, military budgets also rose sharply. In the total Latin American picture, however, these increases were at

	Army	*Navy*	*Air Force*
Argentina	107,000	21,500	19,000
Bolivia	15,000	600	2,000
Brazil	90,000	8,000	9,200
Chile	20,500	8,000	13,000
Colombia	10,000	1,500	200
Costa Rica	has only a small police force		
Cuba	19,000	2,000	2,400
Ecuador	no data		
El Salvador	6,000	400	500
Guatemala	21,000	1,000	400
Haiti	4,500	nil	400
Honduras	2,500	nil	1,200
Mexico	41,000	2,500	3,500
Nicaragua	10,000	nil	1,300
Panama	has only a police force		
Paraguay	5,800	400	nil
Peru	10,000	2,500	5,000
Dominican Rep.	3,500	3,000	2,000
Uruguay	3,000	1,450	200
Venezuela	10,000	2,240	5,000

least partly counterbalanced by sharp declines in Mexico after 1938, in Bolivia following the 1952 revolution, and in Costa Rica following the abolition of the army in 1948.

According to the *Inter-American Year Book* (New York: Macmillan, 1940), pp. 512–541, the armed forces' percentages of the national budgets were as follows: Argentina – 18, Bolivia – 30, Brazil – 24, Chile – 26, Colombia – 16, Guatemala – 19, Costa Rica – 19, Cuba – 22, Dominican Republic – 17, Ecuador – 22, El Salvador – 21, Haiti 24, – Honduras – 19, Mexico – 21, Nicaragua – 11, Panama – 0, Paraguay – 38, Peru – 23, Uruguay – 12, Venezuela – 12.

Although budgetary percentages generally remained constant, the expenses for Latin America's armed forces in absolute figures grew tremendously. This was because total national expenditures, with the rise of statism and big bureaucracies, had risen rapidly. For example, national budgets were several times larger in 1958 than in 1939. To some extent the armed force's increase reflected the cost of modern military equipment.

The resources that annually went into the armed forces' salaries and equipment obviously contributed little to the economic development of a country. Civilian reformers like Arevalo of Guatemala, Paz Estenssoro of Bolivia, and Betancourt of Venezuela found it hard to condone expenditures which seemed so wasteful – wasteful because in their view the armed forces had no commensurate military function to perform: there was no danger of invasion, and the maintenance of internal order was being capably handled by the nation's police forces. In addition, the continued high military budgets served to enhance the political power of the military. Yet these were fixed expenditure items which no government, either civilian or military, could alter. The minister of war or of defence, always a representative of the armed forces rather than of the government, made it unmistakably clear that the military would brook no curtailment in their traditional budgetary share. Whenever a military régime was established there usually occurred a further build-up of the armed forces, with stronger emphasis upon military items in the budget. Only in the four Latin American states, where civilian governments brought their armed forces under control (Mexico after 1938, Bolivia after 1952, Costa Rica after 1948, and Uruguay since before World War I), were substantial reductions made in the military's percentage of the budget.

In the Latin American tradition, military dictators used their office for purposes of illicit enrichment. Almost inevitably military dictatorship led to corruption. Not that civilian governments were clean in this regard, but the record of some military régimes is rather more spectacular. Immediately after a successful revolution the most pressing demands on national treasury came from the new leader's military supporters. This was usually the first stage of corruption. The second came when the problem arose of consolidating power through the attainment of popular backing for the régime. For this purpose funds were needed which would be free from legal control. Established political parties already had resources of this kind, but military régimes did not, and so they naturally dipped into the national treasury.

A new leader did not hesitate for long to join his associates in their peculations; in some cases he set the example . . . The conduct of Venezuela's military dictators was brazen but none the less typical. The corrupt pattern was fixed by General Juan Vicente Gomez, who during his long rule appropriated for himself hundreds of millions of dollars from the public treasury and substantial amounts for his family and military associates. After his death in 1935, his successors, Generals Eleazor Lopez Contreras (1935-41) and Isaias Medina Angarita (1941-5), carried on the dishonourable tradition. Each during his term of office made off with about 13 million dollars, then following the 1945 revolution retired in New York. Yet the young officer who helped to lead that revolution (Perez Jimenez) far outdid his predecessors.

In the five-year period from 1954 to 1959 Latin America's fleeing military dictators carried out of their countries hundreds of millions of dollars. Indications are that Peron escaped with as much as 700 million dollars, Perez Jimenez with more than 250 million, Batista with 50 million in 1944 and 200 million in 1959, and Rojas Pinilla, Paul Magloire and Arbenz with smaller yet sizeable fortunes. Meanwhile, those still in power were providing for their retirement. General Trujillo, in the neighbouring Dominican Republic, had over the years perfected his systematic graft until his annual income was estimated in the neighbourhood of 30 million dollars. In similar fashion, corrupt use of political power has made the Somoza family of Nicaragua one of the richest in central America. But thievery by the heads of state was only part of the story. Under Peron, favoured generals like Humberto Sosa Molina and Franklin Lucero became multi-millionaires. Colonel Pulido Barreto, Perez Jimenez' ordinance chief, amassed millions from parking-meter collections and transportation concessions.

In his book *El Militarismo* (Mexico 1959) Victor Alba calculates that military expenditure per head in Argentina was four times greater than in Mexico; in Chile almost five times greater; in Cuba (pre-Castro) six times, and in Venezuela twelve times. This accounts for the unrivalled rate of economic growth in Mexico. In 1958, according to this source, the situation was in this respect as follows: (see table opposite).

Militocratic appropriation of wealth constitutes the most important form of parasitism in Latin America. It occasions a greater waste of money than that caused by absentee landlordism because at least a part of the profits of the landlords is put into socially useful investments.

Parasitic Involution of Capitalism

The chief concern of businessmen is to make money, and their

76

	Percentage of military expenditure in the budget	Military expenditure per head in dollars
Argentina	25·5	8·82
Brazil	27·6	4·13
Chile	22·3	10·80
Colombia	16·9	2·30
Cuba	16·9	12·31
Guatemala	8·2	2·63
Mexico	10·4	2·12
Venezuela	11·2	25·91

choice of the means to that end depends upon the relative difficulty of various types of activity. So there is no reason to assume that they will choose to behave in ways that are socially useful if socially harmful methods of conducting business bring larger rewards. Many critics of capitalism, most notably Ruskin and J. A. Hobson, have long ago pointed out that neither the happiness nor even the bodily welfare of a nation depends solely on the amount of goods produced, and it is quite clear that many increases in 'real income', as calculated by economic statisticians, are in fact unreal because they make no allowance for such factors as the diminution of free space, air pollution, discomfort engendered by compulsory 'consumption' of transport and so on. These disutilities are at least as important in Latin America as in other parts of the world but they constitute a phenomenon distinct from that which is the subject of the present chapter.

Even before Adam Smith it was generally known that merchants and producers tended to conspire to raise prices; and there can be no doubt that monopolistic practices weigh heavily on the economies of Latin America. However, by parasitic involution of capitalism I mean something wider than monopolistic pricing policies – something that does not come within the purview of the economic theory at all – namely, the tendency to seek profits and to alter market conditions by political means in the widest sense of that word. This tendency is by no means unknown outside Latin America: it is absolutely ubiquitous but its intensity marks off the indigent from the affluent societies.

The easiest method of acquiring wealth is to seize what has been produced by somebody else, and for this reason war and politics have a glamour which productive activities lack. Overt exaction of tribute is (next to unregularized robbery) the simplest and most transparent form of predacity, but in essence this phenomenon is no different from the use of the machine of coercion of the state for preventing the workers from bargaining effectively or for driving a competitor out of business: in both cases wealth is transferred with the aid of coercion. Investments of capital in tax-farming or the purchase of office may be very profitable but socially they are not merely unproductive: their indirect consequences cause a diminution of aggregate wealth. The gravity of the parasitic involution of capitalism resides not so much in the waste it causes as in the discouragement of productive activities subjected to parasitic extortion.

As the societies of Latin America were thoroughly pervaded by parasitism when capitalism began to penetrate them, it is not surprising that it very soon showed signs of parasitic involution. We shall look more closely at this process a little later, but in order to understand it better we must briefly consider the situation in the countries where capitalism evolved in a predominantly productive rather than a predominantly parasitic direction.

In Britain ever since the fall of the Stuarts the state was too weak to act as an overpowering agent of parasitism, and consequently did not offer a particularly profitable field for parasitic investment. A fairly wealthy man could buy a colonelcy in the Army or use his funds for getting himself elected to parliament but the gains obtainable from such posts were usually negligible compared with what success in business could bring. Moreover, in Britain wealth could always open the way to political influence and office but the reverse was less true, whereas in Latin America the connection between wealth and political office was and is perfectly reciprocal. The relatively limited scope for parasitic investment was one of the chief reasons for the early development of English industry. The same was true to an even greater extent in the USA. In France, on the other hand, the possibilities of making money through politics have been on the whole greater than in other fields, and this accounts for the slower speed of French industrialization. In Germany, the state was strong, and therefore offered a wider scope for investment in politics, but it remained under the control of the military nobility and a civil service, imbued with traditions of service which made them fairly immune to graft and thus unco-operative partners in financial manipulation. (Japan was analogous in this respect.) The Prussian government, moreover, extended some protection over the peasants out of concern for them as possible army recruits. Such considerations never carried any weight with any governments in Latin America except that of two Paraguayan dictators, Francia and Lopez.

Taking western Europe and North America as a whole, we can say that where the state was strong it was not in the pockets of capitalists, and where it was more or less in their pockets it was too weak and restricted in its activities to become their chief tool for making money. When these obstacles to parasitic involution no longer operated, new restraints appeared in the shape of democratic government and organized labour which prevented or at least attenuated exploitation. In the United States, where the traditional monarchic and nobiliary constraints never existed, the early establishment of political democracy provided more than a substitute, whilst the abundance of free land greatly enhanced the bargaining power of labour.

The history of Imperial Rome provides the best example of how capitalism may strangle itself through parasitic involution. That there was capitalism in ancient Rome cannot be doubted because, despite the absence of machine industry, all the essential features of a capitalist social structure were present. These were the legal framework appropriate to commercial and financial transactions, highly developed monetary circulation and banking, gainful employment of capital, production for the market carried on in large establishments. However, the large agricultural and industrial establishments were products of mere concentration of ownership, and their methods of production were no more advanced than those employed in very small units. The large industrial establishments consisted of a multiplicity of technically independent small units connected only by their proximity and the fact of being owned by one capitalist: they existed only because capital could be invested in slave artisans. But the biggest field for investment of capital consisted of land tilled by slaves, usury and tax farming, the latter amounting to no more than organized robbery. Within such a structure the influx of gold from the conquered provinces could only stimulate parasitic exploitation, which became so extreme that it seriously impoverished the lands of the empire, and stimulated civil wars which finally ruined them, causing the decay of towns and the disintegration of the economy into isolated self-sufficient domains based on serfdom.

The undisputed dominance of capitalists tends to produce a parasitic involution of capitalism, and thus to arrest its progress, which requires development of production techniques and accumulation of equipment. On the other hand, the subjection of capitalist entrepreneurs is equally inimical to the growth of capitalism because it exposes them to spoliation and makes orderly pursuit of gain impossible. Extreme subjection also fosters parasitism of an interstitial kind: of usurers thriving in the shadow of potentates and satraps – as was the case in the oriental lands. Capitalism tends towards a productive orientation when the capitalist entrepreneurs can neither use coercion for the purpose of parasitic exploitation nor be so devoid of strength as to be exposed to exploitation themselves – in other words, when businessmen are too weak to prey upon the other classes, but too strong to be preyed upon. Such a situation – which I propose to call the situation of equipendency – requires a certain degree of differentiation and segregation between the business élite and the political élite, or at least an influential part thereof. An important implication of the principle of equipendency is that capitalism can function beneficently only in a society where money cannot buy everything, because if it can, then the power of wealth can have no counterweight and a parasitic involution ensues.

The prevalence of graft increases the power of money because it nullifies the force of legal constraints and reduces to impotence even those rulers who might be personally incorruptible; and for this reason the governments of Latin America could seldom oppose the socially harmful uses of wealth. This impotence is not uncommon but in Latin America it assumes more extreme forms than in the more prosperous countries. In these circumstances politics becomes a strictly money-making activity, and capitalist groups invest in it large sums – an expenditure as wasteful but much more pernicious than advertising. Naturally, the situation is not the same in all countries of Latin America – these statements apply with full force to Colombia or Peru but are scarcely applicable at all to Uruguay or Costa Rica.

Bribing officials, paying and arming supporters, buying votes, subsidizing the press, bring rewards in the shape of concessions, permits, appointments, contracts and the leniency of tax-collectors. The nature of such transactions prevents us from discovering the magnitude of the sums involved but we can be fairly certain that they consume a substantial part of the available capital.

Where capitalism has benefited the workers, it has done so by enabling them to obtain higher wages. In Latin America this did not happen because the multiplication of the population kept pace with or outstripped the growth of production, while the arm of the state was continually used to weaken the bargaining position of the workers.

Even when the firms were small it was clear that only by organizing themselves could the workers win improvements in their treatment and pay, or even avoid deterioration of these conditions. Owners of capital enjoy an enormous advantage in bargaining over those who live from hand to mouth. So long as employers compete with each other for labour, while the accumulation of capital outstrips the growth of the population, wages may rise even in the absence of effective unions, but the demand for labour ceases to have much influence upon the wages once concentration of economic control deprives the employees of choice – to put it into more technical language, once the demand for labour becomes monopsonic. Whereas in western Europe the development of the trade unions more or less kept pace with the process of industrial concentration (whilst there was hardly any movement towards concentration in agriculture at all) in Latin America concentration of economic control was always far in advance of unionization of labour. The large estate anteceded capitalism by a long stretch, and capitalism came from abroad in the form of large companies, backed by the power of foreign governments, which faced a pulverized and degraded indigenous proletariat. These companies acquired the position of the only buyers of labour over wide areas.

In the countries of beneficent capitalism wages rose as the trade unions grew in size and strength. Their growth was made possible by a number of conditions of which the simplest and most obvious was tolerance on the part of the governments, the consequence of a fairly democratic state. In the violent atmosphere of Latin American politics there was never much room for such tolerance, and (with the exception of Uruguay and certain phases of the Mexican, Bolivian and Guatemalan revolution) the state has always functioned as the employers' policeman, and (as examples from other parts of the world show) trade unions cannot achieve very much against the police. Repression by state and private police forces still plays an important part in keeping down the wages in most countries of Latin America.

In Northamerica the development of the unions was later than in Europe but until almost the end of the last century the workers had the great advantage of being able to acquire land without any outlay of capital Not all of them 'went West' but enough did so to relieve the pressure on the market for labour and to keep the wages far above those prevailing in the richest countries of Europe. In Latin America such opportunities for escaping poverty never existed partly because tropical lands are less easy to bring under cultivation but chiefly because the land had been pre-empted by the owners of large estates. In Northamerica the democratic institutions prevented foreclosure of uncultivated land, whereas in Latin America such checks were lacking and the emancipation from the control by the Spanish Crown removed the only possible counterweight to the landowning oligarchy.

An owner of a large estate has great power over his employees even if they are legally free to leave: he is the sole buyer of their labour within a wide area, and their only alternative is to migrate to towns if they can afford the expense of travel. The superior bargaining power of the estate owners enabled them to keep for themselves all the fruits of increased productivity: neither the development of coffee production in Colombia nor that of banana growing in Ecuador – to mention only two out of several possible examples – helped to raise the miserable standard of living of the workers. It must be added that as the landowners form a cohesive group interlinked by marriage, they find it easy to conspire to eliminate competition for labour and to keep the wages down.

Until the recent development of the trade unions, the Latin

American wage earners were in an even weaker position than the English workers a hundred years ago because of the greater degree of concentration of control over the industry. Strangely, the situation of the workers is now best in the largest scale industries – the extractive – where the monopsony on labour is complete.* In the mining settlements and on the oil fields there is only one employer, as a rule foreign, and so long as he can rely on unconditional backing from the state, he can keep the wages at the bare minimum: the oil fields of Mexico and Venezuela, the nitrate and copper mines of Chile, the banana plantations of Guatemala, Nicaragua and Ecuador, have witnessed many savage reprisals on recalcitrant workers. Recently, however, the growth of nationalism and of the movements for social reform have made the non-dictatorial governments inclined to take the worker's side against foreign employers. In some countries the governments carried their willingness to protect the workers against foreign employers to unreasonable lengths, making business unprofitable, as was at certain times the case with banana plantations in Honduras. On the whole, however, the foreign firms continue to prosper and, owing to their efficiency and great capital, they can afford to pay higher wages than the native employers.

Although unionization has made great strides during recent decades, it has strengthened only the position of the privileged sectors of the working class, and failed to improve the lot of the majority whose bargaining power is undermined by the rapid growth in their numbers; and so long as the practice of birth control does not take root among them there is no way in which the situation can be remedied. As Francis Place observed a hundred years ago, the limitation of births is the most effective form of strike, but like other forms of strike it is difficult to practise in conditions of abject misery: thus there is another vicious circle.

The situation of the lower white-collar employees is not very different from that of the manual workers: their bargaining position is extremely weak and the pay pitiful. Their nuisance power – that is to say, the power to cause general damage or inconvenience by going on strike – is more limited than that of the

* For the benefit of readers unacquainted with economics: monopolist = sole seller, monopsonist = sole buyer.

manual workers, but this disadvantage is compensated for by the greater respect which they enjoy in the eyes of the police and the higher authorities. The majority of the white-collar workers find entirely unproductive employment in various organs of the state, and their situation is discussed in the next section devoted to bureaucratic parasitism. What, however, must be emphasized in the present context is that Latin American economies have not created a large class of relatively satisfied white-collar workers such as exists in Northamerica or Britain.

A thorough involvement of businessmen in political strife and graft not only provides them with weapons for keeping the wages down but also adversely affects the possibilities of small businessmen who cannot use political influence so effectively as the big capitalists. Particularly important in this context is the stranglehold which cliques of big capitalists have on credit facilities, and which enables them to make enormous profits on usury. In Chile, which is the most orderly country in Latin America, a small businessman cannot obtain a loan from any of the banks. These give them only to a few privileged borrowers who then give private loans at rates reaching 20% per month. The official interest rate stands at about 30% per year.* True, inflation robs the lender of a substantial part of his gains in terms of purchasing power but, as the exchange rate to the dollar has been artificially pegged, he can amass great wealth by converting his profits into dollars. The cornering of credit facilities largely accounts for the high degree of concentration of control over industry and over property in general, and is connected with the phenomenon of inflation which offers great scope for making large profits by various kinds of financial manipulation.

The purchasing power of the people cannot be suddenly increased because it is limited by the amount of goods produced, which in turn is limited by the existing skills, equipment and resources; whose growth depends on the demand for their products. As is well known, economic expansion consists of a beneficent circle of increasing production creating demand for the goods, which in turn stimulates the growth of production and so on; whereas constriction or stagnation creates the opposite vicious circles. To deprive the workers of the benefits of an increase in production is not only unjust, but it also prevents the

* Written in 1961.

expansion of the economy by restricting the market. Transfer of the purchasing power from the masses to the privileged few acts as a brake upon the growth of production because it reduces the market for goods which can be produced cheaply in large quantities, and swell the demand for luxury goods and personal services. Furthermore, it lowers the efficiency of labour by debilitating the workers and depriving them of incentives. There would be some advantage in an extremely unequal distribution of income if the rich invested most of their wealth in expanding production but this is not at all the case in Latin America.

Karl Marx had good grounds for believing that the misery of the proletariat cannot disappear under the capitalist system. The movement of wages at the time when he wrote the Communist Manifesto was in fact downward and many hitherto prosperous artisans were being reduced to the status of miserable wage earners. The so-called Law of the Increasing Misery of the Proletariat was probably a rhetorical exaggeration because Marx must have known that misery cannot go deeper than the subsistence minimum, but the statement that the proletariat would comprise an increasingly large part of the population of capitalist countries was a perfectly valid and simple inference from the existing trends, which had been made by other economists before Marx. The view that the majority of the wage earners were condemned to misery for ever was expounded by many apologists of *laissez-faire*, and found its classic formulation in Ricardo's Iron Law of Wages.

Neither Ricardo nor Marx were wrong in their analysis of the situation which existed at the time. Indeed, without factors which entered upon the scene after the appearance of *Das Kapital* the fate of the working class would not have improved despite the growth of production. The factors which altered the situation, and made Marx's analysis no longer applicable, were four: the rapid increase in production; the decline of the birth rate; the development of trade unionism and the winning of full political rights by the lower classes. The relationship between these trends was that of interdependence, and all of them were indispensable for a radical improvement in the standard of living of the lower classes. The combined effect of these four factors was to prevent the capitalists from appropriating all the fruits of technical progress and to raise the standard of living of the workers. In Latin America the persistence of extremely high birth rates, the late growth and continuous weakness of trade unionism and the undemocratic character of the political institutions ensure the applicability to the present situation there of the analysis which Marx made of the England of a hundred years ago. Functioning under the conditions just described, the system of free capitalist enterprise built a pyramid of upper class luxury upon the foundation of misery of the masses.

Without restraints from institutions rooted in sentiments other than the desire for private gain, capitalism in Latin America has a particularly strong bent towards predation – and therefore self-strangulation – whilst the trade unions, which in more propitious circumstances might have helped to direct it into more productive channels, act as agencies of disruption rather than of orderly and reasonable defence of the interests of the workers, thus stimulating instead of dampening the tendency of the businessmen to seek quick predatory gains to the detriment of long-range, socially useful investment.

The Incubus of Bureaucracy

Nobody acquainted with the realities of the affluent societies could imagine for a moment that the overgrowth and parasitism of the bureaucratic machines is an illness from which only the less developed countries suffer. The malady is ubiquitous but its consequences are graver in poor countries where waste causes severe hardship. In the United States where automation gluts the market with superfluous goods, while depriving a large number of workers of their jobs, a wasteful expansion of administrative services may even have a beneficial effect in that it prevents unemployment. In contrast, in Latin America, where the production does not suffice to satisfy the most elementary needs of the population, and where workers live in dire poverty, any addition to the numbers of concealed non-producers aggravates the misery. In proportion to the population, administrative functions give employment to as many people in the more advanced countries in Latin America as they do in the most highly industrialized countries in the world, despite the much more restricted industrial base. This statement is not quite true of the countries which have very large primitive populations, such as Brazil, Ecuador, Peru, Guatemala and Paraguay, but in the countries where such populations are proportionately smaller (Argentina, Chile, Mexico and Uruguay) the percentage of administrative employees is extremely high. If we take the urban populations only, we find that the ratio between those employed in administration to those employed in manufacturing industry and transport is higher throughout Latin America than in the wealthy countries. As mentioned earlier, the megalocephaly from which most countries of Latin America suffer is due more to the expansion of administrative services than to the concentration of manufacturing industry. The most extreme case is Uruguay whose capital Montevideo contains 34% of the population. In this country, which exports only the products of agriculture, and where industry is little developed the proportion of public employees is higher than in the United States, and if we include dependants, about a fifth of the population depends for its livelihood on government funds.

Although the superfluity of personnel is most obvious in public administration, the administration of private firms is by no means free from this burden. Owing to the miserable salaries of lower employees, the administrative expenses are not crippling, but the social loss must be measured in terms of how much could the production be increased if all the superfluous white-collar employees were more productively employed.

The assertion that administrative services are overgrown is not easy to prove because the concept of hypertrophy is meaningful only in relation to the tasks performed, and we have no yardsticks of administrative productivity similar to those which are used in measuring the productivity of factory workers. The difficulty, of course, resides in the nature of the 'product' of administrative work, which is particularly elusive in case of higher functions. There are certain functions which are fairly simple and measurable: we could, for instance, measure with a reasonable degree of exactness the productivity of the personnel of an office which issues motor licences, but we could hardly regard the number of cases which a judge decides in a week or a year as the measure of his productivity, because speedy dispatch might merely indicate a lack of concern for the justice of the verdicts. However, when a judge is both slow and careless, we can be sure that his productivity is low; and the same applies to other administrative functions.

The absolutely universal opinion among foreign residents in Latin America, and among Latin Americans who know western Europe or Northamerica well, is that administration is inefficient and overstaffed in all the countries of Latin America. Even a quick tour through any of these countries offers opportunities for diagnosing administrative inefficiency when two ticket collectors instead of one can be seen on a small train or several bank clerks have to be dealt with to change foreign currency. It must be emphasized, however, that hypertrophy and the inefficiency of administrative machinery are extremely common ills which are at least as acute in the countries of eastern Europe as they are in Latin America.

As suggested earlier, the vastness of the empire precluded the Spanish kings from creating (even if they had the will and the ability) a very efficient administrative apparatus. Nevertheless by the standards of the age the Spanish colonial administration was not bad, and it was during the period after independence that Latin America became backward in this respect; for whilst in other parts of the world really efficient systems of administration developed, in Latin America the endemic strife ensured the spread of all bureaucratic vices. As appointments remain to this day a matter of patronage, no system of promotion either by merit (in the formal sense – for no more can be expected anywhere) or by seniority has struck root in any country of Latin America, although Chile and Uruguay are nearer to it than Colombia or Ecuador. In consequence the ground is not at all propitious to the growth of the simple virtues of conscientiousness and objectivity, but encourages sycophancy, favouritism and neglect of work. The usual (not only in Latin America) remedy for the shortcomings of administration is the creation of a supervisory or an auxiliary organ which creates more red tape, and adds to the burden on the tax payer. Superfluous officials on inadequate pay and without security of tenure are driven into cut-throat politics, for neutrality and reticence will not ensure permanency; particularly as the scarcity of alternative jobs makes the maintenance of their posts a matter of life and death for all those without private incomes.

In consequence of the extension of the spoils system downwards, politics is not confined to professional politicians and top officials but spreads throughout the civil service and even outside it. It concerns not only those in power but also those who would like to get it. The pressure from the latter is the chief cause of the inordinate swelling of the administrative machinery. Sinecure holders constitute an important (though, of course, unknown) proportion of officials. Many of them do no work whatsoever, and do not even appear in the office, their only connection with the service being through the pay-roll.

The demand for jobs by people with some education of a non-technical kind and a great aversion to manual work enhances the appeal of socialist ideas, because their application entails the creation of a large number of administrative posts, in addition to the existing managerial positions which would be compulsorily vacated by their present incumbents. The desire for the posts occupied by expatriate managers of foreign firms constitutes, moreover, one of the chief reasons for the ultranationalism of the middle classes, which in its marxist guise goes under the name of anti-imperialism. The middle classes of Latin America are primarily the bureaucratic classes, and they train their youth for bureaucratic employment.

Although it was the weakening of the landowning aristocracy that enabled the middle classes to play an important role in politics, the increases in their share of total wealth have been achieved mainly at the expense of the working classes. Sometimes the transfers of wealth from the class of manual workers to that of white-collar workers assume the forms of a cruel joke. For example: social insurance functions in Chile in such a way that, although the contributions are uniformly high, the benefits are so steeply graduated in favour of white-collar employees that their benefits are three times higher in proportion to their contributions than the benefits of the manual workers. Even more important, more than half the contributions go into the costs of administration, that is to say, into the salaries of white-collar employees. So, the system of social insurance, instituted ostensibly for protection of the workers, in fact functions as a tax imposed by the middle class on the working class. In 1956 the white-collar workers, who constitute 20% of the insured, received 80% of the benefits.

Somebody has described the British diplomatic service as a system of outdoor relief for the aristocracy – a diagnosis which fits most diplomatic services of the world. In no other region, however, do diplomats weigh so heavily on the economy of their countries as in Latin America, where the multiplicity and smallness of the states make the cost of maintaining them exorbitant. Whereas in the European capitals one hardly notices the cars of the diplomatic corps, in the capitals of Latin America they attract attention by their number and magnificence, which stand in sharp contrast to the shabby appearance of the general run of vehicles. As on the whole the states of Latin America trade little with each other and cannot fight, the two usual concerns of diplomacy occupy little of the attention of their diplomats who are free to devote themselves to purely decorative functions at exorbitant cost to their poor countries. Their tendencies towards ostentation and living beyond their means are further stimulated by the presence of numerous officials of various international agencies, many of whom do little useful work of any kind and devote much time to intrigues. Latin American politicians, officials and intellectuals fawn on them – expecting that their mighty patrons in New York or Paris or Rome will find for them a sinecure somewhere in the vast international bureaucracy. Hoping to receive a job or a donation, the impecunious intellectuals of Latin America are prepared to accept as their mentors 'experts' with fewer qualifications than themselves who are known to be working for disreputable ends.

Hypertrophy of the bureaucracy is the chief factor responsible for the shift of the employed population from the production of material goods to the services. In Chile, for instance, between 1940 and 1953 the personnel occupied in production of goods increased by 18%, whilst that employed in services grew by 65%. Although the transfer of population from production of goods to services is a normal feature of industrial development, what happened here and elsewhere in Latin America was something different, in spite of the superficial analogy, because the transfer of population was much greater than the growth of productivity in the basic branches of the economy. In highly industrialized economies the rise of productivity of manpower employed in producing goods satisfies more fully the need for the goods with smaller personnel, and with rising prosperity the demand for services hitherto considered inessential grows and attracts personnel released from production of basic goods. In Latin America, with the partial exception of Mexico, the productivity of the manpower engaged in production of goods has not risen generally, and therefore, the multiplication of the personnel occupied in services adds to the burden placed upon the producers of goods. An important condition of this evolution is the fact that an expansion of administrative personnel is the least costly form of creating jobs, and has the added advantage of giving some people the illusion of social promotion; for whereas considerable funds may be required for machines to employ additional factory workers, the minimal equipment of office employees is very cheap.

One aspect of bureaucratic waste which must be mentioned is the extraordinarily generous retirement provision in force in most countries of Latin America. In Argentina state employees can retire on full pension by the time they are 50, and in Chile even at 40. In consequence these countries are full of young and healthy retired men and women, many of whom find another employment for themselves, but all of whom are parasites who, in addition to being a burden on the workers, demoralize them and make them discontented by the display of comfortable idleness, so offensive in the midst of poverty.

As the number of those who profit from bureaucratic hypertrophy is very large, this form of parasitism does not provide the best target for electioneering propaganda, but as an obstacle to economic progress it is no less fundamental than landlordism, and is more important than 'dollar imperialism'.

Economic Imperialism

In contrast to imperialism pure and simple – that is to say, the tendency to expand the area of political control by force of arms – economic imperialism is an elusive phenomenon. A conquest is normally a deliberate act, but control over a country's economic life may pass into the hands of foreigners without any concerted endeavour on their part, simply because they are more willing to engage in commercial and industrial pursuits or possess greater skill. In such a case the outcome may be economic domination but we can hardly describe the spontaneous process which led to it as imperialism. We must remember, however, that a process of economic penetration which began as an unintended product of unco-ordinated activities of many businessmen becomes deliberate and concerted when control over economic activity becomes concentrated in a few hands.

Strictly speaking we could apply the term economic imperialism to all cases of concerted striving on the part of the nationals of one country to extend their control over the economic life of another country, without attempting to become its official rulers. If fully successful, however, economic imperialism ceases to be merely economic because if all the wealth is in the hands of foreigners the national government can hardly avoid being a puppet. And as the history of the British and Dutch East Indies Companies shows, commercial penetration may lead to an outright conquest. Conversely, every conquest (or even extension of a sphere of influence), even if it is motivated by purely strategic or diplomatic considerations, affects the distribution of wealth, and therefore there can be no purely political imperialism, although the importance of the economic aspect varies greatly. For these reasons, the concept of economic imperialism is not a simple one, particularly as it carries pejorative undertones which imply that extension of economic control across political frontiers is always evil.

To the 'liberal' economists all commercial transactions appear beneficial to all concerned, and they see no reason why the benefits bestowed upon a country should diminish when these activities are carried out by foreigners. And indeed if it be claimed that the activities of New York businessmen can benefit California, USA, but can only harm California, Mexico, then some explanation should be given as to how a crossing of the border can make such a difference to the nature of economic activity. The marxists, of course, regard the activities of foreign businessmen as *a priori* detrimental to a country, but they make the assumption that all private commerce is harmful, which is clearly absurd in view of the fact that capitalism is so far the only system which at least in some countries has succeeded in eliminating mass poverty. Both the 'liberal' economists and the marxists are wrong: activities of foreign businessmen may either benefit or impoverish a country, depending on the circumstances under which they take place. It remains true, however, that from a nationalistic standpoint it is possible to regard dependence on foreigners as evil even if it brings economic benefits.

The issues are clearer with imperialism in the oldest sense of the word. Every nation regards a seizure of its territory as a crime, even if the population of the conquered territory benefits economically. Therefore there is nothing surprising in the grudge which the Mexicans bear against the United States for seizing by force half of the territory which Mexico had when it reached independence. True, these territories were sparsely populated and in all probability would not have reached their present flourishing condition had they remained under Mexican rule – it can even be argued that the Mexicans who remained in California, Nevada, New Mexico, Texas and Arizona profited within their lifetime from their forcible incorporation into the United States – but such arguments cannot quench national resentment. Like other nations in similar situations the Mexicans say: we would prefer to see these territories in a less flourishing state but in our own hands.

The conquest of northern Mexico was the only serious territorial loss inflicted upon a Latin American republic. Panama was also acquired by the United States through a thinly veiled conquest: a group of adventurers paid by the US government separated this area from Colombia, declared themselves to be an independent republic, and then concluded a treaty of alliance with the USA, ceding to it the Canal Zone. This was undoubtedly an act of territorial aggression but it did no real harm to Colombia. The territory in question is minute and it constituted a negligible part of the immense territory of Colombia, much of which is still not utilized. At the time, the territory of Panama consisted almost entirely of uninhabited, malaria-ridden swamps which only the construction of the canal made fit for habitation. Left to itself, Colombia would never have been able to put this territory to any use, let alone construct a canal, which was built at the expense and under the direction of the Northamericans by non-Colombian labour imported from Jamaica. The only possible loss which the Colombians have suffered was that had the Northamericans not resorted to a conquest by proxy, the Colombians might have obtained some payment for the territory, or could have leased it in exchange for a share in the profits from the canal. But the net profits from the canal are not so enormous that a share in them could make a decisive contribution to the economic development of Colombia.

The abortive British attempt to conquer Buenos Aires in 1807, and the attempt of Napoleon III to make Mexico into a vassal monarchy under the sceptre of his cousin Maximilian, no longer stir up any national resentment. The same cannot be said about the Northamerican incursions into the Caribbean countries. In comparison with what usually happens when a country is invaded, the actions of the US troops were very mild, but individual soldiers behaved badly. They were all volunteers, and many of them were ruffians for whom the Wild West was becoming too well policed. It is not surprising that such individuals indulged in drunken rowdiness and perpetrated robberies and rapes. However, as the behaviour of the indigenous soldiers was no better, it was not so much these deeds that inspired the hatred of the native populations as their combination with uninhibited manifestations of racial contempt. Even the undoubted benefits bestowed upon the native populations by the Northamerican administrators – such as the installation of sanitation or suppression of anarchy and bloodshed – were resented. In trying to understand situations of this kind we must never forget the psychological maxim – stated by de la Rochefoucauld three hundred years ago – that gifts contemptuously given inspire hatred.

If we regard national sovereignty as the supreme good then all foreign armed intervention must be condemned, but it is neither clear that national sovereignty is the most important ethical value nor that the populations of the central American republics constituted nations in any but the purely formal sense. The Northamerican interventions were certainly not prompted by altruism – the troops went in to protect the assets of wealthy citizens of the USA – but no particular harm was done thereby to the people: in no case has a decent government or a prosperous economy been destroyed by Northamerican troops. When territory was taken from the Indians this was a direct attack on their existence, but the Northamericans never did anything of that kind in the Caribbean. Even on the worst interpretation of their actions and intentions, it cannot be maintained that their direct rule was worse than that of the indigenous dictators. Even when they sequestrated the proceeds from custom duties in order to pay the interest overdue to their financiers, they did not increase the burden upon the population because otherwise these funds would have gone into the pockets of the local tyrants. There is no evidence that the interventions of the US government seriously aggravated the plight of any Latin American country. At most the Northamericans can be blamed for doing nothing positive to help their southern neighbours, but in the days of dogmatic belief in the providential nature of 'free enterprise' a governmental sponsorship of economic reforms would have appeared a blasphemy.

Many Latin American writers and speakers argue as if the figures indicating the amount of foreign investments constituted indubitable proof that their countries are badly exploited. On the other side, the economists of the creditor countries speak as if every loan had to benefit the receiving country. In reality, a loan may be harmful or helpful according to the conditions on which it is given and the use to which it is put. It must be remembered that an investment may be purely formal and fail to produce any movement of real goods into the country in which it is nominally made. Thus many investments in Latin America amounted to no more than making loans to dictators, who put them into their personal accounts in foreign banks, in exchange for unlawful commercial privileges and concessions. The rate of interest on such loans (camouflaged by legal subterfuges) is usually enormous to compensate for the risk of the debtor being ousted from power. Such investments are not merely unproductive but definitely harmful because they facilitate and even stimulate exactions by the politicians. On the other hand, an investment which pays for importation of machinery and materials for building a factory producing insecticides, which will substantially augment agricultural production, unquestionably bestows upon the receiving country a palpable benefit.

Lending at interest for unproductive purposes really amounts to preying on weakness, and the medieval scholars were right in condemning it. Indeed, it is only when the capital is used for increasing production that lending at interest can be socially useful; and unfortunately many international investments do not differ greatly from the harmful usury of a village moneylender who exploits the improvidence of his clients. To this category belong the loans given to the rulers of Latin America for the purpose of buying arms or erecting ostentatious buildings or monuments, or distributing gifts to their friends and supporters. It is impossible to know exactly how large has been the proportion of investments of this kind but it seems that it has been very substantial in the worst governed countries. It may, of course, be said that the use to which a loan is put is the responsibility of the borrower, but it is difficult to absolve the creditors from guilt when they know that the funds will be squandered by the dictator, whereas the money for repayment will be extorted from his unfortunate subjects. Such investments amount to collusion in oppression and exploitation.

The 'surveying companies', which functioned in Mexico towards the end of the last century, provide a good example of purely predatory foreign investment. These companies, whose shares were held mostly by Northamericans, were ostensibly hired to examine the titles to ownership of land, and to reclaim government property which had been misappropriated. In fact two kinds of crime were being committed: firstly, the shareholders of these companies bought the land which they had 'reclaimed' for the government at prices greatly reduced in exchange for bribes; secondly, the 'recovery' was in fact sheer robbery: with the aid of thinly veiled legalistic subterfuges illiterate peasants were robbed of lands which had belonged to their ancestors since time immemorial, whereas speculators who had really misappropriated government lands were left unmolested. As the citizens of the USA played a leading role in committing these crimes, and provided most of the capital invested in bribes, it is not surprising that many Mexicans regarded this as imperialism, despite the participation of native speculators and politicians. True, these operations were conducted by private individuals and not by the US government, but the speculators were receiving 'unofficial' help from various diplomats; and later, when their ill-gotten gains were being confiscated, the US government endeavoured to protect them to the extent of threatening war. So we have here an example of predatory investment which brings nothing but harm and demoralization to the weaker countries. Indeed, this kind of economic imperialism had none of the positive aspects with which colonial imperialism in Africa could be credited. Nevertheless, in order to see the issue in its proper perspective, we must not forget that these deeds of spoliation could not have been committed without the collaboration of Mexican officials and agents, and that on innumerable occasions Mexicans did exactly the same or even worse without any aid or incitement from Northamericans.

Since the times of ancient Egypt mining has been the scene of the greatest degradation of human beings, and among industries operating on an international scale oil firms have the worst reputation for rapacity and ruthless meddling in local politics. The windfall nature of the gains seems to stimulate predatory propensities: in manufacturing large profits can be obtained only by investing great sums and gradually expanding production, whereas in extraction of oil (as of gold) a lucky strike may bring enormous gains. Moreover, the dependence on concessions of land brings the oil companies directly into politics, particularly as the competition among them was centred less around cheapness of production than around the ability to obtain control over oil-bearing fields.

The oil companies which operated in Latin America have much on their conscience. Despite their enormous gains, until very recent times they treated their workers abominably. When dividends of many hundred per cent were being distributed, the workers lived in filthy huts with neither clean water nor sanitation nor the most rudimentary medical care; received salaries which barely sufficed to keep them alive and which in many cases had to be spent in company stores charging exorbitant prices; and were entitled to no compensation when an accident or exposure to unhealthy conditions made them unfit for work. Strikes were brutally suppressed by private police or the troops whose commanders received payment for this service. It is perfectly true, of course, that the indigenous employers treated their workers no better but at least they had the excuse of having less money. In any case, even if we conclude that the oil companies were no worse than the indigenous employers, the fact remains that instead of using a small part of their gains to set a better example, they availed themselves of every opportunity for exploitation.

The present conditions are different: even governments which are on the whole anti-labour are prepared to support the claims of the workers against foreign employers, although they would resist similar claims against indigenous employers. On this point nationalism works in the same direction as communism and socialism. Consequently in the larger states, whose governments are not dwarfish in comparison with big Northamerican firms, the condition of the employees of foreign firms is considerably better than that of other workers: in Chile, for instance, the Anaconda and the other Northamerican mining companies pay wages which are several times higher than the national average, and provide medical services and housing which are also much better than those which ordinary workers have. True, their camps remain as much as ever the foci of industrial unrest but this is chiefly due to frustration generated by isolation and the rather dismal social atmosphere of the mining camps (caused partly by the ethnocentric presumption of the Northamerican managers) and to the strong tradition of loyalty to the communist controlled trade unions and the communist party itself.

In the newer manufacturing industries, created when the power of the labour unions in the United States had already taught the businessmen some respect for the workers, labour relations seem to be good, and indeed better than in most native owned industries. Industrias Kaiser Argentina, for instance, claims to have a better record in the matter of labour disputes than any other large firm in that country.

Owing to mechanization and automation, and the impact of the more liberal spirit of labour relations at home, the foreign companies operating in Latin America on the whole stand now in the vanguard of progress in the matter of working conditions; and indeed this very fact causes some resentment among the native employers. So the foreign employers are blamed for acting badly in the past as well as for being too good in the present.

The oil companies have always meddled in politics. Given the nature of their trade, they could hardly avoid it because they needed concessions of wide stretches of land which they could obtain only from governments. In the struggle for concessions between rival companies the issue depended on influencing a government by blandishments, threats and bribes. According to Romulo Betancourt, it was with the aid of such weapons that Standard Oil and Shell have eliminated their smaller rivals and struggled with each other. By resorting to such means, these companies aggravated or at least helped to perpetuate the gangster-like character of Venezuelan politics. The only argument which could be adduced in their defence is that such methods were necessary in dealing with the Venezuelan dictators and their henchmen; and that companies who refused to enter into criminal collusions would be ousted by their less scrupulous competitors. This argument is strictly correct, but it hardly exonerates the companies from guilt: no really honest person or institution would enter into collusion with criminals because that was the only way of making large profits quickly; and the shareholders and directors of the oil companies could hardly plead poverty as an extenuating circumstance.

Perez Jimenez was one of the worst Latin American dictators in recent times, and what is known about his relations with the oil firms and the government of the United States seems to confirm the standard marxist view of economic imperialism. Under the dictatorship of Medina Angarita the share of the Venezuelan government in the proceeds from the sale of oil amounted to 27·3%. In 1945, after the fall of the dictator and a victory in the first free elections in the country's history, Accion Democratica came to power and raised the state's share to 36%, and just before its fall to 37·6% After the *cuartelazo*, the military junta brought it down to 30%; and when Perez Jimenez established his supremacy he further lowered it to 25·7%. There is no concrete evidence that either the US government or the oil companies helped Perez Jimenez to seize power, but when Eisenhower decorated him with the Legion of Merit, the eulogy of the tyrant contained a reference to his activities before he became 'the president'. After his fall, the elected president Romulo Betancourt succeeded in raising the government's share to 60%.

In 1950 the rate of profit of the oil companies operating in Venezuela was 2·6 times higher than that of other Northamerican firms in Venezuela, and 2·2 times higher than the rate of profit on all Northamerican investments in Latin America. By 1954 Northamerican firms invested in Canada five times as much capital as in Venezuela but the sum of profits obtained in Venezuela was greater. We shall shortly examine the significance and the causes of this discrepancy.

Interference of foreign businessmen in Latin American politics did not begin with the discovery of oil. On the contrary, it goes back at least to the middle of the nineteenth century when Peruvian guano and nitrates were the chief prizes. Later a self-made English businessman named North who succeeded in obtaining control over a very large part of the Chilean nitrate mining, helped (perhaps decisively) the Chilean landowning and capitalist oligarchy to overthrow the president Balmaceda whose etatistic and somewhat egalitarian economic policies, combined with mildly populist authoritarian tendencies, displeased them as well as the British investors.

Self-seeking foreign incursions into Latin American politics did not spread the benefits of free enterprise but it is doubtful whether they wrought much harm upon the nations because usually, if they were successful, they merely led to a replacement of one dictator or clique by another of similar moral stature. When the Northamerican marines intervened in Cuba and other Caribbean countries in order to protect the interests of New York bankers, these countries were ruled by rapacious tyrants; and it is not self-evident that their inhabitants would have benefited had these tyrants been able to retain all the revenue from the custom duties instead of having to surrender a part of it to foreign creditors. Even the argument that the local tyrants would have spent this money locally is not valid because their normal habit was to place a very substantial part of their gains in foreign banks. Sending gunboats to force a Cipriano Castro to pay his debts was certainly not an act of altruism but there is no evidence to suggest that his exactions would otherwise have been any smaller.

It seems that the two most harmful cases of foreign interference in Latin American politics were those already mentioned: the participation of the agents of British investors in overthrowing Balmaceda and the encouragement given by the US government and the oil companies to the military plotters who in 1948 overthrew the first government of Romulo Betancourt. In both cases leaders who were trying to do some good were replaced by money grabbers. On the whole, however, intervention by foreign governments or private pressure groups do not seem to have made Latin American politics more troubled than it would have been otherwise; disorder and looting were rife long before foreign investors appeared on the scene, and in more recent times they were at least as intense in the countries where foreign investments are negligible (as in Paraguay or Haiti) as in countries which have received an appreciable amount of capital from abroad. In preventing desirable reforms the indigenous landlords and military men played a decisive role.*

The majority of businessmen who went to seek their fortunes in the backward countries did not observe the code of behaviour which was customary in their home countries. This was partly due to the mere fact of expatriation which almost always produces a weakening of the social bonds and a diminution of the respect for customs. Of at least equal importance, however, is the corrupting influence of an environment riddled with parasitism and venality: contact men and fixers insist on offering their services in passing bribes or avoiding taxes and tariffs, and some of them have so much power that they can victimize a businessman who does not avail himself of their services. Coerced by threats and insistent soliciting even a businessman used to a higher standard of business ethics often succumbs to the temptation of a short cut to profit. Another important aspect of the situation is that a lawless environment attracts criminals and semi-criminals from better ordered countries where they have less scope for their talents. Cuba, for instance, especially during the rule of Batista, was a haven for Northamerican gangsters and vice merchants for whom life in the United States was becoming too difficult.

The outcome of interaction between a national economy and a foreign company depends not only on the nature of the business and the morality of the partners but also on their relative size. Not even the largest Northamerican company (General Motors) has assets of the same magnitude as the total wealth of Argentina or Mexico; and therefore no Northamerican firm can browbeat a large Latin American country without the wholehearted support of the US government. The situation is very different in the small central American countries where the United Fruit Company has such enormous economic power that it can exercise irresistible pressure upon the weak and indigent governments. As it dominates the economy of several countries, the company can play them off against each other and threaten each of them

* The Japanese ruling class has reacted very differently to the foreign commercial incursions; which proves that the internal factors are of at least equal importance.

with a transfer of business to the others. Later, in connection with the revolution in Guatemala, we shall examine more closely the question of whether the only possibilties are total submission or expropriation. As far as parasitism is concerned, what is decisive is that by controlling the major portion of the most fertile lands, the railways and shipping, and by having a large share in the distributive trades and finance, the United Fruit Company can practise all the usual vices of a monopolist who cannot be challenged. The situation is one of power without responsibility; and it is arguable that it might be better for countries such as San Salvador or Honduras to become entirely the property of the Company because this would make everything an asset of the company, whereas in the present situation their economies are geared to extracting profits for foreign investors from a section of the territory, and every other item of national wealth is regarded as unimportant. These countries would probably benefit if the United Fruit Company were to assume the functions of an official government, like the British and the Dutch East Indies Companies in the eighteenth century, because then the consequences of monopolistic practices would not need to be aggravated by the disorderly parasitism of native soldiers and politicians.

If nationalism did not matter, the small Caribbean countries could gain a great deal by becoming a part of the United States like Puerto Rico because they could then have representatives in Washington who would defend their interests, whilst at present their venal diplomats constitute no counterweight to the lobbies acting on behalf of Northamerican financial and commercial pressure groups.

The foreign mining companies are blamed for inflicting misery upon the peoples of Latin America but these peoples were poor before the companies arrived. Against the accusation that they were and are depriving the indigenous governments of the opportunity to use the natural resources for the benefit of the inhabitants we must set the fact that these governments were (and in many cases still are) incapable of organizing production on the requisite scale. If ore or oil is left under the ground it is of no greater benefit than if it had been carried away by foreigners. What the country loses in the latter case is a potential opportunity to use this wealth more profitably in the more or less distant future. In contrast to the early mining undertakings of the Spaniards, which caused the native peoples great misery, the sins of the Northamerican and European mining and oil companies are of omission rather than of commission: they have certainly not ruined any of the countries in which they operated although they can be accused of doing little or nothing to help. Nevertheless, it must be remembered that they constitute the mainstay of public finance in the countries in which they operate. No doubt the share going to the governments could in some cases be increased, but there are limits to these possibilities. It must be noted, however, that threats of confiscation induce the foreign companies to seek quick gains to the detriment of socially more useful long-term profitability. We have here a case of a self-verifying belief: by acting on the assumption that foreign capital acts to the detriment of the national economy, the governments do their best to ensure that the capital will behave in just this way.

The past cases of expropriation of foreign companies may have been inevitable on political grounds but they produced no direct economic benefits, because mismanagement and corruption have more than absorbed the share which previously went to foreign capitalists. That windfall gains produce no wealth is most convincingly shown by the example of Venezuela. Apart from Kuwait, no country in the world obtains so much money per head from the sale of goods ready-made by nature. If the influx of money from abroad were a sufficient condition of prosperity, Venezuela would be one of the most prosperous countries in the world; whereas in fact it is one of the poorest – much poorer indeed than is generally believed, because the indices of consumption calculated in dollars are swollen by the extremely high prices of goods in Venezuela. The revenue from oil inflated the domestic prices and stultified domestic industries and agriculture by making them unable to compete with the imported products. There is a strong analogy here with the situation in Spain in the sixteenth century and in Portugal in the eighteenth. It might be objected that the Gold Rushes in Alaska, Australia and elsewhere during the nineteenth century produced no such effects, but then, in proportion to the existing stock of precious metals, the increments were small and were not canalized into a country with small total wealth. It seems that the ills wrought by the foreign oil and mining companies upon the countries where they operated stem not so much from the mere fact of carrying away large profits as from the moral effects of this activity upon the economic ethics of the inhabitants, already deficient in this respect.

The employment of foreigners in the highest posts inspires much bitterness against foreign companies; and indeed the propaganda in favour of nationalizing them is largely put out by people who hope to displace the highly paid foreigners. Whether these complaints are justified depends on the circumstances. On the one hand, it is true that national solidarity amongst the expatriates is usually sufficiently strong to lead to a certain amount of favouritism; but on the other hand it is equally true that the countries of Latin America do lack qualified technical and managerial personnel, and that Northamerican and European managers are on the whole more industrious and reliable than their Latin American counterparts. Naturally the supply of suitable native personnel varies enormously from country to country: it is almost sufficient in Chile and Argentina but very deficient in Ecuador or Venezuela. Animosity towards foreign residents appears to be little (or even inversely) related to the need for their services, and seems to be greatest in the countries which need them most. This seems to be due to the greater discrepancy in the ways of living and feeling between expatriates from highly industrialized countries and the inhabitants of less developed lands. As the numbers involved are infinitesimal in relation to the population, the removal of foreign personnel would perhaps satisfy national pride but would not leave much wealth to be redistributed. The roots of friction in this respect are chiefly psychological: putting highly paid personnel from countries with advanced material culture (and particularly sanitation) in the midst of indigent populations cannot fail to generate contempt on one side and envy and resentment on the other.

A comparison of Latin America with Australia, Canada and New Zealand brings us to the fundamental questions of economic imperialism. For if foreign capital were inevitably to bring ruin upon the countries which it penetrated, then Australia and Canada should be among the poorest countries in the world, as they have the highest amount of foreign investments per head. Why should the British commercial enterprise bring prosperity to Australia but poverty to Chile or Mexico? Why should North-american capitalism be beneficent in Canada but maleficent in Venezuela? We can hardly suppose that British or Northamerican capitalists and managers were so much kinder to the Australians or Canadians simply because they spoke the same language (which anyway is only partially true in the case of Canada). True, a common language and a similarity of customs facilitate collaboration, but the ruthlessness with which capitalists have frequently treated employees of their own nationality proves that this could not have been a crucial factor. The true explanation is that in the British dominions circumstances favoured the productive rather than parasitic orientation of capitalism, irrespective of whether the capital was domestic or foreign. There were no conquered peoples, no all-powerful landlords, no dictators, no large armies ready to suppress popular uprisings; and, in view of law-abidingness, the spoils of office did not constitute the most glittering prizes. Politics, therefore, did not offer the most profitable field for investment; and parasitism could not flourish because of the absence of victims; for the workers (particularly in Australia) soon organized themselves into powerful unions; and being neither illiterate nor miserable they ceased in time to procreate excessively, and thus eliminated 'the industrial reserve army'. The absence of despotism and oppression constituted a necessary condition of a productive orientation of capitalism which in turn created the conditions for development of democracy. We have here one more instance of circular causality.

In Latin America, as we saw earlier, circular causality operated in the opposite direction but, although foreign businessmen often took part in predation, their activities were of a less parasitic nature than those of indigenous capitalists.

In the bigger countries neither so-called dollar imperialism nor the minor European variety can be regarded as important obstacles to economic progress. Foreign firms probably do more good than harm in the field of manufacturing. The balance between beneficent and evil effects is rather questionable in extractive industries; but even if the shares of the host governments in the proceeds are not quite sufficient, the loss as things stand at present is small in comparison with the waste caused by corruption and red tape. In agriculture the Northamerican companies contributed their share to soil erosion, but they are no worse offenders than the indigenous agriculturists. The wages which they pay compare badly with those of agricultural labour in their own country but they are still higher than those paid by indigenous landlords. The abuses still perpetrated by foreign firms in the bigger countries of Latin America could easily be eliminated if politicians and officials ceased to seek and accept bribes. The situation in the small countries of central America dominated by the United Fruit Company is different.*

The former European colonies were governed by a civil service which developed some sense of loyalty towards the subjects, and whose decisions were not guided solely by monetary considerations. In contrast, government by a commercial company, exercising its power by bribing politicians and officials, offers very few advantages.

---

* My forthcoming book *Pathology of African Development* offers an examination of neo-colonialism in Africa in comparison with the old colonialism and the dollar imperialism discussed here.

CHAPTER FOUR

ECONOMIC CONTORTIONS

Constriction of the Market

LINKED inseparably to parasitism, but deriving their strength from other sources as well, there are various other factors which impede economic progress. The most obvious is the smallness of the markets, due in some cases to the sparseness of the population and the difficulties of transport, combined with obstacles to foreign trade, and aggravated everywhere by the extremely unequal income distribution. In very small countries the first two factors suffice to arrest economic development: clearly, no large-scale industry could exist by supplying only the markets of Haiti or San Salvador. Such states must either form part of a larger economic community or remain on a primitive level. The area of economic co-operation need not coincide with state borders if tariffs are low, but in most countries of Latin America they are high, often to the point of being prohibitive. This is partially due to the desire to protect nascent industries, but the heavy impositions which fall upon goods not produced in the country indicate that this is not the principal motive. In fact, the chief reason for the heaviness of the tariffs seems to be the ease of collecting them as compared to other forms of taxation. Owing to the prevalence of tax evasion and the resistance of the wealthy to fiscal reforms, the governments would find it very difficult to replace the income lost through a lowering of the tariffs by revenue from direct taxation.

The combination of very high tariffs with administrative corruption and inefficiency encourages smuggling, the prevalence of which has serious effects on the conduct of business as it puts solid firms at a disadvantage. The firms which keep proper accounting and refuse to enter into illegal deals have to pay much more for some of the goods which they require.

In order to overcome the handicaps imposed by the size of the national markets a Latin American Common Market has been proposed, but too much hope must not be placed in this project as Latin America in no way constitutes an economic unit. The tariff barriers in Europe are purely arbitrary and are related little if at all to any obstacles to transport. With very few exceptions, continuity of settlements and roads is complete. Not so in Latin America where the centres of settlement are isolated from each other. Even in minute Hispaniola transport between Santo Domingo and Port au Prince is difficult. It is cheaper to ship goods from Peru to Japan than to Brazil, or even than to send them overland from the southernmost to the northernmost end of the country. Even in the southern part of South America this is true; the freight charges from Buenos Aires to London are smaller than from Buenos Aires to Santiago de Chile. The distance by sea from the Brazilian ports is shorter to Europe than to Ecuador, and Mexico is far nearer to Canada than to Argentina, Chile or Uruguay. So, a lowering of tariffs within Latin America would not produce a great increase in trade, particularly as the national economies are in no way complementary. Why then a customs union for Latin America? Would it not be more profitable for Mexico to have free trade with the USA, or for Argentina to join the European Common Market, or just to have freer trade all round?

There is only one argument against free trade with Europe or Northamerica: it is that such trade would lead to the concentration of industrial production in the more advanced countries, with the less advanced remaining permanently in their role of suppliers of raw materials. On the other hand, a union between countries on more or less the same level of development would lead to more equitable division of labour. This argument, however, can be applied to the relationships between the Latin American countries as well: if it would be harmful for Mexico to have free trade with the USA, why should it be less harmful for Guatemala to have a customs union with Mexico – the community of language would hardly mitigate the effects of economic domination. Argentinian business men exploit Paraguay no less than Argentina was ever exploited by the British, and in all countries the capital cities exploit the provinces.

The argument that free trade is conducive to economic progress is unanswerable so long as we assume perfect mobility of labour and capital, and exclude non-economic factors and considerations. If labour is not as mobile as capital, discrepancies between their movements may cause distress in some regions. It is conceivable though unlikely that income per head in Britain and Argentina treated as one unit would be higher if all the manufacturing was done in Britain and all the agriculture in Argentina, but such a division of labour would require continuous transfer of population from Argentina to Britain, which neither nation would like or even allow. It is certain that mass poverty would disappear from Mexico in one generation if that country joined the USA, and its starving inhabitants were allowed to seek jobs there, but such a solution would encounter such strong emotional obstacles on both sides that it can be ruled out. Emotional obstacles to free migration might be less strong within Latin America but they are by no means negligible, particularly between countries of differing racial composition, and therefore the foregoing argument applies to the project of a Common Market in Latin America as well. (1)

Some freeing of trade would, no doubt, be to the advantage of the countries of Latin America, but there is no valid reason why the lowering of barriers should take place precisely within the area united only by common traditions and language, and neither by economic complementarity nor by proximity in terms of transport. For the minute republics of central America some form of economic integration is a necessary condition of progress, and the same applies to a lesser extent to Uruguay, but most other republics are quite big enough for rapid development: Argentina, Colombia, Mexico, Peru, let alone Brazil are huge in comparison with any European country apart from Russia. Moreover, a small diminution of inequality of income would enlarge the market for local industries more than any possible outlets abroad.

It has been suggested that the proposed Latin American Common Market would bring greater benefits than a mere lowering of the barriers to trade because it would entail the creation of organs of economic co-ordination. This, however, is the most dubious argument of all. It is very unlikely that anyone who cannot manage a corner shop would know how to run a chain store. Likewise, it is very improbable that if we put together a number of countries none of which is governed passably well, a better order will emerge and that they will be able to govern themselves better jointly than they do severally. As far as the quality of government is concerned there is no virtue in size, as can be seen from the fact that the best governed countries in Latin America are fairly small: Uruguay, Chile, Costa Rica. This does not of course, mean that small size ensures good government – there are many examples in central America to show that this is not so – but it does suggest that good government is easier to attain in medium-sized states. It is arguable that Brazil is too big and heterogeneous to be governed effectively. As to the organs which would co-ordinate the economic affairs of Latin America, it is most probable that they would reproduce on a larger scale all the vices which corrode the administration of the individual republics, and add another layer to the deadweight of parasitic bureaucracy. It seems, moreover, that the campaign in favour of the Common Market for Latin America is conducted chiefly by the prospective candidates for jobs in its administrative organs. It must be added that concern for defence against the menace of an invasion (which is the most important argument in favour of a European Union) has little bearing upon the problem of the economic integration of Latin America.

Outside the lilliputian republics of central America, where size really is a severely limiting factor, the chief cause of constriction of the market is the exclusion therefrom of the rural population, which except in Argentina and Uruguay is almost complete. This population buys derisory amounts of goods, and lives under subsistence economy because of the general poverty. Poverty cannot be eliminated so long as production is insufficient, but expansion of production is held back by the smallness of the market constricted by poverty and inequality. We have here one more instance of a vicious circle.

Unless there are forces which constrict it, the smallness of the market is not in itself an insuperable obstacle to the growth of industry: all markets have been small originally and industries have grown nevertheless. A new factory throws a certain amount of goods on the market, but at the same time it pays its employees, shareholders, suppliers, etc., and this money may find its way into the hands of people who want to buy the goods. But because the process of expansion is circular it must be gradual and harmonious: in a commercial economic system an ultra-modern factory, established within a primitive economy is doomed to bankruptcy. A large part of the economic difficulties of Latin America stems from the tendency to jump the stages; to concentrate on grandiose schemes and to neglect more prosaic but more immediately useful investments.

Latin America has the advantage of its countries never having suffered from generalized crises of overproduction, although on many occasions they were severely afflicted by their inability to sell the goods produced for export. The high propensity of the wealthy to spend, which has the grave disadvantage of depriving the economy of the capital needed for investment, has the advantage that the unequal distribution of income does not produce an excess of savings over investments, which on many occasions brought down prices and caused unemployment in the highly developed capitalist countries.

The chief factor which constricts production is the large share thereof which is more or less parasitically appropriated. In order to appreciate its importance we must take into account all the goods and services which would be produced by the present parasites if they had to give something of real value for the commodities which they now obtain more or less for nothing. The circular flow of goods and services cannot acquire the momentum sufficient to carry it into the phase of self-accelerating expansion because too much of it is siphoned off into parasitic or semi-parasitic consumption.

In addition to 'purer' forms of parasitism which have been discussed under separate headings, the exorbitant trading profits require special attention. Distribution of goods is just as essential as production, and the profits of a merchant constitute the price of his services. If he obtains his income by small margins of profit on a large turnover he produces more services – that is to say, his productivity is greater – than if he gains the same amount by high profit margins on a small turnover. In Latin America the latter procedure is the rule.

As in all economic predicaments there is a vicious circle here: if the traders worked on smaller margins of profit, they could sell more and, in consequence, not only could the consumers get more goods for their money but the greater production would generate more income which in turn would swell the demand for their goods, thus further stimulating production and so on. The high profit margins keep the circular flow of goods at a lower volume.

High profit margins are normal among the traders of the pre-industrial world, precluded from working on high turnovers by the undeveloped state of transport, and the persistence of this tendency has been reinforced in Latin America by the atavism of the gold mine-seeking mentality, which produces a preference for a smaller gain here and now over a much larger one in the long run. Businessmen so inclined do not care if they alienate a customer for ever, provided they can extract from him an exorbitant profit once. This bias is connected with a low valuation of work which makes a profit on fewer operations appear more desirable than a profit requiring a greater number. An even more important factor is the instability of conditions. The dangers of wars and revolutions play a considerable role in forming the mentality of businessmen but even more important is the uncertainty caused by violent and unpredictable changes in the policies of the governments, who often suddenly institute or abolish without warning laws, tariffs, taxes, exchange controls, import or export restrictions. Some of the laws and regulations are clearly absurd and impossible to follow, and most businessmen circumvent them – just as they circumvent those which are wise and just; and illegality always implies uncertainty. Moreover, the expansion of governmental control over economic affairs made the businessmen dependent in many ways on the good will of officials (whom they try to influence by arguments, intrigues, bribes and threats); and this means that shifts in ministry personnel have serious repercussions on business prospects, and that the profitability of a venture may depend on the outcome of a struggle for power between bureaucratic cliques. In addition, the expenses incurred in cultivating the goodwill of the officials have to be allowed for.

As the countries of Latin America are dependent on a wide assortment of imported goods, but pay for them by exporting one or two staple commodities, even relatively minor fluctuations in the prices of the latter engender violent general dislocation. Expectation of such happenings discourages long-term planning and sound business practices. The possibility of expropriations introduces a further element of insecurity. Private enterprise can become profitable in a socially useful direction only if it can expect to reap the rewards of building up a reputation for cheapness and good service. Under conditions of insecurity these rewards must seem very uncertain, and not worth pursuing at the cost of forgoing opportunities of making quick and unscrupulous gains. Part of the insecurity stems from the political turmoil due to economic difficulties for which the anti-social conduct of business is partly responsible . . . again a vicious circle.

Selling on credit has helped substantially to widen the market in opulent societies but it has a double-edged effect in the poor countries where defaults are common. If payment is uncertain then the price must include a large premium for the risk. In Chile, for instance, it is quite common to add as much as 60% to the cash price as insurance against default, in addition to what is needed to cover the interest. As it is the customers who pay for it all, this amounts to a tax on the honest for the benefit of the defaulters. Some merchants estimate that about a quarter of the buyers on credit either decamp with the goods or return them in a damaged state. Many of the defaulters are decent people forced into such behaviour by poverty, but nevertheless, knowing that so many have defaulted, those who pay feel a bit foolish. Moreover, knowing how large are the profit margins, many customers feel morally justified in dodging the payment. Such a situation hardly fosters habits of prudence and responsibility.

It remains to be added that as wages are low, shops, offices and workshops abound in semi-idle personnel with the consequence that productivity is low; so that the wages cannot be raised.

Changeability of laws and regulations, combined with prevalence of evasion, favour mushroom get-rich-quick firms, and handicap solid business. Absurdly high tariffs coupled with inability to prevent massive smuggling produce a situation in which practically every merchant is implicated in illegal deals while unrealistic social security laws compel most of the employers to evade them. In Chile, for instance, every employer is obliged to pay the state Social Security Fund a contribution amounting to about 60% of what he pays to the employee. As the benefits to the employee of a given category do not depend on his wage, and as they are negligible and fantastically out of proportion to the contribution, the workers acquiesce in the procedure whereby the employers declare that they pay their employees much less than in fact they do. Indeed, a strict enforcement of the existing social security laws would cause widespread unemployment because many employers could not afford to keep their personnel. More than a hundred years ago economists came to the conclusion that a tax on labour produces unemployment, and this view has been reiterated by a number of Chilean economists who have also pointed out that when the workers do not earn enough to feed themselves properly, it is absurd to divert more than a third of the payment made by the employers into payment for social security, particularly as these payments cause much more unemployment than they alleviate.

These absurd laws can be easily evaded by small employers who do not keep proper accounts, particularly if most of their payments are in kind, while for bigger firms the risks of concealment are greater. Firms employing large numbers of unionized workers, with whom they have collective agreements, cannot evade these laws at all, with the result that the economies of scale are greatly reduced. Domestic service is the form of employment which (to the detriment of general welfare) is most stimulated by these laws, because it is impossible to verify what people pay to domestic servants, most of whose renumeration is in any case in kind. Another arrangement which favours more primitive and less productive forms of business is the turnover tax which the firms which have no proper accountancy easily evade.

The way in which public transport is operated in Santiago de Chile illustrates the pernicious effects of shortsightedness of the legislators, administrators and businessmen. While in London and Paris (where labour is dear) all the buses have conductors, in Santiago (where labour is cheap and the unemployed abound) the drivers have to sell the tickets; and in consequence they need up to three times as much time to cover their routes as they would if they could confine themselves to driving.* Nervously exhausted, trying to make up for lost time by speeding, often counting money while driving, the bus drivers cause innumerable accidents, and their vehicles look as if they came from a battle front. Even from the standpoint of the profits of the bus

---

* This arrangement can work reasonably well even in a big city provided the buses are seldom full and the stops are widely spaced.

companies, a simple calculation would show that the cost of employing conductors would be less than the cost of damage and excessive wear and tear caused by bad driving, not to mention the cost of having to operate more buses than would be required if they travelled with fewer interruptions. From a general point of view we should also include the cost of damages and delays caused to other road users and to passengers, and of injury to the health of the drivers.

The smallness of the market facilitates monopolies, because of which prices are higher and the volume of production lower than they would otherwise be. The prevalence of monopolies is, of course, in no way a peculiarity of Latin America, and innumerable examples of scandalous profiteering can be found in the most highly industrialized countries, some of them worse than those which occur in Latin America: for instance, unlike British-made electric bulbs, Chilean bulbs are not deliberately made to have a short life and last many times longer. Nevertheless, on the whole, monopolies cause even more harm in Latin America than they do in more highly industrialized countries because they operate within poverty-stricken economies, where every restriction of production causes serious hardship, and because the effects of monopolistic practice are aggravated by other circumstances tending to constrict the market. Moreover, the big monopolies of the highly industrialized nations operate on such a scale that reductions in cost of production depend more on technical progress than on expansion of scale, whereas in most branches of industry in Latin America radical reduction in the cost of production could be achieved by expanding its volume.

Gambling

The average Latin American spends a great deal more on gambling in proportion to his earnings than does his European counterpart, and he never saves. The money which remains after the direst necessities have been provided for goes into lotteries and various forms of betting. The rich have their Jockey Clubs and casinos, and licences to run them constitute important items of political patronage. In Buenos Aires the Conservative politicians had a monopoly on roulette until Peron nationalized the casinos. In Brazil the son-in-law of the president Vargas had the biggest casino. But the largest hotbed of gambling in Latin America (if not in the world) was Cuba, particularly during the dictatorship of Batista, where the biggest gambling racketeers, who had to flee from the United States, had congregated.

Lotteries are run not only by the state but also locally by the provinces and the municipalities as well. In this respect Latin America is not, of course absolutely unique: many European states run lotteries, and elsewhere privately-run football pools, horse or dog races perform a similar function. The difference lies only in the importance of the stakes in relation to income. The bulk of gambling in most countries of Latin America is done through privately organized, sometimes legally prohibited, systems of gambling, such as Argentinian *la quiniela* and Brazilian *jogo do bicho*.

Connected with the prevalence of gambling is the paucity of savings. Even before the Second World War, when money was stabler, the saving deposits in Brazil amounted only to one-seventieth of what they were in France, which had roughly the same population. The sum total of saving deposits in Luxemburg, whose population was 150 times smaller, equalled half the amount in Brazil. Calculated in Swiss francs, deposits in savings banks per head amounted in 1937 to: 540 in Norway; 324 in Luxembourg; 297 in France; 274 in Switzerland; 254 in Holland; 20 in Chile and 4 in Brazil. Owing to divergent interpretations of what constitutes a savings deposit, these indices contain a substantial margin of error, but they indicate the order of difference. It must be noted that in the countries where private saving is most intensive gambling is either forbidden or heavily taxed.

In these days of corporate and state investment private saving no longer constitutes the chief means of accumulation of capital but its role is not negligible. What is even more important is the influence of gambling habits on the will to work and to provide for the future by systematic effort.

The Balance of Payments

With the exception of Venezeula, the countries of Latin America live in a state of permanent financial crisis. In spite of massive aid from the USA the net flow of capital is decidedly outward, as the following approximate figures for 1961 show:

Inflow (*millions of US dollars*)		*Outflow* (*millions of US dollars*)	
US private investment	203	receipts of US investors	860
US government aid	721	receipt of investors in other foreign countries	100
non-US investment	315	capital sent abroad by citizens of Latin	
World Bank	200	American countries	700
	1,439		1,660
		net outflow	221

It can be seen that aid does not match the flow of capital from Latin America motivated chiefly by fear of political upheavals.

With the growth of the population and the progress of urbanization, the need for manufactured products has been steadily growing, and it can easily be shown that this need cannot be satisfied by imports. The bottleneck is not, of course, the availability of goods for importation but the difficulty of increasing exports in an appropriate measure, because these consist of raw materials and agricultural produce the production of which is more narrowly limited by nature. In some cases the supply of exportable raw materials actually diminished. Guano, for instance, which for a long time was the most important item in Peruvian exports has been exhausted. Large stretches of land on which bananas were cultivated in central America are now eroded. In some other cases the demand has declined or even disappeared. For example: the Brazilian natural rubber was displaced from the world markets by the output of the Malayan plantations. The nitrates – which formed the quasi-totality of the

Chilean exports before the First World War – became valueless when the Germans invented artificial fertilizers. Another kind of difficulty is illustrated by the situation in Argentina where the growth of the population, and the distribution of purchasing power amongst the wider stratum, have diminished the quantity of meat and cereals available for export. Venezuela is the only country in Latin America where the production of exportable raw materials grew faster than the population during the last thirty years.

Only industrialization can provide manufactured goods for a population which grows more quickly than the quantity of exportable raw materials; but during the initial stages industrialization creates more difficulties than it solves, as it increases the need for the import of machines.

It is often claimed that the situation of the countries exporting raw materials has been aggravated by unfavourable changes in trading terms: that the same quantity of raw materials can buy fewer goods than before. According to one calculation by United Nations experts, raw materials can on average buy only 60% of the quantity of manufactured goods which they could buy in 1873. These calculations, however, are based on so many arbitrary assumptions that their value is exceedingly dubious. They do not take the improvements in quality into account and regard, say, a car of 1920 as equivalent to a 1960 model; and, as more wheat or iron ore is needed to buy a car now than 40 years ago, they conclude that those who sell cars are trading more advantageously in comparison with those who sell wheat. However, even if we reject this conclusion, the fact remains that nobody claims that trading terms have actually moved to the advantage of the countries exporting raw materials. This seems strange in view of the growth of the population, and the fact that the supply of manufactured goods can be augmented more quickly and more easily than the supply of raw materials. The explanation seems to be that the industry is highly monopolistic whereas agriculture is not.

A very unequal distribution of wealth aggravates the balance of payments in several ways: it puts money into the hands of people who are more likely to spend it abroad, travelling or even living there for long periods, as the rich Latin Americans commonly do. In addition, for reasons of snobbery and habits formed long ago, they usually prefer foreign goods and despise local products, sometimes with no justification.

Even in less troubled times many rich Latin Americans kept large sums in foreign banks. Nowadays it seems elementary prudence. In some countries the policy of the government seems to be designed to help them in this matter. In Chile, for instance, by maintaining the exchange rate of the escudo far above its relative purchasing power, the government (in addition to fostering smuggling and injuring domestic industry) incites people to send money abroad by making it extremely profitable to do so: converted into dollars the capital will buy much more abroad than it will in Chile. It must be added that, notwithstanding a chronic trade deficit and the extremely high tariffs, there are no restrictions on the export of capital from Chile.*

The Scarcity of Capital

The insufficiency of capital available for investment is usually considered to be the chief obstacle to economic progress. This, however, is only partially true. Although in a country like Paraguay or Bolivia there is very little wealth available for anything, in the richer countries of Latin America the unproductive use of existing funds constitutes as important an obstacle to economic progress as the paucity of wealth.

In the countries which are now in the vanguard of economic progress, the inequality of incomes was very great during the nineteenth century. This inequality permitted a rapid increase of productive equipment because the rich were willing to save a large proportion of their incomes and invest it in developing production; this was largely due to the influence of the Protestant ethic. The extreme inequality of income in Latin America does not produce equivalent results because of the very strong inclination to lavish spending among the rich.

In Chile 280,000 persons – who constitute 9% of the income-receiving population – receive 43% of the national income; whereas 2,700,000 workers and other employees – who constitute 91% – receive the remaining 57%. The aggregate saving amounted during the recent years to 10% of the national income; 6% being the contribution of the employers and owners

* Written in 1961.

of wealth. This means that the average income of the first category is 8·5 times higher than that of the second, while their rate of saving is 14 times higher; which is low in comparison with the equivalent ratios in economically highly developed countries. The Chilean owners of income producing property consume 64% of their income, save 21% and pay 14·7% in taxes. The same class in Britain consume 30·5%, save 27·4% and pay 42% in taxes. If this class in Chile consumed only the same percentage of their income as their British counterparts, the Chilean rate of investment could double. In Nicaragua, if the 1% who receive the highest incomes would save 10% of their income, the rate of investment would increase by 50%.

Without a change in the mentality of the wealthy classes, indigenous private enterprise cannot develop production sufficiently to raise the standard of living of the masses. The effects of the small propensity to save are aggravated by the tendency (discussed in the preceding section) to place such savings as are made in foreign banks. The combination of these two tendencies creates a vacuum into which foreign firms are drawn; and in which they can make extraordinary profits, owing to the weakness of the competition.

Where this mentality prevails completely, there are only two ways of promoting the growth of industry: one is by inviting foreign capital; the other is by setting up state-owned factories. In the latter case – even if sufficient funds can be raised through taxation – corruption and inefficient management can cripple state enterprise; as has happened with the railways in Argentina and Bolivia, or the extraction of oil in Mexico and Argentina, to mention only the best-known examples.

It remains to be mentioned that development of production is impaired by the channelling of investment into the construction of houses. For the whole of Latin America the investments in this field comprised over 50% of total investment. In Brazil this proportion at times reached 60% and in Colombia 65%. In Venezuela the construction of houses represents 7% of the national product, in the United States 5% and in Britain 4%. The social effects of these investments are determined by the fact that the houses built are mostly designed for the wealthy classes. In Brazil 80% of houses built from private funds were sold to the rich.

Inflation

Inflation constitutes a permanent feature of the economic life of Latin America. Not that it is absent elsewhere; as is well known, a secular trend toward higher prices has prevailed since the Middle Ages; and many European countries have suffered from wild inflation. In Europe very rapid inflation has occurred during and after wars, whereas this has not been the case in Latin America. If we compare only the times of peace, we find that inflation has been much more extreme in Latin America than in Europe. In 1814 a pound sterling was worth 2·55 Brazilian reis; in 1955 it was worth 235 milreis, that is to say 235,000 reis. In 1830 a pound sterling was worth 5·75 Chilean pesos; in 1955 it was worth 1,850, and in 1960 over 3,000. And we must take into account the enormous depreciation in the purchasing power of the pound sterling during this period. On the whole, inflation has been most intense in stagnant economies – in other words, the rate of growth and the rate of depreciation of the currency seem to be inversely correlated. However, it is only a general tendency and there are discrepancies. The rate of inflation has been highest in Bolivia where the total product grew least, and where the product per head declined at the yearly rate of 0·7 between 1946 and 1958. On the other hand, there was no inflation in Cuba whose economy was only a little less stagnant. In contrast Brazil, which had the second highest rate of growth, was fourth on the scale of inflation. In Venezuela, which had the highest rate of growth, the purchasing power of money remained almost constant between 1946 and 1956. It appears therefore that inflation is compatible with either economic growth or stagnation, and is not a necessary consequence of either. The following table illustrates the point. (see overleaf)

What are the causes of this phenomenon? The most important and the most immediate is the printing of banknotes to cover budgetary deficits, although bad organization and management of the banks also play their part. Since the Second World War the budgets of all the republics with the exception of Venezuela always had considerable deficits, which amounted to 10% in Brazil and Chile, and in Argentina was 65% in 1946 and 50% in 1957. These deficits are not incurred in order to finance an expansion of production, but to cover ordinary running expenses.

Country	1946–58 Mean Yearly Rate of Growth of the Total Product	1946–56 Mean Yearly Rate of Increase in the Cost of Living
Venezuela	9·0	4·7
Nicaragua	7·7	6·9
Mexico	5·7	7·8
Ecuador	4·4	3·5
El Salvador	5·8	5·9
Brazil	6·2	15·4
Peru	3·7	12·4
Colombia	4·3	9·6
Costa Rica	5·7	4·3
Panama	3·9	6·2
Cuba	1·8	1·4
Uruguay	1·9	9·1
Honduras	4·2	2·9
Paraguay	2·7	43·8
Chile	2·8	35·7
Guatemala	5·1	3·3
Argentina	1·7	19·8
Bolivia	0·6	63·0

An important factor of inflationary pressure is the extraordinarily large part of government expenditure which goes into salaries and wages: between 40 and 50%. In the USA the government spends only 15% of its budget on personnel, and in France 13·5%. In Chile in 1955 only 2% of the personnel employed by the government were engaged in activities contributing to production. A deficit incurred to finance investment in productive equipment may eventually augment the supply of goods to match the increase in the quantity of money; but, if spent on consumption, it cannot fail to have an inflationary effect.

The tendency towards deficitary budgeting is stimulated by the dependence on the receipts from exports of one or two commodities which, owing to fluctuations in prices, make budgetary forecasts difficult: while the peculiarities of national character accentuate the normal human tendency to count on gains which are not certain. This means that most of the errors in forecasting lead to a deficit. An even more important factor, however, is the structure of power.

Broadly speaking, inflation is the product of a political system in which there is nobody to compel the nation to live within their means. In Spain the prices began to rise faster when Franco's régime grew milder. In Russia the government can even decree a lowering of prices, an impossible feat in a democracy. In the French parliaments before de Gaulle, to mention one of many available examples, a majority could always easily be found to vote additional expenditure but not additional taxation. In Latin America even the dictators have seldom been strong enough to resist clamour for more expenditure than they could afford. A government yields to the pressure of various groups, each of which fights to increase its direct or indirect share in the expenditure, and resists taxation affecting its members. The line of least resistance is to concede their demands and to cover the deficit by printing money, because the reaction of the pressure groups to inflation is to clamour for more money for their members rather than to insist that printing should stop.

The pressures which cumulatively produce inflation have been strengthened by the growth of the labour unions and parties appealing to the lower classes. Inflation is a means whereby concessions can be continually made to the unions and populist parties without increasing the workers' share in real wealth. The marxists maintain that inflation has been deliberately promoted by financial oligarchs with precisely this aim in view – and this opinion might have some basis in fact. Even if it is not engineered, this is how inflation works: if prices rise too quickly, wages cannot keep pace. It must be noted, however, that inflation was common during the nineteenth century, that is to say, long before the supremacy of the oligarchs has been challenged by the mass movements. At that time inflation was a means of alleviating the heavy burden or debt incurred by the improvident but politically dominant landowners, by shifting it on to the entire population.

Once it has acquired a sufficient momentum inflation continues even if the causes which originally brought it into existence no longer operate: interest rates, profit margins, terms of contracts, habits of fixing wages become attuned to its impact. As many examples have proved, to reverse the process is even more painful than to let it continue, particularly as in the circumstances it is the wage and salary earners who are asked to bear the cost. Price control, though sometimes attempted, has never succeeded in Latin America because the administrative machinery is too inefficient and corrupt even in the best organized republics, and the decrees fixing prices have never been accompanied by an effective control and rationing of the supply. The only commodity whose price has occasionally been held down for considerable periods is labour. In consequence, all the attempts at monetary stabilization have exacerbated the conflicts between the classes.

Inflation has important moral effects: it acts as a deterrent to saving and an incentive to spend beyond one's means; it impedes calculation and provision for the future; and it stimulates improvidence and a fatalistic attitude to work and wealth. By making speculation more profitable than steady production or trade, inflation directs the energies of businessmen into parasitic channels. The spectacle of fortunes made by a sleight of hand fires resentment among the poor, and brings more support to subversive movements, which further aggravate insecurity and make it even more difficult to find a remedy based on a consensus of opinion. On the strictly economic side, inflation diverts capital into accumulation of stocks and real property to the disadvantage of productive efficiency.

CHAPTER FIVE

FORMS OF GOVERNMENT

Regulative and Decorative Constitutions

THE most important characteristic of a constitution (or of any law) is the extent to which it is obeyed; and the distinction between regulative and decorative constitutions is of greater importance than the classifications of constitutional jurisprudence. Conversely, we could classify polities according to the degree of constitutional hypocrisy – that is to say, the discrepancy between proclaimed principles and practice.

In no other region of the world have the constitutions been so purely decorative for so long. The basic laws of all the republics of Latin America have been copied from the constitution of the USA with some additions from France. At the time when Asia and Africa were still under the sway of despotism rooted in millennial tradition, when throughout Europe the monarchs by the grace of God were still regarded as the sole founts of authority – when even in Britain the functions of the monarchs had not yet become entirely ceremonial – the constitutions of Latin America proclaimed liberty, fraternity and equality, despite the legality of slavery and the severe property restrictions on franchise. Constitutions providing for representative government could acquire no regulative force in countries where the largest class consisted of slaves and serfs, where the entire pattern of social relations was thoroughly authoritarian, and where the class of economically independent prosperous townsmen (which everywhere constituted the backbone of liberal movements) did not exist. The imported ideology could not alter the fact that only authoritarian governments could function at all, but it did prevent their legitimization and stabilization.

Chastened by the insuperable difficulty of putting something stable in the place of what he destroyed, Simon Bolivar advocated in his later years elective life-long monarchy as the most suitable form of government for hispanic America. It is doubtful, however, whether such a system would have worked even if it had been introduced. In Poland a similar arrangement led to the complete erosion of royal authority and the disintegration of the kingdom. In any case, a number of dictators were virtually monarchs for life, and the chief source of strife was the lack of any accepted rule for peaceful transmission of supreme authority. Some of the dictators have tried to bequeath their positions to their sons and a few succeeded in forming semi-dynasties: the Lopez in Paraguay, the Guzman in Venezuela, the Somozas in the Nicaragua of our time. In early Mexico Augustin Iturbide crowned himself, and Santa Anna intended to do likewise, but both were overthrown.

Why were none of the dictators successful in founding a dynasty? In many republics simply because the forces of disorder, unleashed by the wars of independence, made stable government of any kind impossible. There were, however, more specific obstacles too. The Spanish dynasty retained much of its aura for several decades after independence, so that monarchism remained synonymous with advocacy of the restoration of Spanish rule. In the absence of suitable pretenders the partisans of independence could justify their actions only by espousing republican ideology in the name of which the English colonists threw off the tutelage of the Crown. Moreover, the landowning aristocracy did not wish to be subjected to firm control; and they always opposed the dictators who wanted to be masters rather than puppets, although they did not have enough sense of unity and organization to rule collectively – except in the case of Chile and later Argentina and Colombia. As we shall see in a moment, Brazil was another special case.

The rarity of external wars also militated against a monarchic solidification of autocracy; for very rarely (perhaps only in the case of Lopez in embattled Paraguay) were the dictators regarded as defenders of the nation. Some of the dictators did command true loyalty of at least some of their followers, but it was a strictly personal and untransferable loyalty, and therefore could provide no basis for orderly succession.

The sophisticated political ideology implanted in primitive and chaotic societies has produced unstable autocracies and a complete divorce between words and deeds in the sphere of politics.

Caudillismo

For long periods after independence many countries of Latin America had no government at all; warring bands disputed the ownership of the land, and the capital fell to each of them in turn. When one of the war-lords finally succeeded in subduing his rivals anarchy would subside, but the order thus established seldom survived the death of the tyrant, and usually collapsed even before then. True, a few dictators died from natural causes in the full enjoyment of power, but the usual fate of the Latin American dictators was to be ousted by force and possibly killed in the process. Even dictators of very long standing have suddenly been toppled; as was the case with Rosas in Argentina, Diaz in Mexico and Trujillo in the Dominican Republic, all of whom held absolute power for more than thirty years.

The structure of this type of government is very simple: the chief of the victorious faction installs his henchmen as generals, ministers and officials; and the functions of the government are limited to enforcement of obedience and exaction of wealth. If he is unusually conscientious and farsighted, the dictator may attempt to restrain his followers from ruining the country by following his example, and thus maintain a monopoly on extortion. Nevertheless he has to allow them some latitude in this respect for that is the price of their loyalty. Education is left mostly in the hands of the Church, while foreign firms take charge of such economic development as there is.

Many dictators belonged to old landowning families but this was by no means the rule. Incessant murderous struggles provided many opportunities for climbing the ladder to men of humble origins skilled in warfare and intrigue. Many of them were *mestizos* or mulattos or even pure Indians. As a general rule, the greater the chaos and more brutal the strife, the larger was the proportion of such self-made men among the dictators. Obversely, where struggles were limited by convention, and where the aristocracy achieved a consensus, the dictators usually came from the privileged class.

To give a few examples: Trujillo, the recently killed Dominican dictator, worked as a post office clerk at the age of sixteen and entered the National Guard (a hybrid between army and police) as a common soldier, although in the following year he was made a second lieutenant. Batista was a regular non-commissioned officer for a number of years before he organized the sergeants' revolt. A century earlier, the first 'president' of Venezuela, Paèz, was an illiterate *llanero* (Venezuelan brand of cowboy) who rose up in the ranks of Bolivar's army and became the ruler during the chaos which followed the latter's downfall. Fearless and endowed with matchless strength, he maintained his sway over the wild warriors by challenging those who disputed his authority to fist fights and beating them.

Melgarejo also began his career as an illiterate peasant. He joined the army and, taking part in affrays and battles attendant upon the incessant struggles between factions, he rose high enough to become a dictator of Bolivia. Among the adventures of this ignorant and dissolute tyrant one incident which took place in 1865 throws a particularly lurid light on the nature of political authority in barbarian America. At one point of his rule his rival, Belzú, organized a successful revolt and chased him out of the presidential palace. Melgarejo, however, evaded his pursuers by going where he was least expected: with a few loyal henchmen he entered the palace by the back door, forced his way into the rooms where Belzú was getting ready to appear on the balcony to receive a homage of the populace assembled on the square, killed him, and appeared on the balcony himself. Showing Belzu's dead body he shouted: 'Who is the boss now?' The crowd roared: 'Viva Melgarejo!'

Dictators are often depicted as the defenders of the privileged classes, which is true only in the sense that all of them exploited the poor. Many *caudillos* attacked the aristocracy ferociously, although none of them aimed at transforming the structure of society. Indeed, those who in virtue of their origins felt no attachment to the old families, were too ignorant to conceive the idea of a different social order. Out of revenge or cupidity they despoiled aristocrats, sometimes in considerable numbers, but once they and their principal henchmen acquired wealth, they turned against the poor.

The following extract from the memoirs of Garibaldi, who spent his youth as a roving soldier in South America, vividly illustrate the methods of governing and the policy towards the upper classes of the Argentinian dictator Rosas. Though of aristocratic descent, Rosas had been neglected by his family, grew up as a *gaucho* (Argentinian brand of cowboy) and conquered the capital at the head of a band of *gauchos*.

And then Rosas, all-powerful commenced his course of vengeance against the upper classes which had so long held him in contempt. Amidst the most aristocratic and elegant men, he constantly appeared dressed in a chaqueta and without a cravat: he gave balls at which he, his wife, and his daughter presided, and to which, to the exclusion of the better society of Buenos Ayres, he invited carters, butchers, even the enfranchised slaves of the city. One day he opened the ball himself, dancing with a slave, and Manuelita with a Gaucho.

From that time every man displeasing to him was qualified with the name of Unitarian savage; and he whom Rosas had once designated by that name had no longer a right to liberty, property, life, or honour.

Then, to put in practice the theories of Rosas, was organized, under his auspices, the famous society of MAS HACA, that is to say, more gibbets. This society was composed of all the vagabonds, bankrupts, and sbirri of the city. With this society of MAS HACA were affiliated by superior orders, the heads of the police, the judges of the peace – all, in short, whose duty it was to watch over the maintenance of public order; so that when the members of this society were breaking open the house of a citizen, to plunder the house and assassinate the owner, it was in vain for him whose life and property were in danger to call for assistance; no one was there to oppose the violences that were being perpetrated. These violences were committed in open day as in dark night, without any means of escaping them.

The fashionable men of Buenos Ayres had at that period the custom of wearing their whiskers en collier, that is, extended under the chin. But under the pretence that the beard thus cut formed the letter U, and meant Unitarian, the MAS HACA seized these unfortunate wretches, shaved them with blunt knives, and cut off strips of flesh with the beards, after which they abandoned the victims to the lowest rabble, drawn together by the curiosity of the spectacle, and who sometimes carried out the bloody farce to death.

The women of the lower classes then began to wear in their hair the red ribbon known by the name of the mano. One day the MAS HACA planted themselves at the doors of the principal churches, and all the women who went in or came out without the mano on their heads had one fastened on with hot pitch. Nor was it at all an extraordinary thing to see a woman stript of her cloths and whipped through the streets, and that because she had dared to wear a handkerchief, dress, or any kind of ornament, upon which could be detected the colours of blue or green. It was the same with men of the highest distinction; it was sufficient for them to incur the greatest dangers, if they ventured into public with a coat or a cravat on.

At the same time that persons designated without doubt beforehand, and who belonged to these superior classes of society, pursued by an invisible but well-known vengeance, were victims of these acts of violence, citizens whose opinions were not in harmony, we will not say with those of the dictator, but with the still unknown combinations of future policy, were imprisoned by hundreds. No one knew for what crime he was arrested; that was a superfluous thing, since Rosas knew it: so that the crime remaining unknown, trial was declared useless, and every day, to make room for the prisoners of the following days, the crowded prisons were relieved of the superabundance of their inmates by numerous fusillades. The fusillades took place in the hours of darkness, and constantly the city would be roused up by the nocturnal thunders which were decimating it.

And in the morning, as was never the case in France, even in the most terrible days of 1793, police carters were seen quietly collecting the bodies of the assassinated in the streets, and going to receive at the prisons the bodies of those who had been shot; then the assassinated and the shot were driven away to a large grave, into which they were thrown pêle-mêle, without giving the relations of the victims an opportunity of coming to recognize those who belonged to them, or to render them the duties of sepulture.

This was not all: the carters who took away these deplorable remains announced their approach by atrocious jokes which caused the doors to be shut and the populace to fly out of hearing. They have been seen to cut off the heads from the bodies, and with these heads fill baskets, and then, imitating the cry of vendors of fruit, to have offered them to terrified passers-by, by crying, 'Unitarian peaches! Who wants any Unitarian peaches?'

Interested calculation was joined to barbarity, confiscation to death. Rosas was fully aware that the means of preserving his power was to create around him interests inseparable from his own. Then he pointed out to one party the fortunes of the other, saying, 'That belongs to you!' From that moment the ruin of the old proprietors of Buenos Ayres was consummated, and the friends of Rosas were seen to acquire scandalous and rapid fortunes.

(From *Garibaldi: An Autobiography*, London, 1860, pp. 174–6)

Arguing from the fact that many *caudillos* came from the

lowest classes, and that even some of those who did not nevertheless persecuted numerous members of the upper class, certain writers claimed that *caudillismo* was a democratic force, and Vallenilla Lanz baptized it with the name of democratic caesarism. This contention, however, is baseless, as no *caudillo* did ever do anything to foster the growth of representative institutions. Many of the *caudillos* resorted to demagogy, and some obtained help from the city mob in seizing power, but they never showed concern for the fate of the poor and never attempted to level social inequalities. What the anti-aristocratic dictators did was to stimulate vertical motility: they expelled their enemies from the ranks of the privileged, and brought in some of their formerly impecunious friends who often succeeded in remaining in their new status even after the downfall of their benefactor, and became founders of new aristocratic lineages. Whilst the bulk of the land was appropriated by a small number of families, the trade too undeveloped to provide many opportunities of quick enrichment, and even the higher positions in the Church cornered by the aristocracy or filled by priests from Spain and Portugal, the army constituted the only avenue of social ascent. *Caudillismo* was the agency of neither democratization nor of levelling but merely of reshuffling.

Normally, neither the partisans of the *caudillo* nor his enemies were guided by an ideology, despite frequent professions to the contrary. Usually they were simply bands of men thrown together by chance, and only in the heat of the struggle did they occasionally develop some cohesion. At most they might differ from their enemies in respect of the region from which they came: Venezuela, for instance, was governed for many decades by men from the Tachira province. The absence of commitment to any political principle, and the consequent lack of cohesion, account for the instability of the régimes and for the disorder which almost invariably followed the death of a tyrant. A few dictators (like Gabriel Garcia Moreno of Ecuador) were inspired by the ideal of bigotry and subservience to the Church; a few others (like Guzman Blanco of Venezuela) had some concern for the standing of their countries, and attempted to modernize them, building roads and schools; but the great majority viewed power solely as the means of assuaging their vanity, cupidity and desire for the pleasures of the flesh.

Unstable personal dictatorships were able to remain the prevalent form of government for a century and a half because the peasants were passive, despite sporadic outbursts of rebellion; the urban population was insignificant and the aristocracy lacking in cohesion. Moreover, the economy was so simple that a disorderly government could function without wrecking it. With the development of more complex economic relations, the growth of the urban population, the increasing power of financiers and industrialists, the proliferation of middle-class politicians and the political awakening of the lower classes, the traditional *caudillismo* has ceased to be workable; and at the moment it functions only in the three most backward states: Paraguay, Nicaragua and Haiti. Even in Peru the recent *cuartelazo* brought to power not an old-fashioned *caudilla* but an unstable military junta, not knowing what to do and vacillating between repression and propitiatory gestures towards the oligarchy on one side and the popular parties on the other. Unfortunately, however, the waning of the traditional *caudillismo* need not pave the way for democracy, but may merely augur the advent of more modern totalitarian or semi-totalitarian brands of dictatorship, able to deal with economic complexities and the effervescence of the mass movements, of which the régimes of Peron and Vargas may have been the forerunners.

Landowning Constitutional Oligarchies

With the exception of Uruguay, all the stable parliamentary régimes which functioned in Latin America have been (or are) oligarchic in nature, and were based on the undisputed supremacy of the ruling class, and its ability to keep its internal conflicts within the rules of the parliamentary game. Oligarchic constitutional governments functioned in the past in Argentina, Brazil, Colombia and Chile. At present the political systems of these countries are in a state of violent turmoil, and by no stretch of imagination can they be described as stable oligarchies. On the other hand, a new form of stable oligarchy has arisen in Mexico. It differs radically from the traditional oligarchies in that the ruling class is no longer a land-owning aristocracy but a mixture of capitalist, managerial and bureaucratic elements, whose cohesion is based not on the bonds of kinship – as was the case with the traditional land-owning oligarchies – but on membership of the governing party.

The downfall of the traditional oligarchies was due to outbreaks of uncontrollable strife in their midst and their loss of the ability to control the masses effectively, the two processes being intertwined in manifold ways.

Of all the republics of Latin America Chile has by far the best record of constitutional legality, surpassed only by a few countries in the world. Between 1830 and the present day Chile had only one dictator – Colonel Ibanez – who seized power in 1924. There were, it is true, a few civil commotions – the most serious being the civil war of 1891 – but they were not in the nature of typical Latin American military coups, and the struggles were conducted with some justification in the letter of the constitution. Compare this record with that of France, Germany or Russia, let alone Spain. Such durability of the political order calls for some explanation.

The first factor which must be taken into account is the small size of the country. Although the territory of the Chilean republic is more than twice the size of Italy, only the central part is inhabited, and the area of settlement was even smaller a century ago. Within this central area (which physically is a wide valley) communications are easy, as there are neither swamps nor jungles. The smallness of the territory made it relatively easy to police for, in contrast to Argentina, there were no wide steppes where large bands of *gauchos* could roam; nor were there any self-contained regions, separated from the centre by formidable obstacles to transport, where local potentates could build independent power, as happened so many times in Mexico. Perhaps because the Indian population was always much less dense than in Peru or Mexico, the process of interbreeding produced an almost complete disappearance of the racial and ethnic divisions; and this homogeneity facilitated social cohesion.

In addition to the aforementioned circumstances, the emergence of an extraordinary statesman helped to establish Chile's constitution on firm foundations. Diego Portales was very unlike the usual *caudillos*. He seized power by force at a time of anarchy and resorted to savage punishments in order to keep his opponents at bay, but he was a legal-minded man, honest and sober. His ambition was to do for Chile what the ancient Greek law-givers had done for their cities: to create an order which would perpetuate itself after his departure. When he felt that this had been achieved, Portales retired from politics and went back to his business in Valparaiso. His voluntary retirement was perhaps even more effective than the laws which he promulgated in impressing upon the people – and particularly upon his sucsessors – the idea that authority is something more than personal domination by naked force. The régime created by Portales could be described as a near-autocracy tempered by oligarchy and perpetuated by co-option. Although Portales came into power as a leader of the aristocratic reaction against the self-made generals of the wars of independence who appealed to the lower classes, the fear of disorder and of popular uprisings induced the aristocracy to acquiesce in an autocracy, so long as it was exercised for their benefit.

Chilean political history can be divided into five periods: 1810–30, the period of the wars of independence, military dictatorships and anarchy; 1830–60, semi-autocratic government for the benefit of the aristocracy; 1860–90, the rise of the parties and gradual transition from semi-autocracy to oligarchy; 1890–1920, undiluted oligarchy; 1920 to the present day, acute class struggles fought within the limits of parliamentary party politics, except for the interlude of the dictatorship of Ibañez.

Until the end of the nineteenth century Chilean society was sharply divided into the landowners and the labourers, without an intermediate class of any importance, and so politics remained an aristocratic game. The lower classes were too ignorant, too poor and too timid to meddle in it, and they had no middle-class politicians to lead them. Naturally, the politicians debated and quarrelled: they were divided on the issues of federalism versus centralism, clericalism versus anti-clericalism, the division of power between the president and the parliament, but the fundamental features of the social order were not assailed until the entry into the political arena after the First World War of middle-class politicians. True the most serious civil war which Chile has ever experienced took place in 1891 – that is to say much earlier – but it was not related to any class struggle. It ensued from the opposition of the aristocracy, and particularly of those of its elements connected with commerce and finance, to the autocratic and somewhat egalitarian tendencies of president Balmaceda. The victorious rebels replaced the presidential constitution by a parliamentary government which proved to be thoroughly detrimental to the country because, with the reduction of the presidency to ceremonial functions, there disappeared the only agency which could moderate the tendency of the aristocratic factions to use the state solely for the furtherance of their short-term advantages.

The internal peace which distinguished Chile from the other republics was made possible by the extraordinary prosperity which that country enjoyed during the second half of the nineteenth century. After the conquest of the nitrate-bearing regions from Peru and Bolivia, and before the invention of artificial fertilizers during the First World War, the excise on nitrates sufficed to cover the budget of the state; so that there was no taxation in Chile. Ever since that source of wealth dried up the country has lived in a continuous political and economic crisis. The moral deterioration of the upper class after the removal of the presidential check on its blind greed, the growth of the largely unproductive middle class and the gradual political awakening of the lower classes produced, in combination with the increasing economic stress, an unstable semi-democracy poised precariously on the edge of a precipice.

In comparison with Hispano-American republics other than Chile, Brazil has a good record of constitutionalism, and has suffered only a few brief periods of military dictatorship. This peculiarity was due, above all, to the preservation of dynastic continuity until nearly the end of the nineteenth century. The Portuguese royal family (unlike the Spanish one which was interned) fled to Brazil when the troops of Napoleon occupied its country; and its younger members became so brazilianized that when after the return of the king to Portugal the movement for independence eventually triumphed, a son of the Portuguese king was proclaimed as the emperor of Brazil.

The monarchy did not ensure smooth legality – a number of rebellions took place, and the power of the emperor suffered a progressive attentuation – but it saved Brazil from continuous violence. During the second part of the imperial era particularly, the emperor did not even try to rule, despite the paraphernalia of absolutism: his self-imposed task was to exercise a pacifying and moderating influence upon the regional potentates, and to try to bring about or maintain some concord among them. The Empire of Brazil had more in common with the feudal kingdoms of medieval Europe than with the absolutist monarchies of the eighteenth century.

The equilibrium between the emperor and the nobles was disturbed by the growth of the professional army in consequence of the war against Paraguay. When, by promoting the abolition of slavery, Pedro II alienated the landowners, he became an easy prey for ambitious generals. His exile however, inaugurated only a fairly brief period of *caudillismo* on the Hispano-American pattern. The size of the country and the power of the local magnates were such that the military never attained undisputed supremacy. Moreover, the Brazilian generals were particularly closely connected with the land-owning class. As not much hard fighting took place in Brazil, there were few opportunities for daring adventurers to rise to positions of command through sheer prowess in battle, and such positions were reserved for well-connected individuals. In these circumstances a *modus vivendi* between the generals and prominent civilians was fairly easy to maintain, and in consequence military incursions into politics were relatively rare and not very far-reaching. Until recent decades the republic was governed by coalitions of landowners whose re-alignments constituted the stuff of politics until the appearance in the nineteen twenties of the so-called *tenientes* (lieutenants) – a lodge of young officers connected with reformist middle-class movements.

The absence of powerful dictators was not an unmixed blessing: partly a consequence of the rigid division of the Brazilian society, it helped to perpetuate the chasm, never blurred by dictatorial reshufflings. Whereas Mexico, torn by anarchy and tyranny, had the son of an Indian peasant as president a hundred years ago, nothing similar ever happened in Brazil, where the gulf between the classes remained absolutely impassable until recent decades.

In Argentina a constitutional oligarchy functioned for a shorter time than in Chile or Brazil but at its apogee it was a great deal more stable than the Brazilian. Liberation from colonial rule was followed by anarchy and strife: there was a quick succession of assemblies and presidents, overthrown soon after they assumed office, and most of the country was in the hands of marauding bands of *gauchos*. These bands continued to fight each other and refused to obey the government of Buenos Aires until the leader of one of them – Juan Manuel Rosas – subjugated most of the country. Rosas, the most ferocious tyrant in Argentinian history, maintained himself in power for more than thirty years, and only after his overthrow did the era of relative constitutionalism begin, inaugurated by the constitution of 1853. The oligarchic form of government thus established suffered from more violent upheavals than its counterpart in Chile: the factions were purely personalist, and even the conflict between centralism and federalism was a mere reflection of the struggle between the provincial potentates and the politicians and financiers of Buenos Aires. Despite the habits of nepotism, bribery and misappropriation of public funds, in the later decades of the nineteenth century the oligarchic political system seemed to be acquiring more stability, and constitutionalism seemed to be striking deeper roots. After 1912 the political system of Argentina began to evolve in the direction of democracy but this development was short-lived, and in 1930 a reversion to pretorianism took place.

A constitutional oligarchic régime functioned also in Colombia from the beginning of the present century until the late forties when, as is shown in detail in a later chapter, violence re-entered politics.

Except in Argentina, where the introduction of universal franchise in 1912 was followed four years later by a victory of the reformist and democratic Radical Party, the oligarchies have been able to maintain full control over political life long after the extension of voting rights to the non-property-owning classes.

Methods of 'fixing' the elections depend in the first place on the docility of the lower classes. In Chile in the nineteenth century the labourers and the tenant farmers simply felt that politics had nothing to do with them, and regarded it as a game in which the lords of the land indulged themselves. Voting was regarded as another kind of service which had to be rendered to the owner of the estate. The same was more or less true of all the countries of Latin America where elections were held. In the more outlying rural areas, where the peasants remain passive, the landlords are able to control the rural vote to this very day;

and where there is no opposition, elections can assume an air of festivity. In the 'unspoilt' areas of Brazil the owner of the estate gives his labourers and tenants a great feast, and then leads them in a procession to the voting booths, in front of which his bailiffs distribute the voting papers. A traveller gave the following description of an amusing incident which is supposed to have happened in the state of Bahia. As the bailiff was distributing envelopes with the voting papers, one of the voters wanted to see what was inside, but when the boss saw him opening it he shouted: 'You are not allowed to open it! Don't you know that there is a law which says that voting is secret?'

In rural areas entirely dominated by large estates the laws of the state did not operate at all during the nineteenth century, and hardly operate even today. Naturally, there are great variations in this respect: in Chile the laws are more respected than in Peru or Ecuador; and in Brazil there is an enormous difference between the south and the north. Nevertheless, it is a general rule to which there are few exceptions that where the economic power of the landlords remains intact the elections are very far from being free. In such areas even those who are not his employees are under the landlord's power: he could starve out the shopkeepers and artisans who live in enclaves surrounded by his lands; and the local policemen and minor officials look to his largesse to supplement their meagre incomes, and know that through his influence in the higher circles he could easily obtain their dismissal. Under such circumstances no independent electoral committees can be formed, and if there are any difficulties in getting the peons to vote as instructed, the counting can easily be falsified. Where literacy is a qualification for voting, tests can often be manipulated so as to exclude those suspected of recalcitrance.

Where the local aristocracy is divided into competing parties whilst the electorate remains indifferent, vote buying assumes considerable importance. Often the payments are made not to voters themselves but to persons such as local officials or estate managers who can manipulate the voting.

Such travesties of electoral politics are an inevitable result of an imposition of a democratic constitution upon seignorial agrarian structures which determine the distribution of local power. Similar travesties of the electoral process are, of course, common in other parts of the world. In pre-Franco Spain they used to be known as *caciquismo*. In Brazil the word *coronelismo* is usually employed. To avoid misunderstandings, it must be noted that contrary to what its etymology suggests, *coronelismo* has nothing to do with rule by the military. The word *coronel* came to signify a local potentate because in the eighteenth century a territorial army was called into existence in which the estate owners were supposed to be the colonels. The army existed chiefly on paper, and eventually disappeared altogether, but the military title became the common designation of a local potentate.

Where the rural populations became less docile and less willing to vote as instructed, or where the interference of the urban party machines made outright electoral fraud difficult, the landlords often prevented those whom they suspected of holding subversive views from voting, by intimidating them with threats of dismissal or other form of victimization, or even by violence or threats thereof. Other tricks are employed such as deletion of the names of suspected opponents from the electoral rolls under various pretexts; depriving them of the means of transport which are freely available to supporters and other kinds of harassment.

In view of these electoral manipulations, it may be asked whether these oligarchies can justifiably be described as constitutionalist. The answer is that so long as the peasants do not object to voting as they are told, no breaches of law need take place. The political awakening of the masses has produced on the one hand a movement towards more effective democracy, and on the other, the spread of unequivocally illegal malpractices perpetrated by those who oppose this movement.

Traditional oligarchy ceased to be viable when urbanization disturbed the cohesion of the élite by making it more heterogeneous, made the lower classes less amenable to control, and produced a middle class which provided the masses with leaders. The landlords continued to be able to influence the outcome of elections, but transport improvements enabled party and union organizers from the cities to undermine their power. What is perhaps even more important, the rural sector is steadily losing its numerical importance. In the cities elections can be manipulated effectively by a dictator or a well-organized party machine, but only to a small extent by private individuals, no matter how wealthy. For this reason there are no longer any stable loosely-organized oligarchies. The Colombian régime, which is the nearest approach to the traditional type, is extremely shaky and in fact is in the throes of a bloody class war. In Argentina, Venezuela, Chile and Brazil powerful elements of that system still exist, but they operate in a political arena afflicted by class struggles and invaded by mass movements.

In the whole of Latin America the landowning class dominated society (as it still does in most parts), but only in the few countries discussed in this section did this class acquire sufficient cohesion to rule collectively through parliamentary process; elsewhere it suffered from anarchy or was content to enjoy the fruits of its economic supremacy in the shadow of the dictators.

At present there is only one stable oligarchy in Latin America: the Mexican. It is an oligarchy of an entirely new type, in which the élite, instead of exercising personal dominance, governs through the party machine. In virtue of its organization, the party can fix the elections even better than any aristocratic faction ever could.

Bureaucratic Oligarchy : Mexico

The Mexican political system is in many ways the most perfect example of one-party rule. Not, of course, in the sense that the governing Partido Revolucionario Institucional has more extensive power or is less tolerant of the opposition than other parties which enjoy a monopoly of power, but in the sense of a truly collective exercise of authority. In most monoparty states the cult of personality overshadows the collective authority of the party assemblies. The Nazi party never met or debated but merely cheered and obeyed its leader. The communist parties were for a long time docile instruments of Stalin's will, and even now the collective rule remains without secure foundations. The ruling parties of Ghana, Cuba or Algeria are dependent on the cult of personality.* Moreover, no monoparty régime other than the Mexican has yet been able to devise a mechanism ensuring an entirely peaceful succession to supreme authority. In Russia Stalin, Beria and a number of smaller dignitaries were

* Since this was written the Ghanaian mono-party has been demolished, and the Algerian subjugated, by the army.

killed, and Khrushchev rose through obscure machinations which involved the use of force and had little to do with any legitimized procedure. Perhaps the next succession in the Soviet Union will take place in accordance with such a procedure but up till now Mexico is the only monoparty state which has maintained procedural regularity over several successions to supreme authority.*

The Mexican ruling party was created by president Calles in 1928 under the name of Partido Nacional Revolucionario. It was renamed as Partido de la Revolucion Mexicana and moulded along its present lines by president Cardenas in 1938. It assumed its present name of Partido Revolucionario Institucional in 1945. Though clearly inspired by the Soviet example, the Mexican ruling party became neither monocratic nor totalitarian. One reason for this divergence from the Soviet model was the lack of a clearly defined doctrine, which was both the cause and the consequence of the chaotic course of its revolution. As will be shown in greater detail in a later chapter, no specific ideology but only a vague desire for greater social justice inspired the Mexican revolutionaries. The absence of doctrine made the party more vulnerable to the germs of corruption, but it saved it from the excesses of hunting for deviationists.

The party ensures compliance in the first place through controlling wealth by a far-reaching participation in economic activities. The second and complementary means is intimidation. In the forties, when recourse to violence was most frequent, and the dignitaries moved around surrounded by private *pistoleros,* many opponents of the régime died in mysterious circumstances, often in strange traffic accidents. There are more recent examples of this technique, such as the murder of the peasant leader Jaramillo.

Though not averse to surreptitious or open violence, the post-revolutionary Mexican government has never resorted to massive

* The removal of Khrushchev, which occurred since this was written, was in the nature of a hybrid between a constitutional cabinet crisis and a palace revolution. Its bloodless character and the humane (by Russian standards) treatment meted out to the ousted boss mark an important step towards a civilized constitutional oligarchy. To appreciate its portent we must remember that it was the first time that a head of the Russian state has been removed without bloodshed. The factors involved in this evolution are analysed in Chapter 23 of *Elements of Comparative Sociology.*

terror, in contrast to the bloody régimes of Batista in Cuba and of Perez Jimenez in Venezuela. Since 1938 the ultimate weapon of politics has been used sparingly, and mainly against those who themselves employed force, and those who would prevent the operation of the normal means of perpetuation of the rule of the Partido Revolucionario Institucional – the manipulation of elections. When the counting of votes can be falsified, there is no need to drive the opposing parties out of existence: although this could legally be done with the aid of the recently promulgated Law of Social Dissolution which is so vague that every active opponent of the government could be arrested under it. In many places even electoral fraud is unnecessary, as the illiterate and intimidated peasants can be made to vote in accordance with the wishes of the officials. Often mere economic pressure suffices, for it is well known that only the friends of the government can obtain lucrative appointments, profitable licences, contracts or concessions, and that they find the tax collectors more tolerant. Moreover, the agents of the ruling party can freely use the vehicles, halls, loudspeakers and other equipment belonging to the state to which their rivals have no access. Under the existing laws any newspaper can be suppressed if it publishes 'material tending to degrade the state'. In addition the government has the monopoly on the sale of paper, and can deny it to publications of which it disapproves. Nevertheless, the freedom of expression is greater than under most dictatorships (let alone their totalitarian variants), although there have been dictatorships (such as that of Pilsudski in Poland) which granted an ampler measure of freedom to the press and to writers.

The ruling party of Mexico has never succumbed to monocratic despotism, and it came to constitute a cohesive bureaucratic oligarchy. The president has great power; so great indeed that he appoints a successor who is then duly acclaimed through engineered elections. Nevertheless, in contrast with many other countries, in Mexico a president cannot remain in office beyond his term: presidents come and go, but the party remains supreme. It is possible that with the benefit of advice from Trotsky, the party élite have drawn lessons from those errors of the early bolsheviks which enabled Stalin to build his tyranny. At least partly, however, the party owes its immunity to autocracy to the rectitude of its principal founder, Lazaro Cardenas, who had the power to become a despot, but chose to step down and give an example of the impersonality of office.

The cohesion of the party is largely due to its intricate articulation along functional lines, which attenuates the fissiparous tendencies of local centres of power. Until it was recast by Cardenas, the party was a cartel of military chieftains, each dominating a part of the country. As a counterweight to the army, Cardenas created the industrial and agrarian sectors of the party, consisting respectively of privileged workers incorporated into para-military unions, and of those peasants who had benefited from the agrarian reforms. In 1958 the farm sector had 2,660,000 members; the labour sector 2,113,000; the Popular Sector (consisting of associations of officials, technicians, teachers, merchants, artisans and so on) had 1,848,000. The total membership of the party was 6,621,000. The military sector no longer exists. The whole is enmeshed in a network of interlocking committees and directorates, and has undergone a process of far-reaching bureaucratization. The state and the party machines interpenetrate each other; and decisions are reached (and presidents selected) through obscure manœuvres of bureaucratic pressure groups.

Notwithstanding the monopoly of power enjoyed by the PRI, other parties continue to exist. In contrast to the phantom parties nominally existing in eastern Europe or in Nicaragua and Paraguay, these parties enjoy real independence and actively oppose the government, although they cannot win the elections. Their electoral disability largely accounts for their inclination towards violence, manifesting itself in riots and minor uprisings which (though hardly ever reported in the foreign press) have claimed hundreds of victims during the recent years.

The opposition is inspired either by marxism or by Catholicism. Whereas in other countries of Latin America (with the exception of Cuba) the Church is decidedly on the side of the established order, in Mexico it gives support to revolutionary movements, owing to the anti-clerical origins of the present régime which still affect its relations with the Church. The most violent of the pro-clerical parties is the Union Nacional Sinarquista whose ideology is in many ways similar to that of the Spanish Falange. Other pro-clerical and anti-government parties are Partido de Accion Nacional, Partido Nacionalista de

Mexico, Union Nacional Independiente and Movimiento Social Democrata Cristiano. The multiplicity of the clerical parties is partly due to the fact that they defend the interests of those owners of wealth who are outside the ruling bureaucracy, and at the same time appeal to the impoverished members of the middle class, as well as to the poor, particularly the peasants who are more susceptible to the enchantments of the traditional religion than the urban proletariat. As in communist Poland, the irreligious tendencies of the privileged bureaucracy enhance the appeal of Catholicism to the poor.

The parties which unequivocally espouse the cause of the poor draw their inspiration from marxism. There is the Partido Communista Mexicano, the Partido Popular Socialista (led by famous Vicente Lombardo Toledano who was for a long time the chief agent of the Comintern in Latin America, but who has now adopted a deviationist position), the Movimiento de Liberacion Nacional, the Central Campesina Independiente and various smaller groupings. In addition there are many peasant leagues confined to various provinces.

Practically all the parties of the opposition would like to overthrow the government by force if they could, and are kept at bay by the army and the police, and prevented from winning elections by the previously described means of pressure at the disposal of the government. Nevertheless, they enjoy widespread support, and in truly free elections the adherents of the ruling party would in all probability find themselves in the minority. The chief weakness of the opposition stems from its divisions and the feuds between the parties; and above all from the hatred which the Catholics and the marxists harbour for each other, which has on many occasions led to outbreaks of violence reminiscent of the street battles in which the nazis and the communists used to engage in Germany.

The chief achievements of the present Mexican political system are stability and the reduction of the influence and wealth of the army which have jointly permitted the second highest rate of economic growth in Latin America. Nevertheless, terrible and widespread poverty remains, and it colours the entire political situation. The phenomenal expansion of the economy has permitted a large numerical increase of the wealthier classes, and very substantial improvements in their standard of living;

but it has reduced neither the number of the indigent holders of diplomas nor that of the starving peasants, proletarians and paupers, who are more numerous today than they were in the days of Porfirio Diaz. However, the higher ratio of rich and satisfied to the poor endows the present system with a strength lacking in the pre-revolutionary régime.

Democracy

Democracy in the strict sense of government by the people has never existed outside small groups, and there are no reasons to believe that it will ever materialize amongst larger groups: there are always restricted circles making decisions which the rest of the population carries out. The concept of democracy can be applied only to the relationship between the ruling circle and the mass of the citizens. Defining it as 'government by consent of the majority' does not provide a solution because this allows Hitler's régime at the peak of its popularity to be counted as democratic, for there can be little doubt that after victory over France and before the first defeats in Russia the great majority of the German people adored Hitler. A number of other dema- gogic despots enjoyed wide popular support: the most recent example in Latin America was that of Peron. Even more: in- numerable absolute monarchs, who never courted the favour of the populace, undoubtedly ruled with its consent at least in the sense that it never occurred to the ordinary folk to question the divine right of their rulers. Democracy presupposes the existence of institutions permitting the majority to withdraw their consent and to dislodge the incumbents of power. The definition of democracy as representative government does not add to pre- cision, owing to the vagueness of the concept of representation.

Taking into account a distinction between passive and active consent, we can define democracy as a system of government under which: (1) the posts of supreme authority are elective; (2) the franchise comprises most of the population; (3) the elections are conducted honestly, that is to say without cheating or intimidation; (4) there is genuine competition for votes. The latter condition presupposes that there are at least two political parties, and that there is no cartel-like agreement between them to eliminate competition. It further presupposes that control over economic resources and the means of diffusion of opinion is not so concentrated as to prevent electoral competition. The existence of a system of government which satisfies the conditions specified above naturally presupposes the security of the citizens from arbitrary arrests, tolerance of divergence of views, limitations on the use of authority and a division of powers.

More succinctly we could define democracy as a political system under which the rulers cannot remain in office for long if they are disliked by the majority of their subjects.

Judged by the realistic criteria specified above, only two countries in Latin America qualify as relatively stable democracies: Uruguay and Costa Rica; for even in Chile, notwithstanding its long tradition of constitutionalism, until the 1965 elections the mechanisms of economic pressure described previously enabled the ruling circle to obtain the formal consent of the electorate even if the majority were inwardly hostile.

Uruguay and Costa Rica share with Argentina the characteristic that they bear few traces of conquest and subjugation. The autochthonous populations were sparse, and have been either exterminated or absorbed, with the result that in later times class antagonisms were not aggravated by ethnic and racial contrasts. As the climate attracted European labour, slavery never became very extensive, and the lower classes have never been so oppressed and degraded as in most other parts of Latin America. In Uruguay the additional factor was the importance of cattle breeding, which gives fewer opportunities of intense exploitation of labour than agriculture.

Uruguay acquired fairly democratic and stable institutions at the beginning of the present century but until then it had its full share of the usual Hispano-American *caudillismo* and armed strife, aggravated by struggles for its territory between Argentina and Brazil. As neither of them succeeded in seizing it, the Uruguayan republic grew up on the no man's land. The rise of democracy was preceded by the remarkable educational activity inspired and directed by Jose Pedro Varela. The dictator, Latorre, suppressed, of course, political dissent but allowed Varela considerable freedom in educational matters. Without this unobtrusive effort of enlightenment the democratic order implanted later by Jose Batlle y Ordonez could not have struck root.

Although their aims were radically different, Batlle y Ordonez resembled the founder of the Chilean constitutional oligarchy, Diego Portalez, in valuing more highly the durability of the order which he created than his personal aggrandizement. The constitution which he promulgated in 1913 reduced his powers as president. He even tried to abolish the presidency altogether and to replace it with a collegiate executive on the Swiss model, but was forced to compromise: power was divided between the president and the National Council of Administration – an elected body chosen from both major parties, a third of which had to be renewed every three years. Equally crucial were the establishment of effective local authorities with considerable autonomy, the introduction of the secret ballot and the separation of the Church from the state.

Uruguay's constitution was saved from the usual fate of remaining a mere piece of paper by the attitude of the dominant party to social problems. The Uruguayan government was the first in Latin America to show any concern for the welfare of the unprivileged, and to try to attenuate the hostility existing between the rich and the poor by positive action. Beginning with the presidency of Batlle, there has been a steady progress of legislation on factory inspection, accident insurance, old age pensions, protection of illegitimate children (with compulsory investigation of paternity), free medical care for the poor, holidays with pay, women's rights, including legalization of divorce with a right to alimony. All this does not mean that in the provision of welfare services Uruguay has attained the level of Sweden or even Britain: as described previously, the majority of the rural population lives in misery, and even in the towns only privileged workers enjoy full unemployment insurance. Nevertheless, one needs to recall the existence of a vast army of paupers in the richest country in the world, to realize that the record of Uruguay is respectable even by world standards, and unique in Latin America.

One of the indispensable conditions of this achievement was the success of Batlle in subordinating the army to the civilian authority, and in curtailing its numerical strength. Uruguay's army is the second smallest in Latin America – smaller than the armies of the much smaller and poorer central American republics with the exception of Honduras. Although Argentina's population is less than eight times greater, its armed forces are more than thirty times as large. Nor is it accidental that Uruguay is the most thoroughly secularized state in Latin America; and, unlike Mexico, attained this happy state of affairs without bloodshed. Uruguay's secularization, moreover, is less threatened by outbursts of devotionalist demagogy and violence in virtue of the higher economic and cultural level of the masses. Having been almost uninhabited during the colonial era, Uruguay came into existence without the crushing burden of a vast and immensely rich ecclesiastical body. The relative freedom from clerical domination later permitted the spread of a fairly rational outlook on public issues, which contrasts favourably with the atavistic and blindly impulsive behaviour so common elsewhere. This enlightenment has also led to the acceptance of family planning (practised much more widely than anywhere else in Latin America) in consequence of which the birth rate descended to a level which does not condemn the country to defeat in coping with economic difficulties which remain considerable and stem particularly from the hypertrophy of the bureaucracy, the excessive concentration of the population and resources in the capital, and the consequent neglect of the rural areas.

Costa Rica is the other country where force and economic compulsion play a less important political role than is normally the case in Latin America; and, like Uruguay, it is distinguished by a less poignant inequality between the classes. Equally important, Costa Rica has no army but only a police force of moderate strength. As in the case of Uruguay, the elimination of militocracy was connected with the greater measure of social justice by a relationship of circular causality: a less virulent antagonism between the classes made the upper class less dependent on the army for its survival, and therefore more willing to consent to a diminution of the strength of the armed forces. The consequent lightening of the fiscal burden permitted improvements in the condition of the lower classes, which smoothed the relations between the poor and the rich, and further reduced the dependence of the latter on the military.

A large part of the territory of Costa Rica lies on moderate altitudes and has a climate which attracted Spanish peasants who wanted land to cultivate. Moreover, notwithstanding its name, this territory contained no great riches (and not enough material for serfs) to tempt gold-seeking soldiers. In consequence, the Costa Rican class structure deviated from the normal Latin American dichotomous division of lords and serfs, and was distinguished by the existence of a large mass of fairly prosperous peasants, and the relatively high standing and skill of the artisans and small traders. For this reason, Costa Rica produces simple manufactures in sufficient quality, and is less dependent on their importation from the United States than the other central American republics. On the whole, the vicious circle of parasitism and violence does not operate in Costa Rica to the same extent as in the neighbouring countries, but this does not mean that it is entirely absent: though not absolutely dominant, latifundia and monopolies do exist,

Although the class structure is more favourable in Costa Rica than in Uruguay, the long-term prospects for democracy are less bright because of the very high birth rate and the geographical position. Uruguay has as a neighbour, Argentina, where the cultural and economic pre-conditions of democracy exist, whereas Costa Rica lies in the midst of a zone where they are most conspicuously absent. Being too small to develop independently, Costa Rica cannot avoid entering into a close association with its neighbours; and this might very well lead to a radical political and cultural retrogression.

Mixed Systems

Most of the republics of Latin America do not fall clearly into any of the types discussed in the preceding sections: they are mixtures of oligarchy, *caudillismo* and/or democratic institutions. In itself this characteristic would not, of course, distinguish them from other polities, for the ancient Greek philosophers have already shown that all political systems consist of ingredients of autocracy, oligarchy and democracy, though the dosages differ widely. Polybius regarded the right proportions of these ingredients as the recipe for a successful polity, and attributed to this the victories of the Romans. Likewise, Britain's escape from revolution has been attributed to the balance between oligarchic and democratic tendencies. However, the point about the mixed systems of Latin America is that their ingredients are in violent discord, and that instead of an organic equilibrium they achieve a paralytic stalemate, which prevents a proper execution of governmental functions.

A mixed constitution can function well only if the conflicts involved in the maintenance of the internal balance of power remain within the bounds which permit effective co-operation, which is not the case with the Latin American republics which come into this category. The plutocracies are sufficiently strong to falsify the electoral process and thwart the populist forces, without being strong enough to rule effectively. The labour movements can neither attain power nor substantially improve the condition of the workers, but they are strong enough to inspire anxiety in the upper classes, and to make their actions ineffectual and fumbling. Even the armies, which in the past used to throw up masterful *caudillos*, no longer seem to be able or determined enough to impose their undisputed sway, and instead act mainly as agencies of disruption.

A more or less paralytic equilibrium of forces characterizes the situation in Chile* and Argentina. In Peru and Colombia the aristocracy, together with the military still holds the reins of power but no longer have much freedom of action. Venezuela seems to be moving towards the Mexican pattern but the position is extremely unstable. The greatest confusion prevails in Brazil. Owing to the heterogeneity and size of the country, the Brazilian political parties cannot even be classified according to their ideologies and the same party can stand for opposite programmes in different regions. So long as the aristocracy retained undisputed predominance, its homogeneity and the bonds of kinship provided the cohesion, but at present the cultural, ethnic and economic contrasts between the regions produce such variations in the constellations of political forces that the country is virtually ungovernable.

As pointed out previously, the *caudillos* of old often acted as agents of social mobility but not equalization. During the recent decades, however, the growing strength of democratic currents has led to an emergence of a new brand of dictatorship which courts the favour of the poor by sponsoring structural reforms. As we shall later see in greater detail, Peron was the most outstanding example of this type, but Vargas was another. Getulio

* The Chilean elections of 1965 have given a clear majority to the Christian Democratic Party. The prospects are discussed in the final chapter.

Vargas created the Brazilian Labour Party, organized trade unions, legislated wage increases and various other measures favouring the workers. The landowners, capitalists and generals retained sufficient strength to overthrow him, but not enough to recapture secure supremacy.

CHAPTER SIX

CLASS STRUCTURES

Race and Status

As far as race is concerned the countries of Latin America fall into three broad categories: those in which the majority is of Amerindian descent (Mexico, Peru, Guatemala, Ecuador, Bolivia, Paraguay); those where Europoid elements predominate (Argentina, Uruguay, Chile, Costa Rica); and the predominantly Negroid and mulatto nations around the Caribbean. Brazil and Colombia cannot be classified in this way because they are particularly variegated, and each of their different regions falls into one of these three categories. However, with regard to social situation perhaps more important is the distinction between racially homogeneous and heterogeneous countries. Although it is all a matter of degree, we could say that Mexico, Paraguay, Uruguay, Argentina and Chile have populations in which it is difficult to distinguish races, and where social characteristics are least correlated with physical traits.

The proportions of racial admixture are not without significance because, even if we assume that no mental characteristics are genetically linked to the physical traits which distinguish the races, the character of a civilization is affected by the nature of the initial ingredients (that is to say, traditions); and the impact of a tradition partly depends on the numbers of its adherents.

The most important difference between the nations consisting chiefly of descendants of Europeans, and those with large admixtures of Amerindian and Negro blood, has little to do with genetically determined mental traits, but resides in the fact that the former are less burdened by the heritage of slavery and serfdom, because the immigrants from Europe came as free men and were enslaved only in exceptional cases.

Sociologically speaking, the most important distinction is that between the populations which in their entirety regard themselves as forming a nation, and those who do not. The inhabitants of Argentina, Uruguay, Cuba, Chile, Costa Rica and (with more numerous exceptions) of Mexico regard themselves as forming one nation, whereas in Peru, Guatemala, Ecuador and Bolivia important parts of the populations are classified as Indians, and do not have any clear notion of nationhood. In Brazil and Venezuela there are also sizeable groups without national consciousness. In the latter states there remain Indian tribes which have not yet been subdued, and which are being exterminated or reduced to servitude. Some of them are very fierce and kill any stranger who comes near them.

The barrier that exists between the Peruvians and the Indians of Peru bears very little relation to racial differences, but is chiefly a matter of culture. It is not a question of class because the miserable and mostly illiterate urban proletarians are not counted as Indians. The distinction rests upon language, clothing and the membership of a tribe or a village community: an Indian who learns to speak Spanish well, dresses in town clothes, and leaves his ancestral village ceases to be regarded, or to regard himself, as an Indian. The appellation *el Indio* describes a cultural and social condition – not descent or racial features.

There is thus a radical difference between the colour bar in Northamerica and the divisions between the Peruvians or the Guatemalans and their Indians. A Northamerican Negro speaks the American brand of English as his native tongue; and if he is well educated, he speaks and writes it better than most of his europoid compatriots. He may be wealthy, educated, well-mannered, occupy a high office and be distinguished from his compatriots of similar economic position only by a trace (perhaps very slight) of African ancestry. This is enough to cause him great difficulties and humiliation. If we applied the Northamerican racialist criterion to Latin America, and classified as Indians and negroes all individuals who show a trace of Amerindian and African descent, then (outside Argentina and Uruguay) we would find few people who would fall into neither category. Even in Chile most people show traces of Amerindian blood.

The permeability of the frontier between the Indian and 'the national' accounts for the absence of nativistic movements in

Latin America. To be sure, there have been many uprisings of Indian tribes, but there has never been any tendency for these tribes to merge into, say, an Indo-Peruvian nation as opposed to Spanish-Peruvian, analogous to the process of merging of the South African European nation. As soon as the native tribes and village communities lose their identity, they merge into the territorial nation – become Mexicans or Peruvians – and their resistance to oppression loses its ethnic colouring and assumes the character of pure class struggle.

The problem of the Indians has often been, and is still being, raised but all who raised it proposed only one solution: integration. When in Mexico the monument of Cortez was demolished and the revival of Aztec themes dominated the art, the aim was not to eject from the nation the presumed descendants of the Spaniards but to eliminate the vestiges of the division into conquerors and conquered. Thus there has never been any parallel in Latin America to the emergence of new nations in Africa, where the new educated classes are integrating the tribesmen into purely African nations in opposition to the European masters or their shadow. There can be no Indian intelligentsia or middle class in Latin America because any Indian who enters the middle class ceases to be an Indian, and will not be handicapped on the grounds of his racial traits.

One of the important consequences of this situation is that there can be no nativistic nationalism into which social discontent could be diverted. The factor of race neither cuts across class divisions nor complicates their antagonisms; which is also one of the reasons why the marxist interpretation of society appears so convincing to Latin American intellectuals.

The absence of colour bar does not mean that there is actual racial equality: in all countries of Latin America the proportion of people with Europoid racial characteristics increases with height on the social ladder. The close relation between high status and Europoid features is perhaps least marked in Mexico and Bolivia – the countries that had undergone social revolutions which destroyed the privileges of the old upper classes, and gave to numerous individuals of humble origin the opportunity of far-reaching social ascent. The more frequent incidence of Europoid features amongst the rich than amongst the poor is chiefly a heritage of the conquest, but it has been reinforced by the selective nature of immigration from Europe. Except in Argentina, Uruguay and Southern Brazil, most immigrants from Europe came as businessmen or technicians, and therefore entered directly into the middle class or higher; and even many of those who came poor were able to rise higher in virtue of advantages derived from an upbringing in an environment less conducive to improvidence.

The correlation between Europoid features and high status has a certain self-perpetuating force, because the positive valuation of Europoid features helps their possessors to rise on the social ladder or to maintain themselves on a high level. But it is only a matter of opportunity – not of automatic classification into a higher caste, as in South Africa or Rhodesia. In contrast to South Africa, where the chief task of the welfare services is to prevent 'the poor whites' from falling below the minimum prescribed for a white man, nobody in Latin America has ever made any efforts to prevent the social degradation of individuals with Europoid features. The brothels of Rio de Janeiro used to contain blonde girls from Poland; and some of the Polish peasants who emigrated to Brazil fell into debt bondage, or were captured and put into slave compounds together with the negroes. This, incidentally, was happening several decades after slavery was declared illegal. So it is evident that the Brazilian planters had no deep feelings about the dignity of the white man.

In Brazil pure Negroes are fairly common in the middle class, but there are none among the land-owning aristocracy, although many Brazilian aristocrats would be classified as Negroes in Northamerica. There are few Negroes in the higher reaches of the Brazilian society primarily because social capillarity is generally low, except to a certain extent in São Paulo. The class barriers are more fluid in the south, which is undergoing rapid industrialization, than in the north where the patterns of social life are still determined by the legacy of the division into masters and slaves; and it is in the north that the majority of Negroes live. There is a Brazilian saying that 'a poor man is a Negro and a rich man white', which roughly summarizes the situation. The majority of the very poor are Negroes, dark mulattos or *mestizos*, the rich are predominantly of European descent and the rest are a mixture of shades.

On the whole the African was more severely handicapped in

rising in status than the Amerindian, which does not mean that the mass of the conquered Indians were treated better than the imported African slaves. Actually, although there was not much to choose between their fates, the latter was perhaps slightly better treated because he had been bought, whereas the Indian serf was (and often still is) 'a free commodity'.

In Indo-America (in Peru and Ecuador to a greater extent than in Mexico, Paraguay and Bolivia which have become more homogeneous racially) most people in the upper classes are of predominantly Spanish descent, while the majority of the poor are of predominantly Amerindian blood. The half-way *mestizos* predominate in the intermediate strata but are present in the highest and the lowest strata too. Moreover, even in the highest aristocracy there are individuals of purely Amerindian physical type. And even Indians in the social sense have been known to rise to the highest dignities: the greatest Mexican statesman of the nineteenth century, Benito Juarez, was an Indian, as is the only living Mexican of comparable stature, Lazaro Cardenas. Many dictators in Venezuela and elsewhere were Indians, despite their Spanish names. Though very exclusive socially, the aristocracy of Peru is very far from racial purity. Colombia is probably the country where the descendants of the Spaniards preserved most nearly their 'racial purity'. In some districts of Colombia there are even peasants of pure Spanish descent.

The absence of anything resembling a colour bar as known in English-speaking countries calls for some explanation because it was certainly not due to the kindlier treatment of the subject races by the Spaniards and the Portuguese. Like other social phenomena, interbreeding acquires a certain momentum of its own: once it has occurred on such a scale that the individuals of intermediate shades constitute the majority, any barrier based strictly on physical features is bound to cut across social affiliations, and become thereby unenforceable. The mechanism of heredity is such that siblings of racially mixed ancestry exhibit various dissimilar combinations of traits, thus qualifying for different racial categories. Such cases have caused a great deal of suffering in South Africa but they were never sufficiently numerous to throw the whole principle of the colour bar into confusion. When the overwhelming majority falls into these intermediate grades, the social barriers must be based on criteria other than physical features. This explanation raises the question of why interbreeding took place in Ibero-America on a larger scale than in English colonies.

The difference in the extent of interbreeding stems primarily from two simple demographic facts. The first is that the colonizers of Northamerica came in family groups, whereas the early Spanish and Portuguese settlers came without wives. Even in the eighteenth century, when the conditions of life in the chief cities of Ibero-America resembled those of Europe much more than was the case immediately after the conquest, very few women came from Spain and Portugal. As they lead a more secluded life, the Iberian women were probably less inclined to travel than their cousins from northern Europe, particularly as the journey to most parts of Spanish America was longer and more dangerous than to the north Atlantic coast. Moreover, it seems that the fertility of the European women in the tropics, and the survival rate of their offspring, were lower than the corresponding rates for the *mestizos*. Naturally, there are no statistics on this point, but several physicians have written about it, and it is unlikely that their views on such a simple and unideological point should be entirely baseless.

The distinguished Brazilian sociologist and historian, Gilberto Freyre, attributes the complete lack of revulsion against dark skin to the impact of the Moorish domination of the Iberian peninsula, which implanted in the minds of its inhabitants an association between darkness of the skin and high status. One must also remember that in the matter of skin colouring the Iberians do not differ greatly from Amerindians, and are somewhat nearer to the African than are the English or the Dutch. These factors, however, could only affect the extent of interbreeding because, given the fact that the colonizers came as single men, fairly extensive interbreeding could not be avoided. Similarly, although puritan gravity could, perhaps, have reduced the practice of polygamy (and, therefore, the rate of interbreeding) it could not have prevented it altogether. Even the puritanical colonial officials of Victorian England could not entirely control their concupiscence and so, it would have been very surprising if young adventurers, ready to risk their lives against tremendous odds for the sake of gold, were inclined to self-restraint.

Without polygamy the Spanish conquest of America would have been ephemeral. The men who came from Spain overran only the chief cities of the Aztecs and the Incas, and it is even doubtful whether their legitimate descendants could have maintained themselves there once the Indians ceased to be overawed by the horses and firearms. However, the numbers of the dominating group were rapidly swollen by the products of concubinage. Nearly all the Spaniards had large harems, often running into dozens and sometimes even hundreds, with even more numerous progeny. These children of the Spaniards were baptized and brought up in the Christian faith, given Spanish names, and many were recognized as heirs by their fathers. The conquest of the interior was their work, and it was they who gave to the empire the firm foundations. Polygamy played just as important a role in the iberianization of America as it did in the arabization of the Near East: in both cases the numbers of the conquerors were inadequate to impose a new identity upon the conquered peoples which would outlast the severance of political links. It must be emphasized, however, that massive procreation through non-legalized polygamy would not have buttressed the Spanish rule to such an extent had the Spaniards been inclined to disown their illegitimate offspring. The custom was (and still is in less urbanized areas) that, although illegitimate children rank in precedence below the legitimate and are usually neglected, they are regarded in principle as heirs, not only by their fathers but also by society in general. It remains to be added that this mechanism of iberianization did not cease to function in the early days of the empire; on the contrary, it works to this day in the more outlying regions, because the wealthy men of Latin America have never abandoned the habit of concubinage.

The Catholic Church played a paramount role in fostering the fusion of races. It could never force the soldiers and planters to treat their subjects less cruelly – nor did it ever seriously try to do so – but it insisted on gaining converts, and urged the Spaniards to marry their native concubines. The Protestant Churches have facilitated the maintenance of racial segregation for two reasons: one organizational, the other doctrinal. The Catholic Church, being a centralized and autocratic institution, could disregard the wishes of its flock: the priests could be ordered to include Indians and Africans in the ecclesiastic community whether it suited its European members or not. In any case an inclusion in a strictly hierarchical community does not represent the same challenge to social inequality as does an inclusion into a demo-cratically governed Protestant Church. The Catholic hierarchy, moreover, readily condoned infringements of the Command-ments but took its missionary activity seriously, and insisted on equal obedience from all races. The latter feature was a special manifestation of the general tendency of an autocracy to level the rights of its subjects. The crucial feature of Protestantism was the demolition of ecclesiastic autocracy; and, in virtue of their democratic constitutions, the Protestant Churches had to bow to the prejudices of their members. Secondly, the essence of Protestantism was direct access to the Bible; and the insistence on its literal interpretation could not fail to stimulate racialism, in view of the abundance of doctrines of racial purity in the Old Testament.

The ratio of conquerors to their victims plays a decisive role in determining the extent of miscegenation. In North America the European settlers lived in greater density and were much more numerous than the nomadic tribes with whom they came in contact. Even if they had killed all the men and taken all the women, they could not have surrounded themselves with harems such as those of the Spanish conquerors. On the other hand, the Spaniards were more numerous in proportion to the native popu-lation than were the Englishmen who directed the conquest of India. The latter were so few that no amount of polygamy could have enabled them to alter palpably the racial composition of the enormous native population. Most of the British and Dutch travellers to the East were concerned with trade, and for this reason they travelled to and fro more often, and did not lose contact with their home countries so easily. Moreover, many of them made considerable fortunes, whereupon they left the colonies, whereas among the Spaniards it was usually only the very high officials and those who found gold who went back.

The turmoil which was endemic at the beginning of the empire and after its collapse made the maintenance of social divisions based on race more difficult than was the case under the more regular conditions of political life in the southern states of the USA. In the free-for-all fights tough adventurers could rise meteorically regardless of their race, whilst many old-established families were despoiled.

The fact that a darker skin colour constitutes a substantial but not overwhelming obstacle to social advancement is illustrated by the following table. The same applies to other countries with racially mixed populations but there are considerable differences of degree. Despite the absence of statistical data on this point, we can be sure that in Colombia, for instance, the connection between whiteness of skin and wealth is much closer than in Cuba. This also seems to be the case in Brazil.

INCOME OF THE RACES IN PRE-CASTRO CUBA*

Income bracket	White	Coloured
Less than 30	37·4	46·6
30 to 59	42·8	41·4
60 to 99	13·4	9·4
100 to 199	4·7	1·7
200 to 299	0·9	0·4
300	0·8	0·5
Total	100·0	100·0

* Source: Federico Debuyst, *Las Clases Sociales en America Latina* (1962)

It would be an exaggeration to say that racial discrimination plays no part in generating social antagonisms in Latin America. Nevertheless, its role is relatively minor because racial differences (in the strict sense) correspond only vaguely or not at all to the line which divides the rich from the poor. The conflict between the Indians and 'the whites' rests essentially upon the division between the land owners and the labourers and share-croppers, or the townsmen and the peasants. There is plenty of oppression and exploitation in Latin America – no less than in racialist countries like Rhodesia or South Africa – but people are exploited not on account of their race but because of their social position; and anybody who is defenceless and poor will be exploited regardless of his features.

Income Distribution

As this topic has been touched upon many times in the previous chapters I shall confine myself here to a few additional remarks. On the whole the transformations of the class structure have increased the ratio of those who live above the poverty line to those who live below it; but they have neither diminished the absolute numbers of the latter nor led to improvements in their condition. The increments of productivity brought benefits only to the more opulent, and permitted multiplication of their numbers.

The following table summarizes the situation in Mexico in this respect. The class divisions are based here on strictly economic criteria; the middle class is the one whose percentage in the total population equals its percentual share in the national income. Those who collectively obtain a share of national income larger than the ratio of their number to the total population constitute the upper class; those whose share is smaller than the ratio of their number to the total population constitute the lower class. It must be noted that this classification is the only one proposed so far which is based on economic criteria that are not purely arbitrary or convential.

PERCENTAGES OF FAMILIES AND PERCENTAGES OF NATIONAL INCOME*

Classes	Mexico				USA				Britain	
	1950		1957		1935		1952		1952	
	F.	I.	F.	I.	F.	I.	F.	I.	F.	I.
i. Lower	70	31	65	25	47	18	40	15	40	17
ii. Middle	18	17	19	18	35	33	40	39	40	39
iii. Upper (marginal)	7	12	11	20	11	18	10	15	10	14
iv. Upper (top)	5	40	5	37	7	31	10	31	10	30
TOTALS	100	100	100	100	100	100	100	100	100	100

Notes: F = Families   I = Income

* Source: Ifigenia M. de Navarrete, *La Distribucion del Ingreso y el Desarrollo Economico de Mexico* (Mexico, D.F., 1960).

PERCENTAGES OF INCOME ACCRUING TO THE RICHEST FAMILIES*

Countries	Years	% of Families	% of Total Personal Income
USA	1929	5	30
	1935/1936	5	27
	1944	5	21
	1950	5	21
UK	1880	5	46
	1910	5	43
	1929	5	33
	1938	5	31
	1947	5	24
Mexico	1950	5	40
	1957	5	37
Southern Rhodesia	1946	5	65
Kenya	1949	3	51
Northern Rhodesia	1946	1·4	45
Italy	1948	10	34
Puerto Rico	1948	10	41
India	1950	20	55
Ceylon	1950	20	50
Mexico	1950	10	49
		20	60
	1957	10	47
		20	61

* Source: Ifigenia M. de Navarrete, *op. cit.*, pp. 87–8.

CLASS STRUCTURES

We can see that the lower class has lost proportionately: between 1950 and 1957 its relative number diminished by 5% but its share of income diminished by 6%. The upper class grew from 12% to 16% but its share of income increased from 42% to 57%. In the USA the upper class (thus defined) constituted in 1935 18% of the population and obtained 49% of income; in 1952 the corresponding figures were 20% and 46%. In Britain in 1952 the upper class amounted to 20% of the population and absorbed 44% of income.

Between 1940 and 1950 the income per employed person increased in Mexico by 47% but its distribution became even more unequal. The number of agricultural wage earners diminished by 25% but their real wages declined by 10%. The urban wage earners increased by 108% and their average real wage diminished by 6%. Between 1950 and 1957 the average income per family rose by 23% but the poorest 20% of the population suffered an absolute as well as a relative setback as it share declined from 6·1% to 4·4% of the national income. The next 30% on the economic scale have lost relatively but retained roughly the same real income. (2)

The table on page 162 permits some international comparisons.

It must be noted that in countries where income tax evasion is usual real inequality of incomes is even greater than the statistics suggest.

Profiles of Stratification

In view of the arbitrary nature of the criteria on which they are based, estimates of the numerical strength and proportion of social classes constitute only a rough outline of the real situation; nevertheless, they do reveal the points of radical contrast and point out some important factors of social dynamics. So let us consider the fragmentary data which are available on this matter.

CLASS COMPOSITION OF THE URUGUAYAN SOCIETY IN 1958*

Upper Class	54,460 Persons	..	2%
Middle Class	795,700 Persons	..	31%
Lower Class	1,749,840 Persons	..	67%
Total:	2,600,000 Persons	..	100%

	Rural		Provincial Urban		Montevideo	
Upper Class	11,080	2%	34,380	3%	9,000	1%
Middle Class	160,660	29%	275,040	24%	360,000	40%
Lower Class	382,260	69%	836,580	73%	531,000	59%
	554,000	100·0%	1,146·000	100·0%	900,000	100%

* Source: Carlos M. Rama, *Las Clases Sociales en el Uruguay* (Montevideo, 1960), pp. 110–1.

EVOLUTION OF SOCIAL CLASSES IN ARGENTINA, 1914–47*

Social Classes	1914	1947
Middle Classes	33	40
Employers and self-employed	19	19
Professionals	1	1
Rentiers	2	2
Clerical	11	17
Retired	—	2
Popular Classes	67	60
TOTAL	100%	100%

* Source: Gino Germani, *La Estructura Social de Argentina* (1955).

SOCIAL CLASSES IN BUENOS AIRES*

	1895	1914	1936	1947
Middle classes	35	38	46	48
Employers and self-employed	17	14	16	14
Rentiers	3	2	3	2
Professional	5	6	9	—
Clerical	10	16	18	32
Popular Classes	65	62	54	52

* Source: Federico Debuyst, *op. cit.*

EVOLUTION OF SOCIAL CLASSES IN MEXICO*

Social Classes	1895		1940	
	Absolute Numbers	Percentage	Absolute Numbers	Percentage
Total population	12,698,330	100	19,653,552	100
Upper	183,005	1·44	205,572	1·05
Urban	49,542	0·39	110,868	0·57
Rural	133,464	1·05	94,704	0·48
Middle	989,783	7·78	3,118,985	15·87
Urban	776,439	6.12	2,382,464	12·12
Rural	213,344	1·66	736,494	3·75
Lower	11,525,541	90·78	16,329,022	83.08
Urban	1,799,898	14·17	4,403,337	22·40
Rural	9,725,643	76·61	11,925,685	60·68
Total population Urban		20·68%		35·90%
Total population Rural		79·32%		64·10%

* Source: José E. Iturriaga, *La Estructura Social y Cultural de Mexico* (Mexico, 1951).

MEXICO: CLASS AND OCCUPATIONS, 1950–6*

Classes/Categories	Estimates, 1950			Estimates, 1956	
	Numbers	Per-centage	Pro-portion	Numbers	Per-centage
UPPER					
Managerial			All	77·4	
Professional			$\frac{1}{3}$	137·7	
Sub-total	124·5	1·5		215·1	2·0
MIDDLE					
Stable					
Professional/Technical			$\frac{2}{3}$	274·6	
Office workers			$\frac{1}{2}$	452·8	
Small tradesmen			$\frac{1}{3}$	456·7	
Sub-total	830·0	10·0		1,184·1	12·0
Marginal					
Office workers			$\frac{1}{2}$	452·8	
Small tradesmen			$\frac{1}{3}$	456·7	
Artisans			$\frac{1}{3}$	662·3	
Sub-total	1,535·5	18·5		1,571·9	16·0
Sub-total	2,365·5	28·5		2,755·9	28·0
TRANSITIONAL					
Small tradesmen			$\frac{1}{3}$	456·7	
Artisans/semi-skilled			$\frac{2}{3}$	1,325·5	
Miners/petroleum labour			All	42·2	
Service employees			$\frac{2}{3}$	619·6	
Sub-total	1,760·0	20·0		2,443·0	24·8
POPULAR					
Service employees			$\frac{1}{3}$	309·9	
Manual/day labour			All	383·8	
Agriculturists			All	3,559·0	
Unknown, etc.			All	194·0	
Sub-total	4,150·0	50·0		4,446·6	45·2
ECONOMICALLY ACTIVE	8,300·0	100·0		9,860·6	100·0

* Source: Howard F. Cline, *Mexico – Revolution to Evolution* (1962), pp. 116–21.

OCCUPATIONS AND CLASSES IN THE FEDERAL DISTRICT, MEXICO
IN 1956* (THOUSANDS OF EMPLOYED)

Categories/Classes	Number	Percentage
UPPER		
Managerial; directors	77·4	0·7
MIDDLE/UPPER		
Professional/Technical	412·3	4·2
Office workers	905·6	9·2
Small tradesmen	1,370·1	13·8
Sub-total	2,688·0	27·2
TRANSITIONAL		
Artisans/Semi-skilled	1,986·8	20·0
Miners/petroleum workers	42·2	0·4
Service employees	929·4	9·1
Sub-total	2,958·4	29·5
POPULAR		
Manual/Day labour	383·3	3·9
Agricultural	3,559·0	36·1
Semi-employed; unspecified	194·5	2·6
Sub-total	4,136·8	42·6
ECONOMICALLY ACTIVE	9,860	100·0

* Source: Howard F. Cline, *op. cit.*

SOCIAL STRATIFICATION IN COLOMBIA*

The Rich	2%
The Middle Class	13%
The Poor	79%
The Destitute	6%

SOCIAL STRATIFICATION IN THE RURAL AREAS OF COLUMBIA*

THE UPPER CLASS consisting of: 1%
Absentee estate owners
Resident estate owners
Successful lawyers and physicians
Businessmen
High ranking ecclesiastics
Officials and officers
Idle rentiers

THE MIDDLE CLASS   14%
Small merchants
Small industrialists
Medium agricultural proprietors
Lower officials and officers

THE POPULAR CLASS   80%
Artisans
Peasants
Labourers

THE DESTITUTE CLASS   5%
Paupers
Beggars

SOCIAL STRATIFICATION IN THE URBAN AREAS IN COLOMBIA*

THE UPPER CLASS   3·5%
Big businessmen
Rentiers
Politicians
High officials and officers
Successful lawyers, physicians and architects

* Source: adapted from *Estudio sobre las Condiciones del Desarrollo de Colombia* (Mission Economia y Humanismo, Bogota, 1958).

THE MIDDLE CLASS   12·5%
    Smaller businessmen
    Officials and officers
    Higher private employees
    Lawyers, physicians, etc.

THE POPULAR CLASS (The Poor)   77%
    Lower white-collar   47% of the class
    Artisans   15% of the class
    Manual wage earners 37% of the class
THE DESTITUTE CLASS   7%

Combining the preceding estimates with those given by British, Northamerican and Australian writers we obtain the following proportions (which should be regarded only as a very rough approximation):

PERCENTAGE OF CLASSES IN THE POPULATION

	Upper Class	Middle Class	Lower Class
USA	3	40	57
Britain	3·3	31	65·7
Australia	2	24	74
Argentina	0·7 (?)	39·5	59·8
Uruguay	2	31	67
Mexico	2	28	70
Colombia	2	13	85
Brazil	2	15	83

The foregoing statistical data show that the size of the middle class in Argentina and Uruguay is of the same order as in the most industrialized countries of the world: in Argentina it is as large as in the USA, and in Uruguay as large as in Britain. Chile appears to be only a little behind Uruguay in this respect. At the other end of the spectrum stand Colombia and Ecuador, the central American republics (with the exception of Cuba and Costa Rica), Paraguay and Bolivia. In Brazil the middle class appears to be only slightly bigger than in Colombia, but the situation there varies widely according to region: the social structure of the south resembles that of Argentina, whereas in the north the middle class seems to be even weaker than in Colombia.

A comparison of data for different periods demonstrates a rapid growth of the middle classes throughout the continent. However, what the preceding tables do not bring out – but what can be deduced by confronting them with the statistics of occupations – is the change in the occupational composition of the classes. In the upper class the commercial, industrial and bureaucratic elements have grown rapidly whilst the number of big landowners has remained fairly stationary. Naturally, the former comprise a far larger proportion of the newly rich, and have greater influence in the cities, while the rural areas remain under the sway of the aristocrats. Only in Mexico and Bolivia – the countries which have experienced profound revolutions – do the newly rich appear to constitute the majority among the owners of latifundia.

As in other parts of the world, the middle classes have undergone a transformation from independence to dependence: instead of consisting mainly of self-employed professionals and owners of shops, workshops and farms, they now consist chiefly of employees. In the rural areas the independent sector of the middle class (consisting of owners of middle-sized farms) outnumbers the dependent sector, but in most countries the rural middle class is much smaller in relation to the entire rural population than the urban middle class is in relation to the urban population. The only exception is Costa Rica. Moreover, the rural middle class constitutes the largest part of the rural population precisely in those regions – Uruguay, around Montevideo, the Buenos Aires province and the southern Brazil – where the total rural population is small in comparison with the urban.

Among the lower classes the numerical balance between urban wage earners and agricultural labourers has been continuously and rapidly changing in favour of the former.

The Middle Class and Stability

In a famous passage in *Politics*, Aristotle put forward the theory that a large and prosperous middle class constitutes the chief force of stability and a bulwark against revolution. Many centuries later this view was repeated by Jean Bodin, and it has come to be widely accepted ever since. Marx also assumed it to be self-evident and based his prophecy of the coming of the revolution on the prediction of the inevitable polarization of the capitalist class structure, involving a proletarianization of the middle class.

In Latin America we see that a rapid growth of the middle classes, far from bringing peace and stability, is accompanied by an aggravation of revolutionary ferment. Does it mean that the principle of the stabilizing influence of the middle class is wrong? Not quite, provided it is suitably qualified.

The first qualification is that the effects of the existence of a phenomenon differ from the effects of its coming into being. Aristotle himself has pointed out that changes in the relative numerical strength of the classes often lead to revolution. The periods of internal peace which a few Latin American countries have enjoyed resulted from an exceptional (for this continent) cohesion of the aristocracy. The challenge to their dominance presented by the growth of the middle class inevitably exacerbated the struggle for power. In Argentina this factor (in conjunction with the impact of the economic crisis of the thirties) led to an overthrow of the seemingly well established parliamentary régime and its replacement by a ferociously pro-élitarian military dictatorship. A few years later, however, a group of officers of lower middle class provenience (alienated for this reason from the aristocracy) infiltrated the upper rungs of military hierarchy and under the leadership of Juan Peron gave to the régime an anti-aristocratic and pro-proletarian twist, thus producing a new kind of political system: a populist semi-fascism. In Chile during the last half-century politicians of middle-class origin have been using the proletarian masses as a battering ram for breaking into the charmed circle of wealth and glory; and in doing so have brought the country to the brink of a revolution on several occasions.

Students of Latin American affairs often speak of the rise to power of the middle class, but strictly speaking this is a contradiction in terms, for a class which seizes power places itself automatically on the highest rung of stratification. What the so-called dominance of the middle class means in reality is firstly that among the power élite there are many individuals of middle-class origin; and secondly, that governments sometimes adopt measures favouring the middle class – as a rule, however, at the expense of manual workers rather than of the rich.

When Jean Bodin speaks about the stabilizing influence of the middle class, he refers to the division of wealth; the implication being that the middle class can exert such an influence only if it is prosperous, which is not the case in Latin America. Penurious, embittered and clamorous, the Latin American middle classes are ready to support dictatorial movements. Their revolutionary potential, however, is diminished by a chasm in their midst between those who resent the privileges of the élite more than they fear or disdain the workers, and those who feel the opposite.

Until the present century the middle classes in all countries consisted chiefly of economically independent agriculturists, artisans and merchants who had neither the opportunity of seizing power nor any direct interest in who might wield it, so long as they had peace and security of their possessions. Moreover, whereas the middle class to which Aristotle refers were largely parasitic, in modern times people placed on the intermediate rungs of the social ladder were on the whole playing essential roles in the production of wealth. Although the Latin American middle classes comprise substantial numbers of managers, technicians, active businessmen and agriculturists, their bulk consists of incumbents of or aspirants to posts in grossly overgrown machines of public administration, in addition to a large number of superfluous lawyers. They do not contribute enough to production, but stake large claims to consumption, which they expect to be satisfied by some political sleight of hand.

Vertical Mobility

For many years now the eugenists have been deploring the fact that the upper classes were not reproducing themselves at the same rate as the lower. However, such an inequality of reproduction rates can lead to a deterioration in the general level of potential ability only if the distinctions of rank correspond in a substantial measure to differences at least partly dependent on biological heredity, which may be the case in a meritocracy but not in a society where the status depends almost entirely on an accident of birth. In view of the lack of accurate information, any opinion on this point must remain purely tentative, but it does seem that it is in the societies which are furthest removed from meritocracy – where, that is to say, there are least grounds for supposing that the upper classes contain a larger pool of genetic endowment – that the rich reproduce themselves faster than the poor, as appears to be the case throughout most of Latin America, especially in the more backward countries. Without bestowing any possible eugenic benefit, the greater reproduction rate of the upper classes gives rise to a situation where more people descend than rise on the social ladder – where, in other words, the déclassés outnumber the parvenus.

Owing to the absence of statistical data, my assessment of the trend of mobility must of necessity be impressionistic, even though the few other observers who have given thought to this matter arrived at similar conclusions. There are, however, deductive arguments which support this view. In countries where only people with incomes well above the average can feed themselves adequately, and where only the wealthy can afford good medical attention, the death rate must correlate inversely with status to a marked degree, and the upper class must reproduce itself much faster than the lower unless its birth rate is much smaller. In Latin America only in the most highly urbanized areas in the south does the birth rate tend to be lower in the higher strata; elsewhere it is equal or even greater than amongst the poor; possibly much greater if we take into account concubinage, which is largely a perquisite of wealth.

In view of the significant (though only approximate) correlation between race and status described previously, the widely noted phenomenon of the whitening of the population lends further support to the foregoing assessment of mobility. It may be, of course, that this whitening is purely illusory and repre·sents no more than an alteration in the criteria of statistical assignation. This is more likely in the case of the Amerindians who are distinguished by their way of life rather than by physical features; but as far as the negroids are concerned, the criteria of assignation are more purely racial because these people have no separate culture to keep them apart from their less pigmented compatriots. The same is true of the *mestizos*. Unlike Peru or

Guatemala or Mexico, Brazil has no large sectors of the population following the Amerindian way of life, and for this reason the statistics indicating the whitening of the population are more likely to correspond to some change in the genetic composition than to represent a mere passing of the cultural barrier.

DISTRIBUTION OF POPULATION IN BRAZIL*

	1940	1950
Europoid	54·8	56·9
Afroid	14·7	13·3
Amerindian	0·5	0·4
Mestizos	10·0	9·5
Mulattos	20·0	19·9
Total	100·0	100·0

* Source: adapted from Federico Debuyst, *op. cit.*

Taken alone, this table might fail to convince but it acquires additional plausibility when coupled with the following figures:

Afroid birth rate 316 ⎫
Mulatto birth rate 334 ⎬ Coloured death rate 25·5
Europoid birth rate 333   Europoid death rate 15·9

In Rio de Janeiro the infant mortality was 228 for the afroids and 122 for the europoids.

Vernon Lee Fluharty describes the problem of vertical social mobility in Colombia in the following words:*

It is true that the industrializing cities have their share of white-collar workers, public officials, and bureaucrats, and professional men of second category downwards. They are neither upper crust nor proletariat. Even in the large industries there are sons and relatives of the Great Families who are far below the rank of capitalist or entrepreneur. Therein lies the trap, the distinguishing characteristics of Colombian society. For a very high percentage of these people are the sons, the grandsons, and the great-grandsons of the people who once perched atop the apex of the social pyramid. Thus, most of the middle class are

* The Dance of the Millions. . . .

members of proud old families. They retain the prejudices, the basic beliefs, and the frames of reference of the class from which they are sprung. They try to emulate the mode of living of that class, and set their standards by those of the very top.

It is the rare child of the masses who, with the limited educational facilities open to him, can rise above the 'ignorant, illiterate, disease-ridden, malnourished, ill-clothed, poorly-housed, poverty-stricken, landless, dissolute mass which constitutes the bulk of the Colombian population.'

This peculiar character of the Colombian middle class arises from the dynamics of social mobility and the birth rate. In the United States, the capitalist-managerial class does not reproduce itself: that is, births are highest on the lowest economic levels. Hence, it becomes necessary to 'elevate' from the lower classes enough capable ones to fill the deficit left by the small birth rate among the managing classes.

In Colombia, the process runs contrariwise. Upper-class families have as many children as do the lower, and the survival rate of the well-born is much higher. Thus, there is a gain of white of the upper classes over the lower ranks, in a percentage sense. The upper class gains on the lower. Moreover, the upper-class Colombian generally leaves a numerous posterity, all to the manor born, all sucked and nurtured on its concepts, standards, and prejudices. Most of them will marry early, and generally they will reproduce by the time they are twenty-five. Frequently one sire may live to see one hundred of his descendants. The writer has been present at *reuniones de familia* where the numerous *parientes* ran well over two hundred, not counting *primos segundos*.

It is clear, of course, that not all these aristocrats and near-aristocrats can maintain even a precarious footing on the topmost rung of the economic ladder. Fortunes in lands, stocks, and chattels can be divided and subdivided only a limited number of times; *fincas*, so cut up, cease to be productive, and stocks to be worth much. Hence, second, third and fourth sons, grandsons and great-grandsons, are pushed down the *economic* ladder by the inexorable pressure of mathematics. But as they go, they take with them the rights, perquisites, and prejudices of the top *social* rung, often coupled with a resentment against fate and a longing for their lost birthright.

Such people never can identify themselves with the proletariat, or even with the genuine 'bootstrap' middle-class person. On the whole, they are people who feel that they were meant for better things, and they are against any scheme or system or ideology which preaches egalitarianism or levelling, for this denies that they will ever again achieve their lost world.

The déclassés have played a prominent role in the revolutionary movements in Europe. In Latin America the numerous illegitimate sons of the élite constitute an additional source of revolutionaries, of whom Fidel Castro is an example: an illegitimate son of a parvenu landowner, who demoted his half-brother and other relatives by nationalizing their estates. Equally important as the psychological is the purely numerical aspect of this phenomenon: that is to say, the contribution which it makes to downward mobility.

The excess of the reproduction rate of the upper classes over the increase in their wealth severely restricts the opportunities for social ascent, which has several far-reaching consequences. In the first place, it ominously lowers the level of ability of the administrative and managerial personnel by excluding many gifted potential recruits and including many mediocre but well-connected individuals. Secondly, this limitation of social mobility leads to an accumulation of frustrated ability in the lower classes, thus accentuating their rebelliousness: as on the whole people obey more willingly those leaders who surpass them in relevant skills and ability than those who do not — especially in an epoch when belief in the hereditary transmission of magical powers no longer holds sway. As a further consequence, the present ruling élite could easily be replaced by a new one recruited from below, which improves the prospects of creating a new social order through revolution. In a relatively meritocratic state such as Sweden or even Britain it would probably be quite impossible (or at any rate extremely difficult) to find amongst manual workers enough people of sufficient potential ability (let alone actual skill) to replace the present incumbents of the higher ranks in public and business administration without a disastrous fall in quality. This, however, was the case in neither Russia in 1917 nor in China in 1949 nor in Cuba in 1958; nor would it in all likelihood be the case in other countries of Latin America with the possible partial exceptions of Argentina and Uruguay.

Apart from the countries in the throes of revolution, the capillarity of the channels of ascent appears to be greatest in regions undergoing rapid industrialization and commercialization: that is to say, in the areas around Buenos Aires, São Paulo, Mexico City, Santiago, Bogota and Caracas. However, even there (with the probable exception of the Argentinian and the

Uruguayan centres) the downward flow seems to be of considerable magnitude. The aristocratic origins of large sections of the middle classes infuse into their outlook a nostalgia for ancestral glories and a contempt for the lower classes. Industrialization helps in this matter less than might be expected because it is directed chiefly by immigrants and expatriates. In this respect also Latin America contrasts sharply with North America where the recent immigrants used to do the hardest manual jobs whilst the conquering captains of industry and finance came mostly from long-resident families. In Argentina the development of industry and trade was almost entirely the work of the Italian, British and German immigrants. The same is true of Brazil, except that the British played a smaller role here, and of Chile where the Italians were less important and the Germans more. The native population remained on the whole apart from this activity, and it appears that its mobility was on the average downward, whilst the reverse was the case among the immigrants.

In southern South America the immigrants were generally assimilated rapidly, but in the tropics the large-scale industry, trade and finance were run entirely (and still continue to be run to a very large extent) by expatriates who lived apart from the natives and normally returned to their country of origin. The ethnocentric exclusivism of the expatriates no doubt helped to perpetuate and extend their quasi-monopoly on business, but they acquired it in the first place chiefly because of the small inclination and aptitude of the natives. Anyway, the fact remains that industrialization did not open to the natives as many opportunities of social ascent as would have been the case if they had taken the leading role. In consequence politics remained the chief opening for the native-born upward strivers, with all that this implies for the formation of the national ethos.

CHAPTER SEVEN

FORCES IN THE POLITICAL ARENA

Pretorianism

THE forces which defeated the royal armies were motley crowds of volunteers, few of whom shared Bolivar's and San Martin's concern for liberal ideals. Hatred for the Spanish colonial administration was the only common conviction, and once the Spaniards left, there was no ideology left – not even nationalism – because the embryonic nations were too amorphous to inspire deep devotion. So there were sparsely populated territories over which roamed warring bands, which here and there succeeded in establishing a semi-permanent sway. These recruited *ad hoc* bands had neither standard equipment, proper uniforms, nor systematic training. Their commanders – no drawing-room officers but rough men who had proven their mettle on the field of battle – fought for division of the spoils and personal supremacy unhampered by ideological considerations.

During the first two or three decades after independence the armies functioned as agencies of social reshuffling rather than as props of the established order: the rich were not especially attracted to a life of danger and exertion, and as in the hour of danger military prowess mattered more than family connections, many men of humble origins became commanders of armies and eventually presidents.

When life became more regular and the republics acquired some shape, the armed forces began to acquire the character of regular armies, particularly in the better ordered countries. This process was slow, and it was not until towards the end of the nineteenth century that the armies of the more progressive republics came to resemble their European counterparts. Chile led the movement of professionalization, helped by a German military mission, and by 1880 Chile, Argentina, Mexico and Brazil had regular national armies, although in the more backward countries like Guatemala and Bolivia the armies still retained the character of marauding bands. The movement towards professionalization was stimulated by the coming of new weapons and by conscious imitation of the European models. Artillery in particular required more elaborate organization of supply and greater technical preparation, and made it more difficult to seize power by organizing a band of *gauchos* in the pampas and marching on the capital. The revolutions did not cease but thenceforth there were usually fights between different factions of the officer corps, and for this reason they were less drawn-out and bloody.

With the abatement of warfare in the more progressive countries prowess in combat began to matter less and military life became less arduous, and the privileged classes began to reserve for themselves the higher military posts. In consequence the officer corps became in most countries an appendage of the landed aristocracy. The rank and file were naturally recruited from among the poor. Even in those countries which had laws prescribing universal conscription, in practice only the peasants were liable to be called up. Usually illiterate rustics were preferred, as they were regarded as more dependable than the city dwellers who might have their own views about politics.

Integration of the officer corps with the land-owning aristocracy, in combination with the consolidation of civilian political institutions, produced a certain decline of pretorianism in the second half of the nineteenth century. Apart from Chile where this process was already accomplished by 1830, government became predominantly civilian in Argentina by 1860, in Uruguay by 1890, and in Colombia by 1900. In Brazil the continuity of the monarchy prevented the worst excesses on the Hispano-American pattern and, although the military frequently caused a considerable amount of trouble, it was only during the brief period after the monarchy was abolished and before the aristocracy had organized republican institutions that pretorianism dominated Brazilian politics.

The trend away from pretorianism was limited to the economically more progressive countries: Central America, Ecuador, Bolivia and Paraguay were not affected. In Mexico Porfirio Diaz crushed his rivals and succeeded in maintaining order for more than three decades, but this was a military dictatorship.

The influence of the military upon Latin American politics receded until the 1920's. The prosperity of the region was growing and the changes in the social structure did not yet call into existence mass movements offering an open challenge to the established order, except in Chile, which had been ruined by the collapse of the nitrate market, and of course Mexico.

As Edwin Lieuwen says in *Arms and Politics in Latin America* p. 122 ff,

at the time of World War I, the fraction of the total area and population that was dominated by the military was declining, and by 1928 only six Latin American countries, containing but 15% of the total population, were ruled by military régimes. Then, abruptly, following the onset of the world depression in 1930, there occurred a striking relapse into militarism [i.e. pretorianism].

A rough measure of this phenomenon, though not always foolproof, was the number of presidents in uniform. Brazil, with its civilian traditions, managed to avoid it. But in Argentina, to take a different example, after nearly half a century of civilian rule, eight out of ten presidents between 1930 and 1957 were generals or colonels. To take a single year, in 1954 thirteen of the twenty republics were ruled by military presidents. In those countries which had never developed a civilian tradition in politics, like the republics of the Caribbean and Central America, the military tradition not only continued but was even reinforced.

The armed forces reassumed the political prominence which they had in the earlier parts of the nineteenth century but their role was now much more complex and ambiguous, owing to the entry of new forces into the political arena, and to the changes in the social roots of the officer corps. As the urban middle classes grew in number and importance, they began to send some of their sons into the army, and these men did not feel the same attachment to the cause of the Church and the landed aristocracy.

The social identification of the new-type officer with the urban groups was probably the fundamental cause of the junior officer uprisings that occurred in Latin American's armies in the second quarter of the twentieth century. In general, the ideological conflict was between the old and the new generation, between the generals, on the one hand, and the majors, captains and lieutenants on the other, with the colonels often pulling in both directions (Lieuwen, p. 126).

The struggle for spoils was, of course, nothing new. What was new in relation to the preceding decades was the willingness of the younger officers to enlist the support of the lower classes, frequently resorting to crass demagogy. In this respect, some of the more radically disposed officers, like Peron in Argentina or Arbenz in Guatemala or Busch in Bolivia, resembled Bolivar in the earlier stages of his career and other populist generals of the wars of independence, like the Chilean Bernardo O'Higgins. But in contrast to these early populist *caudillos*, the recent populist pretorians rose to power with the backing of officers' secret societies such as the Lodge of the Holy Cross in Bolivia, the Group of United Officers in Argentina or the Patriotic Military Union in Venezuela.

The fruits of the reforms sponsored by populist officers have not been very impressive. Many of them resorted to demagogy as a tactical weapon in the struggle against the established rulers, but once in power they betrayed their lowly supporters, and devoted themselves mainly to building private fortunes. Such was Ibanez in Chile – the first demagogic military dictator in the twentieth century in Latin America outside Mexico – such also was Sergeant Batista in Cuba who at the beginning of his political career had the reputation of being a communist revolutionary. Other pretorianist reformers were overthrown by officers (often older and senior in rank) devoted to the defence of the upper classes. This was the fate of Colonel Rafael Franco of Paraguay, of Colonel Arbenz of Guatemala, of General Rojas Pinilla in Columbia (although his populism was purely verbal), of Major Osorio in San Salvador, and of Colonel Busch and Major Villaroel in Bolivia who were both murdered. Peron might also be included in this category but his case is more complicated.

From the point of view of the extent of the influence of the armed forces upon politics, the countries of Latin American can be put into five categories.

I. The countries under military dictatorship of the traditional type: Nicaragua, Paraguay, Guatemala, Peru. Here we have the old-time triple alliance of the generals, the landowners and the Church.*

* Since this was written the Dominican Republic and Brazil have rejoined this group, while Peru has nominally left it.

II. The countries where the armies remain in the background of the political arena: Chile, Uruguay, Mexico, Costa Rica. In Costa Rica the army has been abolished and it would have to be re-established before a revival of pretorianism could take place. In Mexico the officer corps is integrated with, and closely supervised by, the ruling party. It seems therefore that only a violent split within the party could put the army back into its role of the arbiter of politics which it played until about 1938; particularly as the Mexican army is smaller in relation to the population than the armies of other republics, with the exception of Costa Rica and Uruguay. In Chile the army has the longest tradition of keeping out of politics but, despite this restraint, it has preserved its independence from civilian authorities, and it cannot be assumed that it would remain passive under all circumstances. The low pay of junior officers on the one hand fosters left-wing sympathies, but, on the other, it discourages from military careers men without a private income, and consequently helps the conservative elements to retain their predominance. It seems probable that the commanders would use the army against a government (even if duly elected) which would try to demolish the present social order, although it is not impossible that such an intervention might cause a split in the army, or even a civil war.

III. Countries in acute turmoil, where the armies are actively interfering in politics but are suffering from internal dissensions, and where their influence is at least partly counterbalanced by the power of civilian parties, labour unions and other pressure groups: Argentina, Brazil, Ecuador and Venezuela.

In Argentina the army has recently deposed President Frondizi and put a puppet president in his place. Nevertheless no military dictator has emerged. The country was in fact without a government because the army would not allow civilians to govern but was itself incapable of ruling because it was torn by strife between various factions of officers. In the main it was simply a struggle for personal advantage, with the displacement at the top accelerated by a curious discrepancy between glory and power, as the most powerful position seemed to be that of the commander of the Buenos Aires garrison, and a promotion from there to the post of minister amounted to a loss of real power. Although there is no absolute correspondence between membership of personalist cliques and ideological sympathies, the latter are not completely without influence, and there seem to be three main ideological groupings in the Argentinian army at the moment: (a) the partisans of a traditionalist, clericalist, élitist, anti-labour dictatorship – popularly called 'the gorillas'; (b) the protagonists of populist or socialist military dictatorship; (c) constitutionalists who are in favour of the withdrawal of the army from the foreground of politics. These cross currents are complicated by rivalries between the army, the navy and the air force. After much squabbling between the factions, the last grouping has won and a civilian president (Ilia) has taken office after a victory at the polls. Nevertheless, owing chiefly to the continuing economic crisis, his position remains gravely imperilled, and a return to military rule could still occur.

In Brazil Janio Quadros – a reformist president with somewhat socialistic leanings – was not courageous enough to withstand the threats of conservative generals and resigned. Subsequently a coalition of conservative deputies and generals would not allow the vice-president Goulart to take over until the constitution had been amended in such a way that the president lost most of his powers. Eventually Goulart succeeded in recovering the lost prerogatives but, after a period of stalemate when nobody really governed Brazil, he was finally ousted by the generals. The actions of the army were characterized by hesitancy due to internal divisions: there are strong radical, socialist and communist groups in the armed forces, and (despite the bloodless success of the recent coup) it is far from certain how the soldiers would behave if ordered to fight in a civil war.

The armed forces of Ecuador are split into feuding factions, the air force having a reputation of being left-wing. As always, the presidential succession is determined by coups of military cliques.

In Venezuela there are communist as well as ultra-conservative military cliques; and both permanently threaten the reformist government of Accion Democratica under the leadership of Romulo Betancourt.* Threatened by well-organized combat groups equipped from Cuba, Betancourt is forced to rely on the army for protection, with the result that the conservative officers

* Now of President Leoni.

have prevented him from carrying out many of the reforms which he planned.

IV. This category has only one member: Colombia, where the army plays a crucial role in politics, as it is engaged in continuous warfare against the rebels, but nevertheless remains a docile servant of the landed oligarchy – at least since the overthrow of the dictator, Rojas Pinilla.

V. A totalitarian régime where political commissars and the political police keep the army well under control: Cuba only . . . so far.

Pretorianism* feeds upon itself by means of a vicious circle. Its excesses have always been and still are one of the chief causes of the predicament of the republics of Latin America. Pretorianist incursions prevented a consolidation of civilian governing institutions and kept the countries in permanent turmoil. The strife and the weight of military parasitism condemned the nations to misery which made the achievement of political consensus and stability impossible, which in turn invited (or even necessitated) military intervention in politics. On several occasions the army intervened to maintain or restore order, and to stop the fighting between armed civilian groups such as the White Guard and the Red Militia in Chile; the pro-Prestes partisans and the Integralistas in Brazil; the fascist Gold Shirts and the labour militia in Mexico or the Liberals and the Conservatives in Colombia. At present, in addition to circumstances of long standing, the fear of communist subversion induces the upper classes (or at least important sections of them) to cherish more than ever the protecting wing of the army, and to tolerate pretorianist abuses, but a number of circumstances diminish the efficacy of the Latin American armies as organs of internal security.

Up till now common soldiers have remained the blind tools of the officers. Only in the early thirties, when the depression brought discontent over loss of pay and deterioration in food and quarters, did the rank and file become restless, and even then only in a few places. In 1931 the soldiers of one of the Peruvian regiments made an abortive attempt to seize the govern-

* For information about this phenomenon in other parts of the world see *Military Organization and Society*.

ment, and the sailors mutinied in Ecuador with equal lack of success. There have been, of course, other minor mutinies but they broke out over day-to-day issues and the mutineers had no political aspirations, except in Cuba (which seems to have a monopoly on unique revolutions) where in 1933 the non-commissioned officers under the leadership of Sergeant Batista overthrew their superiors and became the rulers. The docility of the rank and file is chiefly due to the general apathy, illiteracy and political indifference of the recruits, drawn by preference from the most ignorant sections of the peasantry. However, urbanization and industrialization are reducing the pool of such conscripts, and political awakening spreads even faster than literacy, as even illiterates are now exposed to political propaganda through the radio. The younger officers are also affected by ideological currents, and many of them are closely connected with the discontented sectors of the middle classes; so that their obedience cannot in all circumstances be taken for granted. The generals are aware of these possible weaknesses, and this is why they have been showing a great deal of caution and hesitancy during their recent political intervention in Argentina, Brazil and Venezuela. However, in Peru, owing to the larger proportion of ignorant peasants in the population, the generals have been able to carry out the recent putsch without meeting much resistance. It is relevant to point out that, though they would seem unbearably rough to most readers of this book, the living conditions in the barracks appear to the great majority of the Latin American soldiers as the height of luxury.

In varying measure, all the armies of Latin America are debilitated by corruption and indiscipline. If we tried to rank them in this respect, we would probably have to put the Chilean army at the top as the least addicted to these vices, and the Argentinian at the bottom – at least at the moment. Indeed, as far as Argentina is concerned, it seems that the venality and indiscipline of its soldiers are the chief cause of its troubles.

Fidel Castro's revolution in Cuba has demonstrated how weak an army can be, even if well armed and in possession of the requisite technical skill if it is corroded by corruption. Castro's partisans were able to defeat the bigger and better armed professional army of Batista, because the soldiers were engaged in peculation and fraud, and were completely devoid of any sense of honour, duty or even solidarity. Examples of modern totalitarianism show that a well-organized machine of terror cannot be overthrown from within so long as it remains austere, ideologically committed and led by capable men, but none of these attributes pertains to the Latin American armies of today. It follows that as a bulwark against communist subversion these armies are not very dependable, although military dictatorships might establish and maintain themselves for a considerable time; but, being incapable of solving their countries' basic problems and even aggravating them, they can merely stave off the danger temporarily.

The Church

The helplessness of the Cuban Church in face of the encroachments of the marxist régime offers an astonishing contrast to the dogged resistance of the Church in Poland, where its sway is perhaps greater now than it was before the imposition of the communist régime. The position of the Church in Cuba was not radically different from what it is in many other countries of Latin America, and it follows that the Church cannot be regarded as a strong barrier against the spread of communism.

None of the factors which strengthened the hold of the Church over the minds of its flock in Spain, Italy, Poland, Ireland and Northamerica ever operated in Latin America. In Spain centuries of warfare against the Moors produced a confluence of religious faith and patriotism, which was further strengthened by participation in religious wars and by the idealization of overseas conquests as missionary activity. The golden century of Spain was when she was the chief champion of the Catholic faith, and the nostalgia for the bygone glory links to this day religious devotion with national pride. Moreover, the clergy were always very numerous in Spain, and its lower ranks recruited from the popular strata, while ecclesiastic posts in Latin America continue to this day to provide an outlet for Spaniards and Portuguese in need of employment. Thus the widely spread economic interests vested in the maintenance of the ecclesiastical establishment reinforced the religious slant of the national pride and counteracted in some measure the resentment caused by the inclination of the Church to take the side of the rich against the poor. Furthermore, in spite of being so much nearer to the centres of industrial civilization, Spain was much less exposed to penetration by foreign business than the more important countries of Latin America and so its traditional way of life was better shielded from the corrosive forces of commercial civilization.

A nation nearly half of which casts its votes for the communist party can hardly be regarded as a stronghold of Catholicism, but at least the Italians satisfy their national pride as well as deriving some economic benefits from being masters of the Church, and this brings some measure of moderation into their anti-clericalism.

In Northamerica, dominated by the Protestants who hold most of the wealth, the Catholic Church was regarded by the poor Irish, Italian and Polish immigrants and their descendants as their haven. As the clergy had neither great wealth nor close connections with the upper class, they kept the confidence of their flocks and often tried to help and protect them; this is one of the reasons why these sections of the population remained impervious to socialist ideas.

Ever since the end of the Middle Ages Poland was surrounded by enemies of different faith: it fought Mohammedan Turks, Orthodox Russians, Protestant Swedes and Prussians. During the century of partitions only the Catholic Austrians treated the Poles moderately well, while the Russians and the Prussians persecuted them. Catholicism came to be regarded as a mark of membership of the nation, and the Church as the chief guarantor of national existence. The coalescence of allegiance to the Church with the national will to survive was strengthened by the sufferings inflicted by the nazis and the Russian communists.

In Ireland the situation was very similar. The Catholic clergy were the natural leaders and defenders of the Irish peasants and workers against the Protestant English landlords, officials, employers and usurers. Its concrescence with nationalism and class resentment brought religious devotion to the point of fanaticism.

None of the factors which enhanced the moral stature of the Church in the countries mentioned above ever operated in Latin America. The early association with conquest and slave raiding gave the Spanish-American Church (and to a slightly lesser extent to the Portuguese-American Church too) a predatory stamp which it retained for a long time. True, some of the early missionaries took the fate of the natives to heart, and became their sole defenders. Bartolomeo de las Casas and several other friars wrote impassioned pleas for a better treatment of the Indians; and our knowledge of the cruelties perpetrated by the Spaniards is derived chiefly from their works. Actually, as far as protests against barbarity are concerned, the record of the Spanish clergy of the sixteenth century is outstandingly good, for we must remember that much frightful butchery has been committed elsewhere without any protest from ecclesiastics. However, priests of such purity ceased to appear after the initial period of missionary zeal, when the stabilization of colonial rule created an ample supply of rich prebends and attracted to America many clerics by no means distinguished by their self-abnegation.

During the three centuries of colonial rule the Church became an indispensable ally of the Spanish Crown: not only because it helped to subjugate the Indians by teaching them the virtue of obedience, but also because the centralized ecclesiastic administration was crucial in containing the centripetal tendencies of the Spanish settlers, which might have broken up the empire into independent domains. In addition to the action of the Church through its own machinery, the clergy supplied a substantial proportion of the principal officials of the colonial administration: it was indeed a common practice of the kings to send a bishop as a plenipotentiary when the situation was particularly unmanageable. In order to forestall separatist manœuvres (as well as out of deference to the powerful pressure groups at the court) the higher posts in the Church – like the higher posts in the administration – were reserved for peninsular Spaniards, to the great annoyance of those born in America. In return for its services the kings gave the Church their total support: they prohibited the entry of Jews and Protestants, hunted down heretics and delivered them to the Holy Inquisition.

Closely collaborating with the lay authorities, the Church naturally took their side against any rebellious subjects, and for this reason all movements of popular resistance had an anti-clerical bias. In this respect the situation in the Spanish and Portuguese colonies was not greatly different from that in Spain and

Portugal, except that as the American communities were acquiring a consciousness of their separateness, embryonic ethnocentrism was becoming an additional source of anti-clericalism.

The peninsular affiliations of the Church determined its attitude during the wars of independence, in which the Church unequivocally took the side of the monarchy, condemning rebellion as sinful and even excommunicating the rebels. Even when independence was already a fact, the bulk of the clergy supported the belated attempts of the Spaniards to re-establish their rule. The victory of the insurgents did not destroy the Church, as the social and intellectual prerequisites of a Reformation were lacking, but it seriously undermined its strength: instead of the concrescence of nationalism with bigotry – as was the case in Ireland, Poland and Spain – the opposite association took root. The anti-clerical bias of nationalist reformers further stimulated the antinational tendencies of the clergy. These tendencies were particularly strong in Mexico where the higher ecclesiastics lent their support to Napoleon III's attempt to conquer the country and to impose upon it his relative as a puppet emperor. In addition to these historical antecedents, the large number and prominence of the Spaniards among the clergy perpetuated the dichotomy between nationalism and religiosity, though in a diminished form. This dichotomy was particularly serious in Cuba where until the end of the last century the clergy collaborated with the Spanish colonial authorities in stamping out the movement for independence, and where, until Castro deported them, Spaniards constituted more than two-thirds of the clergy.

In addition to the Church's anti-nationalist record, other circumstances, similar to those which prepared the ground for the Reformation, fed anti-clericalism in Latin America: these were the enormous wealth of the Church and the profligacy of its clergy. After the confiscation of the royal domains, the Church remained the biggest landowner, and appetite for its lands stimulated some anti-clericalism even among the traditionally clericalist aristocracy. As to profligacy, it seems that the clergy of Latin America were the most licentious in the world. Dispersed over enormous distances which made effective supervision impossible, living in a hot climate which stimulates sexual appetite and in a social environment where massive concubinage was the norm, holding sway over illiterate and superstitious people, most of the priests freely indulged in fornication, drunkenness and gluttony. As the clergy remained deeply attached to the traditions of the Holy Inquisition and were inclined to arrogate to themselves total power, many rulers, who were entirely indifferent to social justice and not at all anti-religious, had to attack them to defend their own authority. Moreover, by immobilizing enormous real property and hoarding precious metals, the Church acted as a brake upon the development of business enterprise and incurred the hostility of circles connected with commerce, which was one of the sources of the anti-clerical bias of most liberal parties.

Naturally, the relations between the Church and the State varied in accordance with the different circumstances in the republics and the personalities of the dictators and politicians. Some *caudillos* were devout and subservient to the Church. The most extreme case of this kind was Gabriel Garcia Moreno who, though an absolute ruler of Ecuador, regarded himself as an administrator of a papal fief, and even issued a decree in virtue of which every instruction from the Pope automatically had the force of law in Ecuador. Garcia Moreno substantially added to the already excessive wealth of the Church, made piety a condition of holding public office, and fiercely persecuted heretics, until his death at the hands of conspirators in 1875. On the other hand, Antonio Guzman Blanco (who alternated as dictator, elected president and grey eminence of Venezuela towards the end of the last century) is an example of an anti-clerical *caudillo* who was nevertheless conservative as far as the privileges of his class were concerned. His régime resembled somewhat the so-called enlightened absolutism of the eighteenth-century Europe: an authoritarian government, imposing economic liberalism and secularization, fostering higher culture, reducing the wealth of the Church and breaking its stranglehold on education.

In so far as the political divisions in nineteenth-century Latin America had any ideological basis, they were related to the divergencies between the traditionalists (i.e. conservatives) and the modernizers (i.e. liberals) who wished to make their countries more like England or France. In this conflict the attitude to the Church was crucial, and in most countries the liberals succeeded in jettisoning a substantial part of the heritage of Iberian clericalism; with the consequence that, except for Colombia and Ecuador, the legal framework is more secularized than in Spain, Portugal or Italy: in most countries non-catholics can hold public office and state-maintained education is non-denominational. The most anti-clerical, however, were the governments which actively sought to promote social justice. José Batlle Ordoñez, the founder of Uruguayan democracy, introduced civil marriage and divorce, strictly lay education, and even went as far as to forbid printing the word *dios* (God) with a capital D.

Anti-clericalism assumed the most extreme forms in Mexico. During the wars of independence the Church unequivocally took the side of the Spanish Crown, although among the lower clergy there were individuals who not only fought for independence but even identified this cause with that of social justice. Hidalgo and Morelos – the two great national heroes – were in fact simple vicars but the hierarchy excommunicated them and handed them over to the Spanish troops to be executed. The establishment of the republic brought about a conflict about the privileges of the Church. The Spanish Crown had extensive powers over ecclesiastical appointments but the Church maintained that these were the personal prerogative of the king, and could not be inherited by a republican government. The struggle for power which ensued also had an economic side: the Church was by far the biggest landowner in Mexico, owning perhaps as much as one-third of the best lands. Its possessions were not limited to rural estates: in Mexico City at the beginning of the last century the ecclesiastic establishments took more than half of all the rents. With the advent of the republic a new political class came into existence – many times larger than the corps of colonial officials, and comprising many *arrivists* in search of fortunes – and the property of the Church became the most obvious target. Upstart politicians and military men, knowing that they could not expect to remain in office for long, were in a great hurry to acquire estates and join the ranks of the landed aristocracy. On the economic side the conflict between the Church and the state which intermittently raged in Mexico can be regarded as a struggle for land between the ecclesiastics on one side and the lawyers and the military on the other.

The common concern for the maintenance of that social order in which their privileges were rooted had kept the conflict between the politicians and the lawyers within certain bounds, but this limiting factor disappeared with the revolution which brought in its wake the most severe persecution ever experienced by the Church in Latin America. The Mexican revolution was the most extreme, but by no means isolated, manifestation of a combination of anti-clericalism with social revindication. In other parts of Latin America too, the centuries of collusion in the oppression of the poor brought upon the Church the enmity of all those movements and organizations which took up the cause of the poor. Naturally the Church still has considerable influence but this is far greater among the rich than among the poor. A favourable attitude towards the Church is almost a badge of social respectability, and among the poor even those who go to church often blaspheme and curse the priests. The connection between religiosity and status is reflected in education: in those countries where there are both state and catholic schools and universities the latter contain a much greater proportion of students from wealthy families. This situation is in no way willed by the Church, but is the product of the simple fact that where there is separation of Church and state, the education provided by the former has to be paid for, whereas that provided by the latter is usually free. Nevertheless this selective intake accentuates the association of religiosity with privilege. There are groups among the Catholics which are trying hard to break the identification of religion with the defence of privileges, which they deem to be suicidal for the Church, but the menace of the revolutionary movements which stimulates these endeavours also produces a flight of the privileged classes into the arms of the Church, and thus reinforces this identification.

During the nineteenth century anti-clericalism was espoused by the liberal parties, supported by important sections of the privileged classes and was not necessarily opposed to the existing social order. Indeed, the attitude towards the Church was the only truly ideological issue which agitated the politics of traditional Latin America, and it constituted the chief bone of contention between the liberal and the conservative parties. The rise of mass movements for social revindication altered this, and caused the disappearance of upper-class anti-clericalism. This has happened even in Mexico where consolidation of the post revolutionary upper class coincided with a jettisoning of anti-clericalism.

Association of clericalism with the defence of injustice is further evidenced by a comparison of the republics which stand at the opposite ends of the scale: the control of the Church over culture and education, and its political influence, is greatest in Ecuador and Colombia, the two larger countries of Latin America where exploitation of the poor is most extreme; it is least extensive in Uruguay, the only country in the region which can be described as a relatively stable democracy or perhaps even as a welfare state. It must be emphasized, however, that the Uruguayan anti-clericals never advocated, let alone practised, persecution of the catholics. They opposed ecclesiastic prerogatives, and instituted a separation of the Church from the state, while allowing perfect freedom to practise any religion. According to various opinion polls, practising Catholics constitute only a little over half of Uruguay's population, but this does not mean that the Catholic faith has fewer roots in Uruguay than elsewhere because in the clericalist republics many people go to church without believing, and secondly, a very substantial part of the Indian peasants have not been completely converted and their allegiance to the Church remains ambivalent.

The astonishing thing about the Church in Latin America is its failure to christianize the peasant masses. With the exception of the Jesuit missions dissolved in the eighteenth century, (and to a lesser extent the Dominicans and the Franciscans), the clergy have been always concentrated in the towns, and the villagers seldom saw a priest. The contrast with the traditional village life in Europe, centred around the church, is striking. This fact is connected with the numerical weakness of the clergy. On the eve of Castro's revolution there were only 700 priests in Cuba, two-thirds of whom were Spanish. In Brazil there are only about 6,000 priests, more than half of whom are foreigners, mostly Portuguese. In the USA there is about one priest for every thousand Catholics. In Brazil there is one for every ten thousand. In contrast in Spain this ratio is many times higher, and not so long ago amounted to 1:100. The relative paucity of the clergy is both the consequence and the cause of the weakness of the

Church in Latin America in comparison with Spain and Portugal. (3)

The statistics of illegitimacy provide a good idea of how small is the hold of the Church over the masses. As mentioned earlier, more than half the births in Latin America are illegitimate. In Argentina and Uruguay the proportion is much lower, but in the Caribbean area it is as high as three-quarters, the record being held by Haiti with over 80%. Even in well-ordered Chile, this proportion was 60% until recently, and is now 40%. The high proportion of illegitimacy is due partly to the disordered family life caused by migrant labour and the legacy of slavery and serfdom, but a great many births registered as illegitimate occur to quite stable couples who did not bother, or could not afford, to go through the ceremony of marriage.

Among the differences between the countries it must be noted that the Brazilian clergy, though by no means free from the blemishes of their Spanish-speaking brethren, were and still are less addicted to intransigence and persecution, reflecting the somewhat milder disposition of the Brazilian as compared with the Hispanic nations with the exception of Chile. The peculiarity of the Argentinian clergy, on the other hand, seems to be their anti-semitic leanings.

There are many Catholics in Latin America who would like to break away from the terrible heritage and discreditable alliances, but the infusion of marxist ideology into an increasingly violent class struggle leaves them little room for manœuvre.* But even if the Church took up unequivocally the cause of the poor it would still be unable to compete with the communists for their allegiance, and would lose the support of the privileged classes. Perhaps, only after the masses have had an opportunity to experience the benefits of communist rule, and the clergy have been purified by martyrdom, might a revival of genuine religious feelings be possible . . . provided that it will not be then too late.

Recalcitrance of the Masses

Walter Bagehot attributed the smooth functioning of the British

---

* Since this was written the Chilean Christian Democratic Party has won extraordinary victories, the significance of which is discussed in the last chapter.

parliamentary system to the deferential attitude of the British people, and regarded the critical attitude towards authority as an important cause of the disorder which plagued French politics. This view is not without foundation, and it is certain that complete lack of respect for authority is just as fatal to democracy as excessive reverence. The great problem of political sociology is that of the conditions which permit the attainment of a golden mean in this respect.

As child psychology amply demonstrates, a respect for authority and a sense of duty take root only in cases where authority is exercised in accordance with recognizable rules. Another condition is that authority be used for furtherance of aims regarded as collective, that is to say at least partly for the benefit of the governed. The prototype of all authority regarded as legitimate is that of the father who may be severe but who cares and protects. Paternalism has always been acceptable to most people so long as it is genuine, that is to say, so long as it includes a real concern for the welfare of the subordinates.

As the etymology suggests, perfect paternalism can be found only in parent-child relationships, because only in such relationships is absolute power likely to be used for the benefit of the ward. Nevertheless a streak of true paternalism can sometimes be found in other relationships of authority, and it may suffice to instil loyalty into the hearts of the subjects. When one reads of the petitions which on various occasions have been submitted to kings one sees a touching and usually misplaced faith in royal benevolence. During the Spanish rule in America the Indians were inclined to believe in the good will of the kings, and on various occasions an appearance of a messenger (whether real or false) of the king, bearing a promise of rectification of the wrongs, sufficed to induce the crowds of rebellious peasants to disperse.

A lack of respect for authority makes it exceedingly difficult to govern by moderate methods, because in such a situation leniency is likely to be abused and to lead to anarchy. This is the normal consequence of a long period of misrule.

Owing to the enjoyment of long periods of constitutional government, political office is more respected in Chile than in any other country in Latin America. Chile has had a number of mediocre or dishonest presidents, but it was never ruled by a dissolute and blood-thirsty bandit like the Venezuelan Gomez or the Dominican Trujillo. However, during the last few decades the growing acerbity of political strife has been gradually eroding this Chilean heritage. In any case, in comparison with the nations speaking Germanic tongues even the Chileans have a scant respect for authority. The Venezuelans represent the opposite pole in this matter as far as Latin America is concerned. Venezuela was the only country in that continent where independence was followed by an uprising in the backlands which destroyed the upper class: the cultured and intellectual Bolivar was succeeded by the illiterate *gaucho*, Paez. Since then the country has oscillated between anarchy and tyranny.

With the exception of the USA and Switzerland, all those countries where representative government has functioned without interruption for several generations have been monarchies. The permanence of the living symbols of authority tends to inspire in the actual wielders of power a more impersonal view of their office, whilst the obligation of making ritual obeisances to the titular head of the state has a sobering effect on their vanity. Moreover, the presence of a monarch who has neither the power nor the need to rob makes it more difficult for the politicians to do so. It seems that the honesty and conscientiousness of the last Brazilian monarch contributed to his fall, for he was regarded as an encumbrance by the generals and the politicians determined to satisfy to the full their vanity and cupidity. It does not follow, of course, that monarchy constitutes a guarantee of public probity – apart from many other historical examples, a glance at Ethiopia or the Arab kingdoms shows that this is not the case. Nevertheless it remains true that constitutional monarchy is the only political arrangement under which a gradual reduction of social inequalities and a movement towards democracy has taken place; for it must be remembered that neither Switzerland nor the United States (with the exception of the South) were burdened by profound class cleavages during their formative years.

Setting a country plunged in misery on the road to a better future cannot be easy even for the wisest government, if the citizens firmly believe on the basis of their past experience that all rulers steal, and regard every call for sacrifice as a confidence trick.

As the quantity of goods produced cannot be increased by

passing a decree, it is very difficult to win the allegiance of the masses by showing them that something is being done for them. Where there are large and loosely-integrated estates, they can be broken up and the land divided; but where they are so highly integrated that their division would cause a catastrophic drop in production, or where (as in Haiti and the Dominican Republic) most of the land is already occupied by small peasant holdings, no immediate and palpable benefits can be bestowed upon the masses, and their confidence can be gained only on credit. Peron won popularity by using funds of foreign currency accumulated during the war, but no Latin American country has such a margin now.

People often live according to their reputations, and politicians who are despised have little incentive to act honourably. Their bad behaviour in turn confirms popular distrust and stimulates recalcitrance. Without a moral basis, government must rely on naked force, and even a leader with the best intentions (such as Romulo Betancourt) found it extremely difficult to break out of this vicious circle. As the Chinese proverb says: He who rides a tiger cannot dismount.

Any leader who wishes to make the people more amenable to his guidance must give visible and unquestionable proof of austere living; although by doing so he would not automatically ensure the success of his policies. Satiated Northamericans can take a vicarious pleasure in the mansions and yachts of their celebrities, and sedate Englishmen do not begrudge their social superiors their castles, but in Latin America the climate of opinion is very different: all privileges are regarded as ill-gotten. A conversion to a less cynical view of public office requires a conspicuous example of worldly asceticism. Latin America would benefit greatly from the influence of the English and Northamerican Puritans ... had they not disappeared, whereas contacts with the Puritans' hedonistic and materialistic descendants do not help.

Labour Movements

In the highly industrialized countries the trade unions have saved capitalism from self-destruction by restraining capitalist accumulation. Without them the predictions of Marx would in all likelihood have been fulfilled. If the entrepreneurs and the rentiers were able to increase their share in the proceeds from business activities, the process of accumulation of capital would have been accelerated, while the growth of the demand for mass-produced goods would have been slowed down because the increase in the aggregate earnings of the wage earners would have been slower. The slowing of the growth of demand for mass-produced goods would have reduced the returns on investment into productive equipment, and this conjunction of circumstances would have produced either a parasitic involution of capitalism or crises of over-production or both.

Some economists have tried to prove that the activities of the unions made no difference to the ratio of the revenue going into profits and interest to that paid out in wages, by showing with the aid of elaborate calculations that this proportion has remained constant in Britain and Northamerica during the last hundred years. However, even if we assume the correctness of these calculations we need not accept the conclusion because, although the said ratio may have remained constant, the rate of interest has decreased: in the prosperous countries the physical amount of productive equipment has greatly increased in relation to the labour force; and, if the relative shares of labour and capital remained the same, this proves that labour is more cheaply 'served' by capital than in the earlier period. Moreover the relative shares could have changed in favour of capital; and the example of the totalitarian countries, where no trade unions function, shows that the wages can be kept down even when the rate of growth of productive equipment exceeds considerably the rate of growth of the labour force. However, in economies based on authoritarian planning this situation cannot lead to crises of overproduction and unemployment, as it would in any economy based on private enterprise.

We must not conclude from the foregoing account that labour unions can obtain improvements in the standard of living of the workers regardless of circumstances, or that the only important factors are their numerical strength and cohesion. The unions have been able to affect the general standard of living favourably only where the production (above all of staple commodities) grew faster than the population. The pressure from the unions was a necessary (but not sufficient) condition of development of the productive forces of capitalist economies because it prevented the accumulation of capital from overtaking the demand for goods, and also because, by making labour dearer in relation to the cost of equipment, it made labour-saving devices more profitable. But what can be the results of this pressure when, owing to the influence of other factors, it fails sufficiently to stimulate the growth of productive forces: when the population grows faster than production; or at least than production of articles of mass consumption – above all, of food and housing – as is the case throughout Latin America? The first possibility is the acquisition by the unionized minority of sectional privileges, at least partly at the expense of less fortunate workers and of paupers.

Exclusivist tendencies are common in labour organizations. In Northamerica, for example, a number of unions enforce the colour bar and relegate the negroes to ill-paid jobs or unemployment; with the result that there are many times more negro professors than locomotive drivers. However, in the rich USA the discrimination is practised by a majority against the minority, whereas in the poor countries of Latin America it has to be directed against the majority, and the unions which have succeeded in raising the economic position of their members have created a semi-hereditary labour aristocracy. In Mexico, for instance, entry into employment by the state-owned oil enterprise (Petroleos Mexicanos) or the railways is practically reserved for sons of employees. The vested interest of the privileged unionized workers (who form about 5% of the total working population) constitutes one of the most important factors which enable the Mexican power structure to persist in spite of the acute poverty of the masses and widespread disaffection amongst the intellectuals and the students. Even in Chile, where (except during the short presidency of Aguirre Cerda) the unions never had intimate connections with the ruling circles, the concern for the differential advantages on the part of the workers in the most modern industries weakens the revolutionary impetus of the labour movement.

An exclusivist tendency has manifested itself on many occasions in the hostility of urban workers towards peasants. To take one of the most striking examples: during the Mexican revolution the urban workers, moved by their fear of the savage rustics, fought beside the troops of General Carranza against the peasant army of Emiliano Zapata.

The Mexican unions represent the extreme form of the tendency which characterized to a marked degree the trade union movement in other countries of Latin America, with the exception of Chile: namely, creation from above, that is to say, by politicians who were not workers. In Argentina as well as in Brazil the spontaneous development of the unions (mostly led by immigrants from Spain and Italy) was slow until the dictators inflated their ranks, emasculating them at the same time. Peron helped the unions, in order to use them as a counterweight to the army. In Brazil Vargas built up the unions and organized the Labour Party which controlled them. These developments differ radically from anything that happened in Europe.

The labour movements of western Europe grew independently, and at no time did they owe their strength to protection by the government. On some occasions (which except in Sweden have been brief) – such as during the governments of the Labour Party in Britain, or at the time of the premiership of Leon Blum in France, or at the beginning of the German Republic when Ebert was the Chancellor – the union leaders had direct influence upon the Cabinets; but the relationship between the unions and the British Labour Party or the French Socialist Party or the German Social Democratic Party dated from long years of uphill struggle: they were, so to speak, the two arms of the workers' movement, growing in spite of hostility or even persecution by the government. On the other hand, the position of the unions under Peron or Vargas differed radically from the complete subordination of the Nazi Arbeistfront or the so-called trade unions in the communist countries: neither Peron nor Vargas have succeeded in controlling the unions to the point of being able to use them for enforcing industrial discipline and goading the workers to greater efforts. Castro may be able to do it, but until the advent of his régime only Trujillo in the Dominican Republic had succeeded in subjugating the unions entirely. The Mexican unionists support the government but have to be placated by privileges, and enjoy considerable autonomy. It must be noted that exclusiveness and the striving for invidious privileges do not preclude the espousal of communist ideology and efforts to apply it to everything except one's own backyard.

Vargas, Peron, Cardenas, and to a lesser extent some other leaders of the state, have deliberately involved the unions in politics, but the economic situation has made this trend inevitable in any case.

When general improvements can be obtained through bargaining and strikes, the unions tend to become non-political; but when industrial action brings no gain, the unions inevitably gravitate towards direct involvement in politics, seeking either sectional advantages or the overthrow of the social order. Which of the two latter alternatives will materialize depends on how wide is the membership of the unions: the wider it is the less feasible is the pursuit of sectional privileges and the stronger the attraction of subversive action. Apart from the internal tendencies of the unions, their orientation depends on the general political climate: when the struggle between the parties is very bitter every large organization will sooner or later be drawn into the arena.

Repression by the organs of the state compels the unions to engage in subversive activities for the sake of survival, even where they were originally founded as apolitical associations for mutual aid. Although repression has often been motivated by greed and lust for power on the part of employers who could have afforded to make concessions, even employers and rulers of good will may be driven to it if the supply of goods is not large enough to satisfy the basic needs of the workers. As in other matters, a vicious circle operates here: poverty leads to violence directed against the workers, who become thereby ever more resentful and unco-operative or even bent on sabotage, and thus put yet another brake upon the growth of wealth.

The striving of workers for better conditions of existence gravitates towards violence not only in response to repression but also in consequence of the fruitlessness of peaceful means of pressure. When the cities throng with unemployed, full of resentment against their more fortunate employed fellows (and therefore willing to be 'blacklegs'), and when the workers have no reserves enabling them to sustain a long strike, the strikes cannot have much efficacy. Only highly specialized workers who cannot be easily replaced, and whose stoppages can create great and immediate dislocation, have any bargaining power at all.

The violence and massive vandalism, which usually accompany strikes in Latin America, are due to despair inspired by the futility of the strike weapon, in so far as they are not a simple reaction against violent suppression. (4)

Recourse to peaceful strikes requires the acceptance of an appropriate code of behaviour by both sides, willingness to compromise and to be reasonable, which need to become traditional to be effective. Thus, the mere speed of industrialization militates against good labour relations. The employers cannot divest themselves of the seigniorial disdain for their underlings and resentment at any manifestations of independence on their part, whereas the great majority of the workers (particularly to the north of Uruguay and Chile) are at best only a generation removed from illiteracy and servitude, full of gross superstitions, improvident, unruly and lacking in self-control, and easy prey to demagogues. Naturally, we can hardly expect the miserable workers to behave more responsibly than their social betters: when succession to the presidency is settled at gunpoint, the workers would have to be superhuman to be able to contain their actions within the limits of 'fair play' as understood in England or Sweden. The behaviour of the strikers often confirms the worst suspicions of their opponents; and, fearing their destructive propensities, even those employers who in a more propitious social setting would be willing to compromise, call for repression: another vicious circle. (4)

There are few exceptions in Latin America to Adam Smith's dictum (the first formulation of which is wrongly ascribed to Marx) 'that the state exists for the protection of the rich against the poor'; and the repression of labour would in all likelihood be more severe if a mechanism had not come into existence which permits the making of concessions to the workers, while depriving them of the fruits of such concessions: namely, inflation. It seems that mild inflation constitutes a necessary condition of the fairly smooth working of a combination of capitalist economy with representative government. It alleviates the burden of debt and interest (which otherwise would bring the economic system to a standstill) and it permits the occupational organizations to function and to retain the loyalty of their members by regularly winning nominal victories, without which they might become embroiled in internecine struggles. Rapid inflation, on the other hand, permits co-existence of elective government with extreme exploitation of the employed by the owners of the wealth.

Where the population grows more rapidly than the production of basic commodities, the numerical expansion of the labour unions accentuates the tendency towards violence, because (as pointed out earlier) the larger the labour movement, the less profitable the striving for sectional privileges. For this reason, the most revolutionary of all have everywhere been the peasants' leagues, even when led by a scion of the upper classes like Francisco Juliao.

In such circumstances it is hardly surprising that the communists are extremely powerful in the unions throughout the continent. With the exception of Argentina (where they have to compete with the *peronistas*) they are unquestionably the most dynamic element in the labour movement; and through closed members, fellow-travellers and sympathizers they exercise powerful influence even in those unions which they do not control. The politicians and employers, or the agencies of the rich Northamerican labour organizations, may cajole some of the leaders away from extremism, but this makes no permanent difference because such leaders eventually go over to the side of the bosses and are replaced by fiery demagogues newly risen from the masses. The buying of leaders does not prevent the drift of the movement towards subversion although it can unquestionably slow it down. The bias towards subversion and sabotage on the part of the mass unions (that is to say, other than those confined to small privileged sectors) is a product of misery and despair, but it has by now acquired a certain independent momentum as one of the forces which block the way out of the mesh of vicious circles.

Anti-yankism

Under the heading of 'Imperialism' I have tried to give an analysis of the problem of whether (and to what extent) the peoples of Latin America have benefited or suffered from the activities of foreign firms on their territory. Here I shall speak only of the roots of this powerful current of opinion which are not directly related to economic grievances – which are irrational or, so to speak, psychological. The simplest of such stimulants is envy, and it is not surprising that impecunious Latin Americans resent freely-spending Yanks.

Moreover, the egalitarian customs of the Northamericans aggravate instead of lessening this feeling because the wealth of unrefined individuals stimulates more resentment than that owned by persons of outward distinction. The upper classes, on the other hand, feel that wealth in hands of people without appropriate manners undermines the basis of the social order. The hostility against the Yanks is further stimulated by the incongruence between relative wealth and relative social status; a rough farmer from Illinois, who cleans his combined harvester with his own hands, may have much more money to spend than a genteel estate owner from Chile. So, simple envy of greater wealth combines with resentment against the newly rich who place little value on decorum as understood in Latin America.

The effects of incompatibility of manners are aggravated by the fact that, owing to the unique affluence of the USA and the relative cheapness of living in many countries of Latin America, many Northamerican tourists come from social categories whose counterparts in other countries would not dream of foreign travel. No wonder, then, that they are found wanting in gentility. Even worse: coming from a much wealthier and better organized country, where the standards of hygiene are far higher, they despise their hosts, and many do not refrain from voicing their feelings loudly. Being interested in the picturesque, they look for sights which the local residents would prefer to hide, stare from their comfortable cars at emaciated peasants trudging painfully on foot, and cannot help flaunting their wealth. Even those local inhabitants who are not so poor do not always enjoy being looked upon as if they were exhibits in a museum or a zoological garden.* Similar complaints about Northamerican tourists can be heard in Europe, but to be just, we must remember that the Spaniards and the Italians feel offended in identical ways by tourists from Germany and other countries of northern Europe. In fact, massive contacts between individuals from countries (or even regions of the same country) of widely disparate economic levels must generate a considerable

---

* It is significant, however, that domestic servants usually like working for Northamericans best, for Europeans next, and least of all for their compatriots.

amount of ill-feeling. The fact that the Northamericans are disliked most heartily in those countries of Latin America which they visit in greatest numbers shows how untrue is the notion (propagated by international organizations, travel agencies and schools of languages) that intensification of contacts between individuals generates friendship between the nations. The Soviet policy of restricting foreign travel not only limits the risks of contamination of Soviet citizens by bourgeois decadence, but also allows the inhabitants of foreign lands to cherish a romantic view of the Soviet man; for the sight of opulent Soviet bureaucrats, dining and wining in expensive restaurants, and the experience of having to clean their shoes, carry their luggage and haggle with them over tips, would cool somewhat the enthusiasm for the Soviet way of life amongst sufferers from capitalism.

The official propaganda of the USA does not improve matters: it consists mainly of telling people how nice life is in the United States, thus adding fuel to the already strong fire of envy, particularly as the majority of those whose appetite for the American Way of Life is whetted thereby can neither obtain a visa nor buy a ticket. Being thus debarred from the distant paradise, they are not even told how to bring about a similar condition at home. They hear, of course, about the virtues of free enterprise but they can see with their own eyes how this works in their countries, whereas the communist therapy has not yet been tried outside Cuba.

Never before has the world seen a powerful state distributing gifts instead of exacting tribute, but despite this generosity the Northamericans continue to be disliked. Justifications for this apparent lack of gratitude are not difficult to find: it can be argued that instead of giving presents the Northamericans should be paying more for the copper, coffee and other raw materials obtained from Latin America; and it is a fact that the loss of earnings due to drops in prices have in many instances greatly exceeded the amount of aid received. A verdict on whether the Northamericans were and are paying enough for what they buy can be given only on the basis of a number of debatable assumptions about the ethical aspects of international trade. Thus political sympathies decide which view is adopted, and the anti-yankists can say that the subsidies amount only to a small part of the wealth sucked out of their countries. Furthermore, there is the argument, not devoid of validity, that self-interest rather than generosity lies behind the professed desire to help, that the aid to under-developed countries is merely a new form of the old practice of buying allies, and that any feelings of gratitude would be irrelevant. When Che Guevarra told the Latin American delegates to the conference at Montevideo that they should be grateful to Castro for the gold which they were receiving from the USA, he was not far from the truth because it is a fact that the generosity of the USA is prompted by the fear of communism conquering Latin America in the wake of economic collapse. Indeed, altruistic generosity and· gratitude are rare enough between individuals, and are almost entirely absent from the relations between nations. Lack of gratitude, however, need not amount to the definite hostility which is due to the inclination (noticed three hundred years ago by de la Rochefoucauld) to hate the benefactor who shows condescension or who is merely suspected of secretly harbouring such feelings.

In considering the feelings of the mass of Latin Americans about the financial aid from the USA, we must take into account the unpleasant fact that much of it never reaches the people for whom it is destined. For instance, most of the foodstuffs, blankets, etc., sent from the USA to the starving peasants of Peru, victims of floods and earthquakes, were sold in the shops in towns. As the goods were worth millions of dollars, the principal perpetrators of this fraud could easily be discovered but no prosecutions were instituted. In Chile some officials who stole goods sent as relief for the victims of the terrible earthquake of 1960 have been punished but most of the relief funds were diverted to uses other than helping the victims. The US officials bear a very small share of guilt in such affairs, because their interference in such matters would be regarded as infringement of sovereignty. The result, nevertheless, is that ordinary people, who read in the newspapers about the extensive aid from the US but see little of it, conclude that the whole story is just a lie spread by journalists hired for the purpose.

Outside Argentina and Uruguay individuals of pure European descent form a small minority of the population. Even in Chile, the third 'whitest' country, the majority shows unmistakeable traces of Indian ancestry, So, it is not surprising that the racialism of the Northamericans greatly adds to their unpopularity, particularly among the lower classes where darker types are more frequent. This is particularly true of the Caribbean nations. In addition the communists never tire of branding the Northamericans – and for that matter West Europeans – as incorrigible racialists. Unfortunately these assertions, though exaggerated and one-sided, are not without foundation as many people in Latin American know from their own experience. Although Castro himself is fairly europoid he is regarded by many darker Latin Americans as a fighter against racial discrimination, which greatly adds to his popularity. Northamerican propaganda services in Latin America can profitably be scrapped so long as racial discrimination continues in the USA; for it is no exaggeration to say that one incident like the famous disturbances in Little Rock suffices to nullify a year's work by an army of propagandists, and is taken as a conclusive proof that the vaunted Northamerican democracy is all sham.

It may be worth remarking that oppression of the negroes cannot be explained in economic terms, as it can be in Rhodesia, for instance. In the USA the negroes constitute less than 10% of the population, and their exploitation can add little to the wealth of the rest although it benefits certain marginal groups. For the same reason, and in contrast with the situation in southern Africa, an equalization of political rights could not lead to a reversal of the roles and wreaking of vengeance upon the former masters. In Northamerica racialism provides an outlet of least resistance for the ubiquitous and irreducible dose of normal human nastiness. Moreover, in a highly competitive society, where an economic failure is regarded as evidence of personal inferiority, there are many people who find in racial pride the only prop for their self-esteem, and the only opportunity of satisfying the universal human craving for somebody to look down upon; particularly as these feelings are based on something which cannot be lost in competitive struggle. Racial discrimination in the USA gives to the communists such enormous advantage that it would be surprising if some of their secret agents were not abetting the racialists.

The prestige accorded in the USA to Nordic appearances slightly offends the upper classes of Latin America amongst whom swarthy types predominate. This is one of the reasons of the greater popularity of Latin Europe in those circles. Politically this is not an important factor but neither is it completely negligible.

Among the roots of anti-yankism in Latin America we must include the natural dislike of the stronger, particularly if he has the reputation of being a bully. And it is perfectly true that on many occasions the representatives of the US government, or even of commercial firms, have spoken to the dignitaries of Latin American states in a peremptory and disdainful manner, and compelled them to do things which rightly or wrongly they did not wish to do. The policy of The Big Stick could hardly fail to leave a heritage of bitterness. However, such is the meanness of human nature that a vigorous bully elicits admiration and even a sneaking affection as well as hatred, whereas an ex-bully draws upon himself nothing but abuse. Thus, as the Northamericans began to become more conscientious and delicate in their relations with their southern neighbours anti-yankism gained in force. Finally, nothing helped so much as the Cuban fiasco to build the picture of the Yank as a horrible but decrepit bully who can be insulted as he deserves without fear of consequences, until Kennedy's successful brinkmanship restored the prestige of the United States.

Living in societies pervaded by parasitism, the Latin Americans generally believe that wealth is the fruit of exploitation, and they automatically extend this interpretation to the relations between nations: if the Yanks are so rich then it must be because they robbed and cheated other nations, above all their southern neighbours. As they seldom see economic virtues rewarded, it hardly occurs to most Latin Americans that these Yanks might be so rich because (in addition, of course, to the good fortune of having at their disposal ample natural resources) they have worked and saved hard for many generations. In this way, anti-yankism is fed by an extrapolation of the popular view of the nature of economic relations which fits well enough the facts of communal life as experienced by ordinary Latin Americans.

Anti-yankism is a source of many comforts: by blaming the Yank for all their misfortunes many Latin Americans ward off unpleasant thoughts about their national character, and escape feelings of guilt. The latter point is probably fairly important in the motivation of the people who are on the exploiting side.

Anti-yankism promotes social cohesion because it is one of the few political sentiments which are fairly general throughout the nations of Latin America. Moreover, hostility towards a foreigner drains internal antagonisms of their emotional charge. On the other hand, as every psychotherapist knows, an individual who refuses to recognize his own faults and errors, and insists on blaming others for all his misfortunes, has less chance of cure or self-improvement than a person who is prepared to face the truth about himself. In the same way, harping upon the iniquities perpetrated by the Yanks, which usually goes far beyond what is justified by the facts and assumes the character of an obsession, distracts many Latin Americans from doing something positive for their countries, or even from thinking seriously about what should be done.

The Appeal of Communism

To a thinking or sensitive or merely disgruntled Latin American communism cannot fail to appear attractive. Surrounded by poverty, injustice and corruption, seeing the blatant ostentation of the selfish rich, he cannot be indifferent to the enchantments of a doctrine which promises a better social order. Living far from the borders of the Soviet empire, he has no opportunity of making friends with people who have personally experienced the blessings of the workers' paradise, and he rejects as lies all the statements hostile to communism which he finds in the press. In not accepting such information, the ordinary Latin American is by no means behaving irrationally because he can see with his own eyes how mendacious the right wing press is. It tells him that everything is perfect in the country, and the leading articles are written in a sublime tone of pure idealism which camouflages unscrupulous defence of extortion. During the long reign of Trujillo, the abject sycophancy of the Dominican press equalled if not surpassed the exploits of the journalistic lackeys of Hitler and Stalin; and even in the relatively democratic republics the pro-government press is too apologetic to be respected. However, we should not attach too much weight to the discredit of the right-wing press as a factor which stimulates the spread of communism because in France a quarter of the electors vote for the Communist Party, in spite of the existence of good newspapers and the abundance of refugees from communism.

Seen from afar and without critical verification, the Soviet achievements seem greater than they are. The majority of the Latin Americans – including the intellectuals – imagine that pre-revolutionary Russia was something like Bolivia or Peru. They do not realize, or at least do not bear in mind, that old Russia produced not only great musicians, novelists and poets, but also scientists of the first order: Lomonosov, Mendeleyev, Lobatschevski and Pavlov belong on any reckoning to the category of great discoverers; and nothing equal to their works has ever been written in Spanish or Portuguese. At the turn of the century Russia had engineers, economists and historians equal to the best in western Europe: insufficiency lay in their number not in their quality. (The same, incidentally, was the case with the weapons used during the First World War.) Tsarist universities demanded from their students more knowledge than the best universities in the USA, and their higher degrees were the most difficult in the world. The peasants suffered from sporadic famines but the majority of them were not debilitated by continuous undernourishment, as is the case with the poor of Latin America, with the exception of Argentina. It is clear that the cossack dance, which is probably the most exhausting ever invented, could not have been the most popular dance if the population were seriously debilitated. The rate of growth of the Russian industry at the end of the Tsarist régime was the highest in the world, and if it had been maintained, the Russian industry would have surpassed by now that of the USA. Consumption of meat per head was higher in 1913 than it is today; and after uninterrupted progress since 1945 the real wages had attained by 1962 the level of 1913. Naturally, Soviet industry is immensely larger than the Tsarist was but the level of the starting point has been assiduously belittled in order both to magnify the achievements of the Soviet system and to mislead the inhabitants of the poor countries of Asia, Africa and Latin America into thinking that they are in the same situation as the Russians were under the Tsars, and therefore, that they can easily have an industry like the Soviet if they only adopt communism. Belittling the wealth and the speed of economic development of Tsarist Russia is extremely important, because a true presentation of the initial position at once raises the question of whether the development of Soviet industry took place because of or in spite of the system. I do not wish to suggest that the facts justify opting for the latter alternative; but what matters from the point of view of an analysis of the appeal of communist ideology is that this complex problem is presented in a way which admits neither doubts nor qualifications.

Neither military power nor advanced technology constitute a proof of the human value of a system of government, but they produce an aura which gives a favourable colouring even to its least desirable aspects. Moreover, whatever the moral merits, most people want to be on the winning side, so that the exploits of the Soviet cosmonauts greatly enhance the appeal of communism.

Hostility to commercial occupations constitutes one of the most essential ingredients of communism, and it feeds upon the resentment generated by parasitic involution of capitalism and traditions of disdain for such occupations. In Latin America the disdain for commerce is not nearly so pronounced as it was in eastern Europe and in old China but it does exist and it enhances the persuasive force of communist ideology. This ideology, moreover, attracts support of the badly paid or unemployed members of the class of white-collar employees because it advocates nationalization and general extension of the activities of the state, which imply creation of a large number of bureaucratic posts.

Communism wins adherents much more easily in Catholic than in the Protestant countries. Can this be accidental? One possible explanation is that the Protestant countries are all prosperous whereas all the entirely Catholic countries are poor. The only country in the world which has neither a large number of Protestants nor widespread poverty is France, and there about half of the population is irreligious and the Church is disestablished. There is thus an indirect connection between Catholicism and communism in the sense that Protestantism, by promoting prosperity, prevents the emergence of a social environment propitious to the spread of ideologies preaching violent subversion. There is, however, also a more direct link: Catholicism is an authoritarian creed which inculcates submission on matters of conscience, and such an attitude can be transferred to another object. A person accustomed to letting a priest decide what is right and wrong will more easily submit to a party secretary than somebody who relies on his own conscience or his own interpretation of Holy Writ; and once it is accepted that the Man at the Top is infallible, it is psychologically of secondary importance whether he resides in the Vatican or in the Kremlin. Moreover, Catholicism extols the will to believe what is logically absurd, which is a very good background for a marxist. The psychological affinity between Catholicism and communism is further proved by the fact that many disillusioned communists of Protestant or Jewish background become converted to Catholicism.

Man is seldom a rational animal, and people who change faiths usually do it for purely emotional reasons. So, the process of the weakening of the influence of the Church and of its replacement by communism among the masses of Latin America is only in a small measure due to the progress of scientific education; although it is true that acquaintance with natural science does undermine the readiness to believe in saints and miracles without immunizing against pseudo-scientific political doctrines. Unquestionably the most important factor which stimulates the transfer of allegiance of the masses from the Church to the communists is the resentment against the collusion of the Church in exploitation of the poor.

As far as the intellectuals are concerned, in addition to the usual promptings of discontent, there is the superior intellectual merit of marxism, which wins by default. Allied with the ecclesiastics and the military, the conservatives have been consistently anti-intellectual, and hardly ever attempted to support their case by rational argument. This shortcoming, however, is inevitable because in order to put forth a reasoned case for conservatism there must be something in the country which is worth conserving – that is to say, some features of the traditional order which benefit even those who have no privileges – which is the case only in very fortunate countries. The lip-service paid to the liberal ideals has about as much relevance to the situation in Latin America as has Marx's vision of the communist paradise to the realities of Soviet life. Moreover, the truth about Latin American societies (as about many others) is so grim that the line of least resistance for somebody not suffering personally is to avert his eyes.

Collusion between the Extremes

Even in countries where there are civil liberties worth fighting for, the menace of communist infiltration is often used as a pretext for clamping down on all nonconformists and reformers; and most of the avowedly anti-communist organizations are interested in combating communism only in so far as they can thereby further the preservation of the privileges of the wealthy. We cannot therefore be surprised that in countries furthest removed from the ideals of justice and liberty, anti-communism seldom amounts to more than taking the side of the rich against the poor. The lack of a genuine attachment to professed ideals, on the part of the anti-communists as well as the communists, provides a foundation for a collusion between them directed against all sincere reformers and protagonists of justice.

The habit of branding as communist everybody who opposes entrenched privileges helps the real communists a great deal, as it bestows upon communism a certain aura of saintly martyrdom, makes many people disbelieve the truth about the communist manœuvres, helps the real secret agents to camouflage their activities, and establishes in the minds of a large section of the public a link between opposition to communism and subservience to vested interests.

The collusion in question is not confined to Latin America: there are examples from elsewhere, the best known being the joint attack of the nazis and the communists upon the German social democrats. Although the decisive reasons for it pertain to political strategy, this collusion finds some support in the psychological affinity of ideologies preaching hatred, violence, blind obedience and draconian punishments, and in the hatred which the servants of despotism feel for upright independent-minded people. As is well known, a bigot or a priest almost always prefers a believer in a religion violently opposed to his own to a free thinker; and the attitude of an adherent of a totalitarian doctrine is analogous.

The communists shape their strategy upon the reasonable assumption that the greater the misery, exploitation and disorder, the better their chances of seizing power, and therefore they oppose most violently those willing and able to remedy these evils. They helped Hitler because they thought that he would bring ruin upon the capitalist world and place it at their mercy. They came very near to a fatal miscalculation but in the end their reckoning proved to have been right and brought them an extensive empire in eastern Europe. Equally well calculated seems to be their practice of abetting the Latin American dictators and helping them fight democratic reformists. Their collaboration with Batista has paid them handsomely. Equally astute, though not yet crowned with final success, has been their vehement opposition to Latin America's most promising reformer, Romulo Betancourt, who was prevented from putting much of his programme into practice by having to rely upon the army for protection against the communist terrorists.

On the other side of the fence, the predatory despots and oligarchs have an interest in appearing as the only alternative to communism, which enhances the persuasive power of their clamour for subsidies and arms from Washington, and brings them the support (or at least neutrality) of various elements in their own countries which would favour even a radical assault upon the existing order but justifiably fear the communists. For this reason the communist party has often enjoyed tacit or even open tolerance when all other opposition has been mercilessly stamped out. A ferocious tyrant like Leonidas Trujillo – who cruelly avenged the slightest criticism – refrained from taking effective measures to annihilate the communist party, and for a few years even actively encouraged it. The Peruvian dictator Odria's flirtations with the communists – to mention another example – had a similar background, the common enemy in this case being the APRA. The normal communist response to such advances is to set up two ostensibly independent parties, one of which comes out into the open and collaborates (at least up to a point) with the dictator, whilst the other proclaims its opposition through the mouths of exiles and organizes a clandestine network for future use.

The communists cripple the reformist movements by infiltrating into them and sowing strife and confusion in their midst, discrediting worthy causes by using them as camouflage for their machinations. They have succeeded in perverting not only innumerable political and cultural associations but even the agencies of UNO, especially UNESCO.

The foregoing gruesome picture is lightened by the discord

within the communist ranks between the followers of Moscow and those of Peking. Possibly this rift has averted communist seizures of power in a number of Latin American countries. Unfortunately, however, though squabbling among themselves, the communists may have enough influence to prevent the emergence or victory of sensible reformist movements, thus indirectly helping to perpetuate the misery and oppression of the working classes.

CHAPTER EIGHT

REVOLUTIONS

The Mexican Revolution

THE Mexican revolution which broke out in 1911 was no smaller an upheaval than the Russian although the resulting social order was more like the preceding one than in Russia's case. In the magnitude and duration of the confusion the state of Mexico most resembled that of China after the collapse of the Confucian empire, which also occurred in 1911.

The first resemblance between the Russian and the Mexican revolution was that in both cases the first push was given by moderate middle-class elements attempting to replace a despotism by a constitutional and elective government; and in both cases the overthrow of the conservative autocracy released forces which attacked the entire social order. The crucial difference, however, was that in Russia the attack was directed by a well organized and disciplined party determined to erect on the ruins a society of an entirely new kind, whereas in Mexico the old order was badly mauled but not destroyed by a spontaneous upsurge of the masses without any guidance from a doctrine or a party. Moreover, whereas Kerensky was overthrown by Bolshevik ultra-revolutionaries, his Mexican equivalent, Francisco Madero, succumbed to the treachery of his own general, Victoriano Huerta, who set himself up as dictator in traditional style. The struggle against the usurping general waged under the leadership of Venustiano Carranza created conditions propitious to the eruption of the armed peasantry upon the political arena.

Why did the revolution take such a turn, deviating from the traditional pattern of civil war between rival bands of mercenaries? In seeking for an answer to this question we must remember that peasant uprisings were nothing new in Mexican history: Mexico has always been a conquest state in which the descendants of the conquered race were cruelly exploited and occasionally driven to desperate rebellions. We could, therefore, regard the presence of this inflammable mass as a constant, and try to find out why this particular outbreak achieved a larger measure of success than those which have preceded it. We might seek an explanation in the extent of the breakdown of the containing forces of authority, but this does not seem to be justified because the periods of equally great anarchy which Mexico had experienced before did not occasion a general assault on the land-owning class. The factor which allowed the uprising of the peasants to assume such huge proportions – which prevented its localization to a single province as had been the case in the past – was the mexicanization of the peasants.

The few hundred followers of Hernando Cortez would not have been able to conquer Mexico if its inhabitants were united. Without the succour from the Aztecs' indigenous enemies and the resentful subjects, the Spaniards would in all likelihood have suffered a defeat. Their descendants could continue to rule owing to the persistence of tribal divisions and the variety of tongues. As the rebels neither knew nor cared what their counterparts in other provinces were doing, the outbreaks were confined to a region, and the aristocracy could always muster sufficient forces at the scene of conflagration. The advent of the railways, the expansion of commerce and industry and the growth of towns during the thirty years' peace enforced by Porfirio Diaz, produced a detribalization of a large proportion of the peasants, who came to form a mass much more integrated than a collection of tribes and clans, and possessing a rudimentary class consciousness which made it more susceptible to revolutionary propaganda. As many more of them now knew Spanish, they could form large supra-tribal armies.

The gradual integration of the peasants into the nation was not accompanied by any improvements in their lot: on the contrary, their misery had grown worse. Owing to the peace the population had increased whilst the growth of wealth was almost completely confined to the construction of urban properties and railways, and the expansion of production of exportable goods, none of which brought any benefits to the peasants. Even worse, they were being robbed of their land and in consequence the production of basic consumption crops – maize, wheat and beans

– declined. As described earlier, the Porfirian era witnessed an acceleration of the process of concentration of property in land. The widening of the gap between the rich and the poor – which did not occur where it should have according to Marx's prediction – did take place in Mexico on the eve of revolution. Whilst explosive potential was accumulating below, the traditional land-owning aristocracy was becoming very discontented because of the intrusion of foreigners, chiefly Northamericans. By 1910 foreigners owned about one-seventh of Mexican land. Moreover, the foreign-owned mines and cotton farms were luring away labour from the *hacienda* and generally unsettling the old customs of rural Mexico. The development of the banks – again mainly foreign-owned – led to the growing and very much resented dependence of landowners on financiers, particularly as Mexico was becoming more and more exposed to the consequences of the vagaries of price movements on international markets, owing to its increasing dependence on exports.

The gradually growing class of literate urban white-collar workers constituted another element of revolutionary potential. Unprepared by tradition to make its way in business, and seeing the top positions monopolized by aristocrats and foreigners, it provided an ample supply of ideologues and organizers of the revolution. So on the eve of the outbreak only a small clique of direct beneficiaries remained satisfied with the régime.

The contact with Northamerica undoubtedly made the situation more explosive than it would otherwise have been, and probably accounts for the fact that a revolution of this kind broke out in Mexico rather than in other countries of Latin America where the social situation was fairly similar in other respects. On the one hand, the commercial freebooters from Northamerica were dislocating the traditional patterns of social relations, aggravating the exploitation of the poor and the hatred which the latter felt for the rich, whilst at the same time undermining respect for authority by their manners. On the other hand, the acquaintance with the customs and ideas of a more egalitarian and law-abiding society across the frontier could not fail to stimulate the Mexicans' resentment against injustice and oppression in their own country. What is more, despite the close links between Northamerican business and the dictator, Mexican fighters for justice, such as the brothers Flores Magon or Francisco Madero, not only found in the USA a refuge from which they could conduct propaganda and direct subversion, but also received from Northamerican sympathizers moral and financial support or even arms. In a way, at the beginning of the present century Mexico had already experienced the unsettling and double-edged impact of Northamerica which modern means of transport and communication have spread throughout the continent and beyond.

After these etiological considerations let us glance at the sequence of events. Porfirio Diaz was overthrown without much bloodshed and shipped off into exile, and Francisco Madero assumed the presidency. At no time, however, was he able to control the country completely. Having neither a well-organized party nor an army of his own, he came to rely on the *porfirista* troops whose chief, Victoriano Huerta, finally betrayed and murdered him. The Constitutionalists, who, after a long struggle under the leadership of Venustiano Carranza eventually defeated Huerta, never constituted a unified force. Their camp consisted of numerous armed bands, some like soldiers of a regular army, others more like simple bandits, with many intermediate shades and alternating roles. The biggest chiefs were Emiliano Zapata in the south and Pancho Villa in the north. The former was a true revolutionary although his only doctrine was belief in the irremediable wickedness of the aristocracy from whose exactions his own family has suffered grievously. It was Zapata who first demanded the breaking up of the estates, and who transformed the revolution – which up until that point was more or less purely political – into a class war. Pancho Villa also assailed and despoiled the wealthy but on the whole he behaved less like an avenger of the poor than like an ideologically uncommitted bandit.

The Constitutionalist alliance broke soon after their victory over Huerta. The usual quarrels about power, precedence and division of the spoils were aggravated by the division between the peasants, with their uncouth leaders, and the urban elements led by Carranza. Carranza might very well have lost had he not found an ally in the person of Alvaro Obregon – a man of very humble origins, endowed with a great talent for organizing and generalship. To outbid Zapata, Carranza proclaimed socialist ideas, such as agrarian reform, free education for all, laws protecting labour and fostering its unionization, nullification of foreign contracts and monopolies, civil liberties and government by election. When the Carranza-Obregon coalition finally won, these promises were written into the Constitution promulgated in 1917; although, of course, with the economy in ruins they were unable to implement them.

In 1920 Obregon overthrew Carranza and remained the boss until his assassination in 1928, although he relinquished the presidency in 1924 in favour of his chief assistant, Plutarco Elias Calles. After the death of Obregon, Calles became the ruler, governing through puppet presidents until 1934 when Cardenas – whom Calles installed with the intention of manipulating him – turned against his master and sent him off into exile. Throughout this period the government was based on force of arms with a constant recourse to assassination and bribery. The revolutionary leaders could not resist the tempting fruits of power and fell into peculation and self-indulgence. Little was done to put into practice the noble ideas of the revolution. The only issue into which ideology entered was the struggle against the Church.

The Church had lost much of its wealth and power during the era of Juarez, one of whose chief aims was to break the stranglehold which the Church had not only on the culture but also on the economy of Mexico. Apart from being necessary for modernizing the country, this policy had the additional advantage of providing a source of rewards for liberal politicians. Nevertheless, at the beginning of the present century the Church still remained wealthy, powerful, and in close alliance with the landowning class, and was regaining its former influence in politics. It was inevitable therefore that the revolution had to take an anticlerical turn, particularly as the clergy were not averse to inciting the devout to violent resistance or even to organizing counterrevolutionary attempts The chief bone of contention (apart from sources of income) was control over education, where the clergy were determined to restore their monopoly On the other side, the rulers who had emerged from revolution were able to forget about agrarian reform and social justice, but felt deeply about education. It was clear that, even apart from the considerations of justice, the country could not be modernized without a radical extension and improvement of education. Moreover, in view of the open hostility of the Church, the new régime had to debar the Church from access to schools for reasons of self-defence. On the other hand, the prohibition of religious ceremonies was in the nature of a temporary reprisal and was never effectively enforced.

The struggle between Church and state reached its peak during the ascendancy of Calles. It subsided somewhat under Cardenas, who guaranteed freedom of worship, and almost ceased under his successor, Avila Camacho, who publicly declared that he was a believer. Afterwards the Church continued to regain influence although it is still far from recovering the predominance which it had before the revolution; and the situation in Mexico is very different in this respect from that in Peru or Colombia. Tragically, however, the Church has recovered enough influence to prevent the government from adopting an enlightened policy of encouraging birth control, without which the ideals proclaimed in the Constitution must remain a dead letter.

The reformist impetus seemed to have withered when it was given a new lease of life by Lazaro Cardenas when he assumed the presidency in 1934. It was only then – nearly a quarter of a century after the outbreak of the revolution – that a serious attempt was made to push through agrarian reform. During the six years of Cardenas' rule more land was distributed to the peasants than in all the preceding years. The idea which haunted the revolutionaries from the earliest times was to restore the ancestral village community and to raise its economic and cultural level by providing it with capital and instruction. By 1940 the various communal units (*ejidos*) comprised about half of the crop land and half of the agricultural population, whilst the population of the *haciendas*, which amounted to 3,000,000 in 1910, dropped to 800,000. However, the inertia of the peasants, the inefficiency and corruption of the administration, and, above all, the scarcity of resources, prevented any substantial improvements in the condition of the peasants. Economically most of the communes turned out to be failures, but something was done for the self-respect of the peasants, and the landlords lost their absolute supremacy.

The most important achievement of the Mexican revolution consisted of putting the army, the Church and the landowners into relatively subordinate positions from which they could no longer dominate society and appropriate most of its wealth for parasitic consumption. On the other side of the balance, however, the great expansion of bureaucracy aggravated its own form of parasitism, particularly as little progress was made towards the elimination of corruption, which remains as flagrant as ever. In this respect, the Mexican post-revolutionary régimes compare badly with Castro's Cuba. Nevertheless, the character of the new ruling class (which, being predominantly bureaucratic and commercial was less bound by antiquated traditions than the old aristocracy) permitted extremely rapid economic growth along captitalist lines with a strong admixture of state enterprise.

Although it has done little or nothing towards abolishing inequality, the revolution has renovated the élite, opening access to it to many impecunious but gifted and enterprising men whose energies would have been wasted under the old régime. The hard and brutal struggle for accession has brought to the top men a great deal abler than the aristocrats who occupied most of the important posts in pre-revolutionary Mexico in virtue of their family connections. The increase in vertical mobility and the renovation of the élite may have been the chief factors responsible for the dynamic character of the post-revolutionary society which stands in such contrast to the sleepy though violent ways of old Mexico. Moreover, the diminution of the prestige and security of landed property has helped to redirect the flow of funds into industry.

Partly (as in the case of oil and the railways) in order to wrest from foreigners the control over the key points of the economy, partly to develop essential industries which private capital did not find profitable, and partly owing to the expansionist tendencies of the bureaucracy, the Mexican government embarked upon multifarious economic activities and built an extensive network of pervasive control over private enterprise. Though severely hampered by corruption, red-tape and excessive administrative personnel, the mixed economy of Mexico has experienced since 1940 an extremely rapid growth. Had the population remained stationary, gross poverty would have become rare by now; but, as the growth of the population has even accelerated, it has nullified most of the gains. People who have not enough to eat now constitute a much smaller proportion of the population than they did in 1910 – perhaps one-third instead of two-thirds – but in absolute numbers they are even more numerous than in the days of Porfirio Diaz.

Peron's Semi-Revolution

The rise and fall of Peron was closely analogous to those of ancient Greek tyrants (though it must be mentioned for the sake of accuracy, that those 'tyrants' did not always rule tyrannically: the name designated any illegitimate and autocratic ruler even if his rule was on the whole benevolent). As explained by Aristotle, the poor, being unable to rule collectively in the manner of the oligarchs, and therefore incapable of defending themselves against the rich, supported a bid for absolute power by a man who promised to protect them, but who in the end usually betrayed them, and oppressed the ex-oligarchs and the poor alike.

Until 1916 Argentina was ruled by a small oligarchy of landowners, who drew enormous incomes from the export of meat and wheat to Europe (chiefly Britain), and for this reason cooperated closely with British commercial and financial houses. The railways and industries, of which meat-packing was the most important, were almost entirely in the hands of British companies.

From the beginning of the century the Radical Party (Union Civica Radical) began to challenge the supremacy of the landowning families. It fought for the interests of the rapidly growing urban middle class, from which came its leaders, and was also supported by a large section of the proletariat, quickly expanding in and around Buenos Aires. Soon after a liberally-minded president, Saenz Pena, had removed the legal buttress of the oligarchy by extending the suffrage to all male Argentinians in 1912, a candidate of the Radical party, Hipolito Irigoyen, became the president. During his tenure, and that of his successor, Argentina experienced the most democratic period of its history. Unfortunately, however, the new ruling group could not resist the temptation of illicit enrichment, and its corruption had seriously diminished its efficacy and powers of resistance when the military struck.

Argentina received a fierce blow from the Great Depression: exports and prices fell catastrophically, unemployment and poverty spread, and the struggle between the classes for what remained of the wealth intensified. The big landowners and the officers could no longer bear to leave the Radical politicians to enjoy the bounties of office; particularly as they blamed them for their inability to cope with the economic crisis. In September 1930 the army overthrew the newly re-elected Irigoyen and instituted a régime based on an alliance between the landowners and the officers, who in any case formed largely overlapping circles.

The new conservative régime was more oppressive than the one which existed before 1916 because the economic situation was worse and the opposition more violent. Although the constitution providing for representative government was not abolished, the elections were fixed: the owners of the estates – and to a lesser extent other employers too – blatantly directed the voting of their labourers: the overseers and hired helpers inspected the voting cards, and kept recalcitrant electors away from the booths by intimidation or assault. If these methods were ineffective, the votes were dishonestly counted. Whenever, by dint of daring and endurance, the opposition won an election in one of the provinces, provincial autonomy was suspended and an 'interventor' was put in charge, whose task was to hold new elections and to see that they came out right. Unlike the legal restriction of suffrage in force until 1912, this method of nullifying the effects of the extension of franchise spread deep demoralization which has weighed upon the country till this day.

This régime lasted until 1943 when on June 4 President Castillo was overthrown by the troops. The chief cause of the revolt was the ascension to dominance within the army of a lodge called Grupo de Oficiales Unidos, who objected to the foreign sympathies of the politicians connected with the landowning aristocracy. The landowners whose fortunes were built by exports to Britain were traditionally pro-British, whereas the srmy was always inclined to ape the Germans. Some of the officers became so enamoured of Mussolini, Hitler and their ideologies that they decided to set up a similar régime in Argentina, and dreamt of establishing a hegemony of Argentina in South America.

The purely military régime dropped all pretence of democracy: it disbanded the congress, outlawed the parties, maimed the trade unions by purging them or their independent-minded leaders, re-established compulsory Catholic education in the schools and set up concentration camps. The fruits of extended authority enabled the officers to wipe off their debts, which had constituted a strong incentive to rebellion. The game was spoilt only by the realization that they had backed the side which was losing the war. The Allied victory brought the ideology of the régime into disrepute and encouraged the opposition, which now comprised nearly everybody outside the military clique. The military government began to make concessions, restored some freedom to the press, the trade unions and the parties, and promised to hold elections. Uncertainty about the future stimulated the fissile tendencies within the officer corps, and to the usual tug-of-war of personal ambitions were added divergences of views on how to save the military rule.

Among the more influential members of the officers' lodge was Juan Domingo Peron, son of a small farmer who had known some hard times in his youth. As a military attaché in Rome he had seen the power of Mussolini's and Hitler's demagogy. While most of his senior colleagues favoured an authoritarian régime devoted to the defence of the interests of the rich, Peron, who had been put in charge of the Secretariat for Labour, conceived a new tactic based on cultivating the sympathies of the workers. When his faction acquired more influence the government began to veer from an anti-labour policy parallel to that of Franco towards a form of populist authoritarianism. During 1944 and 1945 Peron, as the Secretary for Labour and Vice-President, had done more for extending and protecting the rights of the workers than the trade unions had been able to do during three decades of hard struggles. He started low-cost housing schemes, decreed annual paid holidays and ordered increases of wages, which did in fact rise faster than the prices during these two years. Most important of all, he helped the workers to organize. There existed trade unions before that time but they were confined to select trades – there was, for instance, a strong union of railwaymen – but only under Peron did the most depressed and backward workers get the opportunity to organize themselves.

In the meat-packing and sugar industries the companies maintained gangs of armed men and spies whose task was to thwart unionization. The workers who attempted to act as organizers were immediately dismissed, beaten up or even murdered. The hours were long, the pay poor, and the workers were bullied by the foremen and the managers. Peron gave the organizers police protection and made it plain to the employers that the unions had the blessing of the government. This support, however, was accompanied by gradual subjugation. Aided by his magnetic personality, a sonorous voice and a histrionic ability, Peron was able to instil into many of the workers – particularly the poorest and the most ignorant – a devotion to his person, thus stealing their following from the union leaders. He created new organizations entirely subordinated to him, and obtained control over most of the older unions. Good government jobs served as bait for union officials, whilst the recalcitrant were pushed out of positions of influence by intrigue, blackmail or terroristic threats. By these methods Peron became the real boss of the General Confederation of the Workers.

Several factors facilitated Peron's conquest of the labour movement. The first was the uncompromising greed of the employers, and the second the sudden numerical growth of the industrial and semi-industrial proletariat. Thirdly, internal quarrels, particularly between the socialists and the communists, gravely impaired the strength of the labour movement. The fourth important factor was that as immigration dwindled, the proletariat came to contain a large proportion of second-generation Argentinians, prone to ultra-patriotism, who regarded the socialist ideas of their European fathers as too foreign. Furthermore, the internal migration, which replaced immigration, brought to the towns large masses of peasants, many of them illiterate, who feeling lost and defenceless were grateful for being organized from above. In addition, the unions were weakened by the bureaucratization and *embourgeoisement* of their leaders who had largely forfeited the loyalty of their followers even before the rise of Peron. So Peron had no difficulty in subordinating the unions to the Partido Laborista which he had created. Opposition to Peron continued among the minority of workers who retained their socialist or communist loyalties, among the students and the anti-authoritarian middle class. But the most powerful of his opponents were those of his fellow officers who, in addition to personal envy, were influenced by their links with the land-owning aristocracy and big business. Their reaction against Peron was an attempt to restore political freedom and parliamentary government as well as the privileges of the rich.

The situation in Argentina in no way fitted into the stereotyped scheme of right and left wings which had been perfectly applicable to French and German politics before the First World War, when the parties which defended the interests of the upper classes also upheld authoritarian ideologies, whilst the other parties fought for the interests of the underprivileged as well as for the cause of liberty and democracy. The rise of the movements advocating authoritarian levelling of social inequalities, and resorting as freely to demagogy as to police terror, confused the issues. There is no justification for classifying Hitler as more right wing than the last Chancellor of the Weimar Republic. Even the activities of Joseph McCarthy fit nowhere on the right-left scale because they formed the crest of the wave of popular intolerance, whipped up by politicians of demotic origins, and directed against Harvard educated upper-class officials, scholars and diplomats. The freedom of dissent was curtailed with popular backing. Peron's *justicialismo* incorporated selected attitudes of both extremes of the pre-First World War European political spectrum. The front line lay between a pro-labour militarist authoritarianism and the anti-labour élite, trying to destroy the budding autocracy and to re-establish constitutional liberties; not so much out of libertarian convictions as for their own protection.

When Peron's senior partner, General Farell, was thrown out of presidency by a coup led by conservative generals, the employers immediately began to disregard the laws protecting the workers, to curtail their liberties and to attack the unions. Peron was jailed but was saved by a massive reaction of the workers of the lowest categories – the so-called 'shirtless' (*los descamisados*). Incited by Peronist agents (among whom Peron's mistress Eva Duarte played the leading role), the labourers from the suburbs of Buenos Aires and even farther afield flooded the capital, camping on the streets and demanding Peron's release. The army could have dispersed them, even though they numbered more than a million, but the generals were not eager to wage a civil war, had doubts about the reactions of the conscripts, and were hampered by the delaying tactics of pro-Peron officers. Peron was released and allowed to return to office on condition that he held elections soon.

Before embarking on an electoral campaign, Peron married

Eva Duarte who had proven herself to be the most effective demagogue in Argentina. Probably since Joan of Arc no other woman had such power over the crowds. Born poor and full of rancour against the upper classes for past humiliations and the snubbings which she received even after she became the wife of the President, she whipped up the hatred of the poor against the rich, and presented herself and her husband as their saviours. Taking charge of welfare and dispensing it in a spectacularly demagogic, though not the most efficient, manner, she gained the passionate loyalty of simple souls who begrudged her neither her ostentation nor her fraudulently obtained wealth, and vicariously enjoyed her success.

In February 1946 Peron won the presidential election, violently conducted but honestly counted, by the biggest majority in Argentine history. He could have governed as a constitutional president but preferred to move towards totalitarianism. He deprived the press of the remains of its freedom: some papers were regularly confiscated, others compulsorily bought and the remaining submitted and sang paeans to the presidential couple. Although the political parties were allowed to linger on, they were deprived of all freedom of action and their leaders jailed or harassed by the police. Many people were shot 'while escaping from arrest', and many others disappeared mysteriously. The universities were thoroughly purged, some losing three-quarters of their staff, who were replaced by incompetent supporters of the régime. In the countryside Peron stirred up the labourers, tenants and sharecroppers against the landlords but did little to promote the much vaunted agrarian reform, apart from parcelling out the estates of a few personal enemies.

Peron's régime never became fully totalitarian. Unlike Hitler or Stalin or even Mussolini, he was never able to obtain complete control over the army. Unable to purge the officer corps, he tried to undermine their authority by appealing directly to the lower ranks; and with this aim he created a trade union for non-commissioned officers. Afraid of direct coercion he played the game of divide and rule and tried to win the officers by generously distributing lucrative posts in civilian administration, trebling the pay and granting profitable exemptions from import duties. As later events have shown, he did not succeed in neutralizing the army, but the demoralization which he spread among the officers was largely responsible for the parlous state of Argentina since his fall.

Why could Peron not become the master of the army as Stalin, Hitler and Franco have done? Stalin's position in this respect was the strongest because the Red Army was created by the party, and its officers remained under the close supervision of the political commissars, so that they never had opportunities for organizing an independent clique. When Hitler came to power the generals retained control over the army but they were brought up in the tradition of faithful service. They interfered in the politics of the Weimar Republic because they had never accepted the parliamentary politicians as their legitimate rulers, and party squabbles gave them a chance of playing the role of the supreme arbiters of politics. They also regarded most of the politicians as unpatriotic, which was not a charge which could be levelled against Hitler, who won for them the opportunity to recreate a large army. Moreover, Hitler had his own machine of coercion in the shape of the storm troopers and the highly selected and indoctrinated janissaries of the SS. Peron had no equivalent bodies at his service, and the army would not allow him to create them. Actually, his attempts in this direction provided the *casus belli* of the military revolt. Peron had only the police, which was good enough for stamping out civilian opposition, but was too weak and corrupt to fight the army. Nor has Peron had the advantage (which Franco has) of having personally commanded the army in its march to victory. Peron played the pro-labour card because he could not rise to the top of the army hierarchy. Furthermore, whereas Hitler – and to a lesser extent other European dictators – profited from the tradition of military discipline, the Argentinian officers were thoroughly permeated by the pretorianist outlook. Perhaps Peron's inability to terrorize the army into submission would have mattered less if he had the moral authority of a De Gaulle, but his magnetic personality could inspire devotion only among simple people who did not know about his embezzlements and licence. The fall of Peron – like that of Batista – shows that in order to be efficient, terror must be operated by a core of fanatics, and that sybaritism and thieving among the rulers fortunately makes a despotism more vulnerable.

As the régime was acquiring an increasingly totalitarian character, the resistance was correspondingly stimulated. In the meanwhile, the death of Eva deprived Peron of his chief magnet for the devotion of the poor. When Peron began to organize a party militia, after an abortive revolt of a few regiments, the officers decided that they must act before it was too late. Peron's quarrel with the Church seriously weakened the régime. His motives in this affair remain mysterious, for there was nothing in his ideology that was essentially anti-clerical. His attack on the Church can partly be attributed to the evolution of the régime towards totalitarianism which had aggravated the eternal friction between the Church and the state. Possibly, facing the threat from the forces of traditionalist reaction, he sought to enlist the support of anti-clerical socialists and communists. It is also possible that the bishops, foreseeing his fall, decided that it was time to come out into opposition.

The landowners, financiers and even the favoured industrialists always resented Peron's flirtation with labour, but they became desperate when the country found itself on the verge of economic collapse. The growing economic difficulties, moreover, diminished Peron's popularity among the poor, whose numbers could have provided a counterforce to the army, as they had on the earlier occasion.

Undoubtedly one can find extenuating circumstances for Peron's disastrous economic policy. In order to keep the support of the workers he had to give them something without waiting for an increase in the volume of production. They could get something at the expense of the more opulent classes but, as is usual in such cases, the actual transfers of wealth did not amount to very much and in the end they were nullified by inflation.* To keep the officers happy he had to buy costly armaments and multiply senior posts, but he cannot be exonerated from personal responsibility on this score because by doing so he was indulging in the normal proclivity of a professional soldier, playing Caesar and dreaming of conquests. On the whole, his management of the economy was shortsighted, wasteful and dishonest, and could continue for ten years only because at the beginning he had come into possession of the large balance of sterling which Argentina had accumulated during the war.

Corruption, always rampant in Argentina, reached fabulous

* The rural population were the real sufferers who had to pay for the concessions to the urban proletariat.

proportions under Peron, when large parts of the economy came under governmental control. According to serious estimates, Peron accumulated 700 million dollars in his personal accounts in foreign banks. The traffic in permits and appointments was enormous. The burden of graft weighed heavily on Argentina's economy, but even more fatal was administrative inefficiency and incompetent planning. By instituting a government monopoly on agricultural produce and fixing uneconomic prices, and at the same time denying to agriculture the permission to import goods necessary for the maintenance of productivity, Peron's government succeeded in causing food scarcity in this country of fabulous abundance of food. In consequence, once the enormous amounts of foreign exchange accumulated during the war were spent, nothing could be exported to pay for the necessary imports, including those indispensable for the working of the newly built industries. Argentinian industry made great strides under Peron, thus continuing the development stimulated by the two World Wars, but many ventures were unviable white elephants; and as the industry never became capable of competing in world markets, whilst remaining dependent on imported machinery and raw materials, the collapse of agricultural exports brought it into severe crisis. Peron's legacy plagues Argentina to this day.

Peron chose to call his régime *justicialismo*, and it cannot be denied that in many ways he has done much to introduce more justice into Argentinian society. He has raised the self-respect of the workers, helped them to organize themselves, extended facilities for free education, introduced social insurance and other measures of public assistance. Had he not squandered money on arms and ostentation, had he been an efficient and honest administrator, he could have put Argentina among the prosperous and stable societies. Possibly a measure of authoritarianism was necessary for carrying out necessary reforms, but he did not need to push the cult of personality to degrading extremes which repelled honest citizens and led to an invasion of all public services by a horde of incompetent and dishonest sycophants. In addition to dislocating the economy his rule aggravated the corruption and inefficiency of the administration; it stimulated appetites whilst reducing the means of satisfying them.

Revolution at Starvation Level in Bolivia

Bolivia is one of the poorest countries in the world. The climate is harsh and the soil arid and poor. The altitude imposes a severe strain on the human organism, as the air is so rarefied that no fires seem ever to break out in La Paz.

Although clear-cut racial differences disappeared long ago, society continued to be divided into the privileged whitish, Spanish-speaking minority and the Indian peasants, most of whom speak Qechua. Throughout the nineteenth century a succession of savage *caudillos*, interspersed with a few more civilized dictators, ruled the country; strife and turmoil never abated for long. The economy continued to be semi-feudal, with mining companies injected into it as foreign bodies. Minerals (principally tin) began to be mined intensively at the beginning of the century, and ever since accounted for no less than 95% of the exports, although they sustained a severe blow from the depression of the thirties, from which they have never recovered. Innumerable local peasant uprisings took place but a true revolutionary situation did not arise until after the Chaco war, into which Bolivia was goaded by North American, and Paraguay by British, oil interests; the object of the dispute being frontier regions presumed to contain oil.

The war brought disaster, and revealed the utter incompetence, cowardice and corruption of the high officers and officials. It discredited the entire ruling class and stirred the Indians out of their torpor, as the conscripts had to be indoctrinated with patriotism later tinged with leftist ideas by the intellectuals. A few years after the war a clique of younger officers seized power. Under the presidency of Colonel Taro, labour legislation similar to the Chilean was introduced, unionization encouraged, and the holdings of the Standard Oil expropriated. This socialistic trend continued under Colonel Busch who overthrew Taro, and ruled until he was murdered when attempting to tax the mining companies more heavily. The two generals who successively replaced him were more conservative and accommodating towards big capital, which in Bolivia is almost entirely foreign. During this period three important political parties, whose ideology can be described as semi-marxist nationalism, came into existence; one of them being

Moviemiento Nacionalista Revolucionario, distinguished by an anti-semitic slant, partly explained by resentment caused by the prominence of foreign Jewish financiers in controlling the Bolivian economy.

In 1943 a coalition between an officers' lodge and the MNR overthrew the government, which had incurred the wrath of the miners by cruelly repressing their strikes, and installed Major Villaroel in the presidency. During the two years of his rule his policy was fairly pro-labour and he sponsored the unionization of the miners; which does not mean, however, that he was a civilized democrat, as he had frequent recourse to assassination. Eventually, he was assaulted by an angry mob and hanged on a lamp-post in front of the presidential palace, while the army refused to defend him. The régimes which followed were subservient to the landlords and the mining companies, which used every opportunity to put the workers back in their place.

On 9 April 1952, there occurred in La Paz one of those rare occasions in which civilian rebels defeat an army in an open battle; although it must be added that the Bolivian army had no tanks, hardly any aeroplanes and not much artillery; while the police took the side of the rebels and provided them with arms. The first act of the victorious Movimiento Nacionalista Revolucionario was to disband the defeated army, reduce the numbers of the police (despite their contribution to the victory) and create an armed workers' militia. Having eliminated the most obvious dangers to its authority, the new government under the presidency of Victor Paz Estenssoro began to introduce basic reforms: it nationalized the mines, expropriated large estates and gave the land to the peasants; though the latter act was largely only a formality because in many regions the peasants did not wait for the new laws but organized themselves into leagues, seized the land and drove the landlords away. This demolition of the edifice built upon the conquest did not make the peasants prosperous but it restored their self-respect, as from then onwards they were no longer treated with contempt. The government made serious efforts to extend schooling, reduce illiteracy, and to instruct the peasants in methods of cultivation. The US government pursued an enlightened policy of giving some aid (about 30 million dollars a year), despite those measures taken by the Bolivians which affected adversely the commercial interests of the US citizens.

On the psychological level the new rulers had some success: they did make the peasants and the miners feel that they belonged to the nation and that the government was trying to do something for them; but little could be done to raise the miserable standard of living of the masses because there was very little to share out. The division of the estates gave to the peasants the feeling of having gained something but it did not increase food production. With primitive equipment and transport the productivity of the miners was very low, and in consequence their real wages could not be substantially increased. Trying to satisfy the expectations they had aroused, the government raised the salaries but the inevitable inflation soon robbed the recipients of any real gain.

Given the tradition of violence and the harshness of the struggle for existence, it would have been miraculous if the government had not resorted to repressive measures. The dispossessed former privileged classes plotted a restoration while the communists (of Stalinist and trotskyite varieties), as well as other competitors of the MNR on the revolutionary side, were trying to outbid it and were preparing for its overthrow. Later dissensions emerged within the Movement itself between those who were running the ministries and the leaders of the newly-established unions who were under pressure from their followers to obtain some improvements for them. As was inevitable, many members of the new élite proved to be far from idealistic and used their power chiefly or only for their personal benefit. Qualified technicians and managers, already rare before the revolution, became even scarcer owing to the departure of those who did not like the new order or were forced to flee.

The very democratization of the government had some adverse results: as the supporters of the new government were more numerous than those of the preceding régimes, the task of rewarding them was even more burdensome. Not only were many people taken into the civil service, thus swelling its size, but the creation of the labour unions, which now comprised most of the working population and came to play an important part in administration and policy making, added new appendages to the heavy body of the bureaucracy. As all the miners who had been dismissed during the preceding years for supporting the MNR or for taking part in strikes were reinstated, while those who had been engaged to replace them remained in their jobs, the number of miners rose by about 50%, although production hardly increased at all, owing to disorder and the breakdown of discipline. The post-revolutionary régime is unquestionably the best that Bolivia has ever had: its leaders are capable men who have made serious efforts to improve the lot of the masses. For the first time continuity of government has been assured and the presidency of Bolivia decided by means of elections instead of a palace revolution. The rule is no longer personal but exercised collectively by the party. True, cheating and intimidation accompany the elections but the leaders undoubtedly have a great deal of genuine popular support, and do not rely on terror, as the traditional *caudillos* did; and, instead of 'cloak and dagger' conspiracies around the tyrant, debates are conducted within the party. The army, resuscitated but not permitted to recover its former size, no longer devours most of the budget, and has ceased to be the chief disturber of public order.

These undoubted benefits are, unfortunately, outweighed by the horrible fact of economic deterioration. While the big nationalized enterprises – the mines and the railways – function badly because of bad management, indiscipline and the deterioration of equipment which is not being replaced, smaller private mines are brought to bankruptcy or near bankruptcy by a combination of labour unrest, harassment by the hostile bureaucracy and disorganization of the markets. The Bolivians are eating their capital while growing in numbers. In these circumstances no progress can be made in the direction of the ideals of the revolution, and there is a great danger of a retrogression towards despotism.*

Reactionary revolution in Colombia

Reactionary revolution can be defined as an overthrow of the legal order, with the aim of re-establishing the privileges of the upper class which have been disappearing or being undermined. Colombia has recently been the scene of such a phenomenon.

---

* Since this was written a *cuartelazo* has taken place and General Barrientos has seized power. The reversion of Bolivia to the traditional pattern of military dictatorship constitutes another proof that there can be no representative government at starvation level.

During the first half of the present century Colombia belonged to the choice minority of the Latin American states with functioning parliamentary institutions. The civil wars and *caudillismo* which had been tearing the country throughout the preceding eighty years had been eliminated at the turn of the century. Having peace, the country developed rapidly: the cities grew, railways and harbours were built, coffee cultivation expanded and foreign capital came in large quantities. Despite this development, the majority of Colombians remained as poor as ever. When the workers began to organize themselves and demand better conditions, the antagonism between the classes became more acute. The strikes were severely repressed: on one such occasion nearly 2,000 strikers were shot. The situation became particularly inflammable during the economic crisis of the thirties, but even during the years of prosperity the Colombian workers had good grounds for feeling aggrieved because at no time had they derived any benefit from the growth of the economy. The rise in the index of income per head, which attained the respectable figure of 3% to 4% per annum during the period between 1945 and 1957, reflects only the growing consumption of the upper and middle classes, whilst the standard of living of the majority actually declined. The effects of the unequal distribution of wealth were aggravated by the phenomenal population growth, which attained the rate of $2\frac{1}{2}\%$ per annum; the population doubled itself in 28 years.

In Colombia the best situated 10% of the population receives 51% of the national income, the next 10% obtain 13%, and the remaining 80% are left with 36% of the income. The rise in the national income, which between 1945 and 1957 attained the high rate of 7% per annum, occurred because the rich bought more cars, refrigerators, radiogrammes, air-conditioning installations and so on, whilst the construction of houses and production of food could not keep up with the population growth. Between 1950 and 1954 real wages declined by 23%.

Colombian politics have traditionally been controlled by two parties: the Liberals and the Conservatives. The Conservatives were clericalist and rather more closely connected with the strictly agricultural old aristocracy, whilst the Liberals were mildly anti-clerical and had closer connections with the city merchants and financiers. However, the connection between party allegiance and class was not very close: the parties had (and still have) the character of feuding clans with few programmatic differences and strong hereditary loyalties. Their leaders were always preoccupied with day-to-day struggles and petty personal squabbles, and never paid much attention to matters affecting the entire nation. On the whole, however, the Liberals were more rational, less *a priori* opposed to reforms, and had a more conciliatory attitude towards the lower classes.

During the presidencies of Lopez and Santos the reformist wing of the Liberal party succeeded in getting enacted a series of measures which greatly alarmed the Conservatives: the workers obtained a legal recognition of their right to organize and to go on strike, and a number of concessions, such as the limitation of working hours to 48 hours a week, whilst the employers found themselves burdened with liability for sickness and accidents. What angered the Conservatives most was the reform of taxation, particularly the introduction of direct income taxation which had hardly existed before that time, although even under the new law the maximum tax on declared net income did not exceed 17%. The Conservatives were not alone in opposing social reforms: they found allies in the Liberal party, and even in its moderate wing which succumbed to dissensions and lost the capacity for action.

In the meantime, the Conservative party was undergoing a transformation in the direction of fascism, under the leadership of Laureano Gomez, who was imbued with the spirit of the Spanish Falange. This development followed the pattern of 'circulation of élites' which Vilfredo Pareto claims to have discovered some decades earlier. According to this scheme two types of rulers, the lions and the foxes, replace each other in an eternal series of cycles. The lions are dogmatic, conservative-minded, firm in the belief in their right to rule, with a strong spirit of group solidarity and a readiness to use violence. The foxes are innovators without any firm beliefs, addicted to anarchic money grabbing, squeamish about resorting to force and therefore inclined to rely on fraud as the means of maintaining their rule. In this particular case the Liberals (foxes), afraid to use force and therefore ruling by fraud, were succumbing to effeteness and corruption, whilst the 'reformed' Conservatives, disciplined and bellicose, were moving to overthrow them. The 'moderate' Liberals tried to compromise but the mood of the Conservatives was too violent for such arrangements to last.

The growing fanaticism and militarization of the Conservative party were largely due to the fear that the policies of the Liberals would lead to a revolt of the masses. And indeed, the policy of flirting with the poor, granting them paper concessions which were disregarded in practice, exploiting them cruelly while being ineffectual about repression, was not one which could be pursued for a long time; particularly as the administrative machine was disintegrating through corruption. Import and exchange controls, instituted during the war, opened vast new fields to graft: the traffic in import and exchange licences made more fortunes than any other activity, even land speculation. The ministers were so deeply enmeshed in bribery and intrigue that they could form no coherent policy of any kind. Some of the younger followers of Gomez may have also been prompted by a motive somewhat nobler than the desire for office and the fear of loss of the privileges of their class: they seemed to regard the militaristic and ultramontane ideology as a means of purifying Columbian politics.

Students of the fascist movements in Europe have noticed the connection between their spread and the distress of the middle class. The same connection existed in Colombia with this difference: there the natural growth of the middle class was even more important than inflation. Indeed, we have here a confirmation of what Francis Bacon said nearly four hundred years ago in his essay 'Of Seditions and Troubles':

> Generally, it is to be foreseen that the population of a kingdom (especially if it be not mown down by wars) do not exceed the stock of the kingdom which should maintain them: neither is the population to be reckoned only by number; for a smaller number that spend more and earn less, do wear out an estate sooner than a great number that live lower and gather more: therefore the multiplying of nobility, and other degrees of quality, in an over proportion to the common people, doth speedily bring a state to necessity.

In the essay Of True Greatness of Kingdoms he adds: 'Let states that aim at greatness take heed how their nobility and gentlemen do multiply too fast . . .'

The birth rate is extremely high in all classes of Colombian society but, owing to their lower death rate, the higher classes reproduce themselves faster than the lower. That this must be so is evident from the survival tables; but the 'whitening' of the population, despite the absence of immigration from Europe, provides additional evidence that this deduction is not mistaken, although here there is the doubt as to the constancy of the criteria on the basis of which people are classified into racial categories. As industrialization is insufficiently rapid to create a very large number of managerial and highly technical jobs, the young men of the middle classes compete desperately for posts in the civil service or as retainers of politicians. In this respect Colombia is not unique, but the situation there is graver than in Chile or Argentina because the reproduction rate of the higher classes is higher whilst the chasm between the classes is even greater and more closely related to racial differences, which make a downward crossing of class frontiers more repugnant.

In 1946 dissension within the Liberal party enabled Ospina Perez to win the presidential elections, whereupon with Laureano Gomez as his grey eminence, he began to move in the direction of a police state, discarding the rules of the game which had contained the squabbles of Colombian oligarchy within the bounds of peace for half a century. In response to this trend the leadership within the Liberal party passed from Conservative Lleras Camargo to populist Jorge Eliecer Gaitan – a lawyer of mixed blood and humble social origin – who had defended the interests of the poor for the previous twenty years, and became the idol of the masses. In contrast with many other Liberal politicians who coaxed the poor in order to use them as pawns in the game against the Conservatives, Gaitan appears to have been a man of convictions. His appeal to the proletariat amounted to a breach of the class solidarity which until then had united the Liberal and Conservative politicians and overridden their quarrels.

The murder of Gaitan in April 1948 unleashed the most terrible riots, during which the capital was partly destroyed: the crowds went berserk, looting, burning buildings, buses and motor cars. This orgy of destruction (baptized with the generic name of *bogotazo* – perhaps in expectation of things to come) revealed the depths of hatred and nihilism in the souls of the poor. Though put down after a few days, this outbreak inaugurated the civil war in which half a million Colombians lost their lives.

The civil war was extremely confused: it was neither a fight between armies nor a clear-cut peasant uprising. Armed bands sprang up in various places and began killing. In some areas anti-government forces were in complete control but there was no front and no regular battles. It was the time for paying old scores: peasants avenged their ill-treatment upon their lords, whilst the lords with their retainers engaged in affrays among themselves and the deputies were exchanging shots inside the parliament, whilst at many points guerrilla warfare merged with ideologically uncommitted banditry. As full and reliable information is unobtainable, it is difficult to be sure about the details, but it seems that gradually the strife was evolving in the direction of a clear-cut class war, with peasant bands fighting the police and the armed retainers of the landowners. The police reprisals were atrocious, involving the burning of villages and crops, and account for the majority of the deaths.

The important feature of the Colombian reactionary revolution, which aligns it with that of Franco in Spain, was its clericalism. All the crimes of cruel repression were justified in terms of the defence of the Faith, and committed with the blessing of the clergy. Neglect of religious practices could bring death upon the apostate, and Protestants were persecuted. Laureano Gomez – who occupied the presidency only for a short time but was the power behind the throne throughout the period of the civil war – was a pupil of the Jesuits; and he put other pupils of theirs, as well as many actual Jesuits and priests, into important governmental positions. The identification of Catholicism with cruel oppression and ruthless defence of unjust privileges is nothing new in the history of Colombia but its consequences are different in the twentieth century from what they were in the past.

Although his admiration for Franco, Hitler and Mussolini led him to outbursts of extreme anti-yankism, Gomez became a great friend of the USA after the war, thus helping to spread anti-yankism among his opponents.

As the bloodthirsty fanaticism of Gomez was ruining Colombia, many of his followers began to waver. And so, when he started a quarrel with the commander-in-chief of the army, Gustavo Rojas Pinilla, the latter overthrew him without difficulty.

The military dictatorship was a considerable improvement over the rule of Gomez. Rojas Pinilla tried to calm the country and call off repression, declaring an amnesty which brought many peasants back to their villages. Nevertheless, many others remained in the bush and continued to fight.

Rojas Pinilla tried to imitate Peron, and subdue the politicians by appealing to the lower classes, but he had no Evita to help him, was too closely connected with the privileged classes and too much an ordinary officer; and so he remained an ineffectual replica of the Argentinian dictator. Moreover, in contrast to Peron, who came into the possession of large funds, Rojas took over a badly damaged country. So, notwithstanding demagogic gestures, the régime remained just an ordinary military dictatorship with the usual abuses of power and graft, and the old economic and social evils continued to afflict the country.

Reconciled in the face of common enemies – the dictator on one side and the rebellious masses on the other – the politicians effected a reconciliation, making an agreement that each party should have a turn at winning presidential elections; and with the aid of some officers overthrew Rojas and re-established parliamentary government under a united oligarchy. While the paupers are multiplying and the politicians amassing fortunes, the guerrillas, now disowned by the Liberals, continue to fight and recently have been coming under the influence of the Cubans from whom they are receiving guidance and aid.

Communism and Dollar Imperialism in Guatemala

The events in Guatemala illustrate poignantly the inevitability of dictatorship in an uncivilized republic. Until 1944 Guatemala had never known any form of government other than *caudillos* who succeeded each other through countless coups. Some were less rapacious and cruel than others, but none – not even Barrios – could be described as really enlightened. The abyss between the Indians who constitute about 60% of the population, and the *Ladinos* (the Latins, that is to say, Spanish-speaking Europoids and *mestizos*), together with the gulf between the rich and the poor, precluded the emergence of any really binding code of political behaviour. The last dictator, Jorge Ubico, was a pernicious megalomaniac. Most of the inhabitants are illiterate and poor. The less accessible parts of the country are still occupied by Indian village communities while the better lands belong to the owners of latifundia, the biggest of which is the United Fruit Company. Northamericans and other foreigners control the finance, trade and the bulk of commercialized agriculture; and they purchase an almost political sovereignty with bribes given to the native politicians who are free to oppress and exploit their countrymen as much as they like so long as they respect the interests of foreign firms.

The wave of public opinion against authoritarian systems (other than those invoking socialist ideals) which swept the world at the end of the Second World War, in conjunction with internal circumstances such as the discontent of the younger officers, led in 1944, to an overthrow of the dictatorship by a movement enjoying a fairly wide popular backing. Soon afterwards the fairly free and honest elections gave the presidency to a returned emigré intellectual, José Arrevalo, who embarked upon far-reaching reforms: he allowed formation of trade unions and political parties, maintained the newly-won freedom of speech and publication, built schools and tried to help the poor by improving the medical services and housing. What is more, he pushed forward an agrarian reform involving the breaking up of many large estates and the distribution of the land to the peasants. This naturally incensed the land-owning class and (which proved even more dangerous) the managers of the United Fruit Company, which lost large chunks of its possessions.

Neither Arrevalo nor his successor in office, Arbenz, were able to increase the wealth of the country. On the contrary, the immediate effects of the egalitarian reforms were a fall in the production of exportable goods and shortages of imported commodities. On the other hand, the expectations of the people were being continuously raised by the propaganda of the parties competing for power. Given the traditional attitude to authority, and given the small administrative capacity of the past and present rulers, it would have been a miracle if the ordinary people had been prepared to tighten their belts and to work for a better future in an orderly and persistent manner. It was only too natural that in the newly formed unions, manned by impatient and ignorant men without any experience of self-government, the power should slip into the hands of the most ruthless and best organized group of demagogues – namely, the communists. Being the only disciplined body in the political arena, the communists quickly attained an ascendancy over other populist parties, and made big strides towards a complete subjugation of the governmental machine through open pressure and clandestine infiltration. On the other side of the fence a counter-revolutionary conspiracy, formed by those who resented the attenuation of their privileges, began to gather strength with the backing of the Northamerican firms and governmental agencies. With an ample supply of funds and arms from Northamerica, and provided by the neighbouring dictators with convenient hideouts, Castillo Armas organized an army (comprising Guatemalan opponents of the régime as well as foreign mercenaries) which entered Guatemala from Honduras and effortlessly overthrew the government of Jacobo Arbenz.* Having installed himself as a dictator, Armas returned to its former owners the land which had been parcelled out among the peasants. The United Fruit Company got back its estates.

There was no replica of the Spanish civil war or of the Mexican revolution: the feebleness of the resistance demonstrated the low quality of the leadership and the lack of conviction and solidarity among the lower classes, no doubt largely due to the gulf between the Indians and the *Ladinos*. Notwithstanding their easy victory, the counter-revolutionaries decided to teach the lower classes a lesson and executed a large number of peasants (possibly several thousand) who had had the temerity to take the lands of their masters.

Castillo Armas was assassinated before he had much time to savour the pleasures of power, but his successor, Ydigoras Fuentes, continued to maintain a ruthless dictatorship, backed by the police trained by instructors from Spain. The rule by a quadrilateral alliance of officers, priests, landowners and foreign capitalists hardly forms a basis for a decent social order; but clearly the alternative was a communist dictatorship which might have been even worse for the majority of the Guatemalans, apart from constituting a strategic menace to the non-communist world. In view of the much lower cultural level, a communist government could not even have done for Guatemala what Castro has done for Cuba. At best, a communist Guatemala

---

* It must be added that his own army deserted him.

could have become something like Albania . . . hardly a workers' paradise.

Cuba

As the pre-Castro income per head in Cuba was the third highest in Latin America, several writers have argued that the success of Castro's uprising had nothing to do with economic distress. This view, however, disregards the crucial fact that Cuba was also one of the three countries in Latin America where (even according to the habitually optimistic statistics of the United Nations) the real income per head declined between 1945 and 1958. And a number of cases show – most notably that of Germany in the thirties – that the process of falling from a relatively high standard of living generates more violent revolutionary and bellicose currents than long-standing poverty. Moreover, the apparently high standard of living was due almost entirely to the unusually large (for Latin America) size of the wealthy and middle classes, as well as the privileged sectors of wage-earners concentrated in Havana.

The usual Latin American chasm characterized the rural districts of Cuba: on one side the latifundia, occupying most of the land, on the other tiny and primitive peasant households. What is more, as in Mexico during the decade preceding the 1911 revolution, the ownership of Cuban land was becoming more concentrated: in 1899 farms of 143 acres or less occupied 50% of the land, whereas by 1946 the latifundia covered an area ten times larger than did the farms of under 26 acres.* Most of the latifundia concentrated on growing sugar for export, but despite their considerable efficiency, the consequence of this specialization was that 29% of the foodstuffs had to be imported without sufficing to provide a healthy diet for the poorer half of the population. The proceeds from the export of sugar went to pay for cars and other foreign goods used by the wealthier third.

Another serious consequence of the specialization in growing sugar was the seasonal fluctuation in the employment of agricultural labourers, many of whom worked only during the harvest lasting about four months. During the decade preceding the

* In contrast to the latifundia in most other parts of Latin America the Cuban estates were not manorial but capitalistic.

revolution unemployment fluctuated between 10 and 20%, rising on occasions to 25%, while another 20% were only partly employed, so that only about 60% of persons of working age had regular full-time jobs. This number included peasant-owners who could barely feed themselves from their tiny farms. Among the rural population only about 11% drank milk, 4% ate meat and 2% eggs, while 44% had never been to school. About 30% of the inhabitants of gay Havana had not enough to eat.

The middle class was large for Latin America, but one of the effects of its growth was that its lower ranks had great difficulties in maintaining their customary standard of living. A considerable number of graduates were unemployed or underemployed, while among those who had jobs many were earning very little; which was the principal cause of the endemic political agitation among the students.

Even before Batista appeared on the scene the public administration and the political parties were utterly corrupt. Batista has surpassed his predecessors in the amount of wealth he had amassed, but his chief contribution to the political scene was terror accompanying extortion, which during the latter part of his rule attained unprecedented dimensions. About 10,000 people died at the hands of his torturers and executioners, whilst a large number of others have been castrated or mutilated in other ways. The development of Castro's régime cannot be understood without taking into consideration the nature of the environment from which it sprang, which did not nourish forbearance and amicability.

Why did Castro's rebellion break out and why did it succeed? The first part of the question is easier to answer: given the circumstances and tradition, there was nothing strange in a group of young men trying their luck in overthrowing a hated régime: what requires an explanation is their spectacular success. Whereas the marxist writers claim for the proletariat or 'the masses' the honour of overthrowing Batista, the anti-marxists maintain that it was the turning of the middle class against the régime which tilted the balance in favour of the minute group of rebels, who in fact came from this very class. As usual in such controversies, both sides are wrong. Certainly, the revolution was not brought about by a mass uprising, but it is equally clear that a subdued hostility of the middle class could not have brought down a well-equipped army 30,000 strong. In any case, Batista – a mulatto ex-sergeant – has never been an exponent of the interests of any social stratum. His régime ministered primarily to the cupidity of the mercenaries and their close allies in the civilian administration, though with due regard for the interests of the wealthy planters and businessmen, particularly if they were Northamerican.

We might usefully distinguish between two types of dictatorship: the classist dictatorship – established and perpetuated by the widespread support of a social class whose interests and ways of life it fosters and defends – and the apparatic dictatorship serving primarily the interests of a military and administrative apparatus which is alienated from the rest of the society. This distinction is not applicable to totalitarian polities, where the apparatus completely enmeshes the entire society, and where the gradation of the ranks within the apparatus constitutes the only kind of stratification. Batista's régime approached the type of apparatic dictatorship, though less closely than does Duvallier's régime in Haiti.

The revolution was certainly not brought about by a mass uprising. Castro's *barbudos* were completely unlike the vast army of peasants which defeated Chiang Kai-shek, or the Bolshevik troops which beat Kolchak, Denikin and Wrangel: firstly, their number was ridiculously small – not exceeding 6,000 even on the day of victory* – and secondly the proportion of students and other people of middle-class origin was much higher. In contrast to the Bolshevik troops, Castro's forces contained very few urban workers, a fact which was largely the result of the attitude of the trade unions who had chosen to defend only the interests of narrow and privileged sectors and cared little for the fate of the peasants and the paupers.

Castro's partisans also differed radically from the peasant troops which sprang up during the Mexican revolution. The latter were much more numerous and were led by uncouth men of the humblest origins, whereas all the leaders of the Cuban revolution had a middle-class background and a fair amount of education. However, it seems that peasants from the regions adjacent to Sierra Maestra formed the majority of the rank and file, at any

* Of which the majority were late joiners. Most of the fighting was done by less than 1,000 men.

rate during the later stages of the campaign. What was even more important was the support given by the peasants who remained in the villages, which enabled the partisans to eat and to hide, and to receive supplies of arms and information about the movements of Batista's troops. It must be remembered that nowhere in the world have guerrillas been able to operate without massive help from the local inhabitants who must be moved by a conviction strong enough to overcome the fear of reprisals and the temptation of generous rewards for betrayal. Without such a backing the *barbudos* would have been caught as quickly as were the incomparably better equipped and much more numerous soldiers of the anti-Castro expeditionary force in 1961.

Castro's victory disproved what the students of revolution believed to be the best-founded sociological principle in this field: namely, that no revolt can succeed without defection from the armed forces or the previous disintegration of such forces. When the French revolution broke out many soldiers took the side of the crowds. The Bolsheviks seized power when the tsarist army had already been knocked out by the Germans. The Chinese communists broke the army of the Kuo Ming Tang before it had time to recover from shattering blows from the Japanese. During the Mexican revolution different sections of the regular army fought each other. The Cuban partisans were the first in modern times to defeat a much more numerous and better equipped regular army. They were, of course, very brave and tenacious, and they had in Fidel Castro a leader of extraordinary ability and courage, but all this would not have been enough if they had had to face 30,000 SS men instead of Batista's mercenaries. It was the lack of the most elementary military virtues among the latter which brought about their defeat.

Batista's officers (following their master's example) were amassing large fortunes and leading truly sybaritic lives. They profited from bribery, lawless seizures of property, smuggling, drug traffic, prostitution and gambling dens. They were mostly the old companions of Batista's first coup – the famous sergeants' revolt when the NCO's, led by the mulatto sergeant-telegraphist, Fulgencio Batista, deposed their officers and took their place. The pre-Batista officers had been bad enough, but they had had some code of behaviour and some sense of corporate solidarity, of which Batista's henchmen had none. As uncouth *parvenus* who acquired riches through a lucky strike, they were lazy and dissolute. Having risen through treachery, they felt loyalty neither to their chief nor to each other, whilst the possession of big funds in foreign banks undermined their will to undergo dangers for the sake of retaining power.* Once the common soldiers (who were equally venal) became aware that their bosses contemplated giving up the struggle for the sake of an equally luxurious but more carefree existence abroad, they panicked and the entire army collapsed.

It is easier to explain why Castro won than why his régime evolved in the way it did. Nevertheless, certain factors are fairly clear. The most understandable element in the situation was the anti-Northamerican bias of the new government. Among the factors which made it inevitable, national pride mixed with racial animosity played an important role, and Castro's rejection of the mighty neighbour could not fail to be felt by the majority of the Cubans as an assertion of the dignity of their nation and indeed race; for it must be remembered that although, according to the official statistics, Negroes constitute only 25% of the population, by the racialist Northamerican criteria the great majority of the Cubans fall under the stigma of racial contempt. To understand the attitudes of the Cubans and the Northamericans to each other we must never forget the disdain in which people of the same colour as most Cubans are held. Resentment among the Cubans was further stimulated by their having to serve crowds of American tourists and to endure their contumely; particularly as many of those tourists were of a particularly unsavoury kind; for whereas the Northamericans who were interested in culture went to Europe, the chief attractions of Havana were its gambling dens and brothels. There was a vicious circle here because catering for tourists tends to warp the character of the local inhabitants and to stimulate dishonesty; and as the tourists came in contact with the less upright of the inhabitants, they found plausible confirmation of their prejudices and in turn reinforced the hostility from the Cuban side, as it is difficult to entertain friendly feelings for a country where one's nation is regarded as a race of crooks and prostitutes.

Racialism seems also to have affected the present political

---

* The better officers, on the other hand, were so disgusted with the set-up that they were also evading fighting.

attitude of the Northamerican public which is much less forgiving towards the swarthy Cuban dictator and his even darker followers than towards the lighter-skinned masters of the Kremlin; although here we must also take into account the fact that (as Adam Smith observed in *The Theory of Moral Sentiments*) the venial sins of the small fry incite more self-righteous wrath than the crimes of the mighty.

In addition to racial antipathy, the mere fact that the revolution overthrew an ally of the USA was bound to give it an anti-Northamerican bias. Despite his earlier flirtations with the communists, Batista received from Washington arms and decorations, and Northamerican firms were among the chief beneficiaries of his régime. True, they did nothing that the native businessmen and capitalists did not do, but they would have had to be disciplined by any government which wished to put an end to corruption and injustice. In view of the subservience of the State Department to big business before the advent of Kennedy, any such attempt was bound to lead to a clash with the government of the USA. Was then Cuba's alignment with the Soviet Camp inevitable? And was it due to the internal forces or to the errors of Northamerican diplomacy? A case can be made out for both contentions which, in any case, are not mutually exclusive: it may be that this alignment was doubly inevitable.

In a famous speech, delivered after he had already become a firm ally of Russia, Castro claimed that he had always been a marxist; but people often antedate their views in order to give themselves credit for foresight and consistency. Supposing he had not been a marxist in the early days, would he not be tempted to claim that he had in fact been one, rather than admit that he was a belated convert? We cannot, therefore, regard his speech as conclusive proof that from the very outset his aim was to foist upon Cuba a communist system. Let us then examine the logic of the situation.

Suppose that Fidel Castro had not intended to join the Soviet camp, what could he have done in the circumstances? He could have held elections – which would have certainly given him the presidency – and then he could have governed more or less as Betancourt did in Venezuela; but this would have amounted to abandoning all hopes of a radical change in social conditions. If he were an ordinary political adventurer, he could of course have established a dictatorship of the usual type, and proceeded to fill his pockets. Given his determination to do something radical quickly, Castro's rule had to be authoritarian because deeply rooted habits of prevarication, venality, mendacity and bickering could not be eradicated overnight by gentle persuasion. What remains to be explained is why this authoritarianism assumed the form of communism. To a large extent the evolution of the Cuban régime was determined by the operation of two universal human tendencies: that the enemies of our enemies become our friends; and that we tend to regard our mighty protectors as worth imitating. Moreover, the appeal of the Soviet model to the Fidelistas was enhanced by the lack of any attractive alternative blueprint for a better society.

Unlike Lenin or Mao-Tse Tung or Hitler, Castro presented no programme before seizing power; and it seems that he had none beyond a vague desire for social justice, although he certainly hated the colonial variants of capitalism. It would have required a great deal of highly creative sociological thinking to devise an original and workable blueprint for a better society; and such a feat could not have been achieved amidst the intellectual poverty of Cuba. The politicking and favouritism at the universities (combined with low salaries and lack of security of tenure for teachers), the heritage of Spanish intolerance and continuing obscurantist censorship, the mercenary character of the press and the publishing houses, crass materialism, all helped to suffocate higher intellect. Northamerican influence contributed to this state of affairs, as it was too strong to permit the development of a higher indigenous culture, and yet too weak to absorb the Cubans completely. This ideological vacuum in combination with intellectual poverty made the aping of a foreign model inevitable. It must be added that totalitarianism has a great attraction for a powerful and relatively benign but not very wise ruler who can easily imagine that all evils will disappear as soon as he brings every activity under his control. Moreover, as Castro wanted to be the liberator of the masses throughout Latin America, he needed an ideology with wide supra-national appeal and a powerful ally from outside, in which matters he had little choice.

Next to the handing over of half of Europe to Stalin, the Cuban expedition was the greatest folly ever committed by the

US government in the field of foreign policy. Arguments could be found for doing nothing, for making conciliatory gestures or, on the other hand, for sending enough troops to destroy Castro's forces; but nothing can be said in favour of making the threat so great that he would accept Soviet aid on any terms. How could President Kennedy – who gave ample proof of his ability a year and a half later – and his advisers entertain the foolish hope of toppling Castro by sending an expeditionary force ten times smaller than his army? Only by falling victim to their own propaganda, which depicted him as an isolated and universally hated despot.

Castro's acceptance of (or request for) Soviet rockets was a natural consequence of the abortive expedition. It is possible, of course, that in any case he would have entered into a close alliance with the Russians for ideological reasons, no matter what the US government did. Nevertheless, the latter's policy ensured that he would do so even if his original intention had been to adopt a diplomatic position similar to that of Nasser or Tito.

Opinions about Kennedy's actions in forcing the Russians to withdraw their rockets from Cuba usually depend on views on the virtues or vices of the Cuban régime, but the two issues are really separate. Even if the state of Cuba were a paradise, a move which would have placed the North Atlantic countries at the mercy of the master of the Kremlin would have had to be resisted by force. Unless they intended to surrender, the Northamericans had to show that they were prepared to fight. That their own errors helped to put them in this dire dilemma was irrelevant to the choice with which they were faced in autumn 1962.

One may heartily acclaim Kennedy's success in forcing the Soviet retreat, and approve the steps to counteract the subversive activities of the Fidelistas in a country like Venezuela, without accepting the picture of Castro as a bloodthirsty oppressor of the Cuban people. In evaluating a political system we must take into account what it has replaced, the alternatives at the time and how it compared with other systems functioning under similar conditions. However, we must not fall into the common error of imagining that by showing that the preceding régime was bad we are proving that the present is good. What we can demonstrate is that Castro's dictatorship is less tyrannical than many others which are readily accepted as members of the 'free world'; and that he cannot be accused of destroying a decent polity. In this respect, he is entirely unlike the Czech communists, who on orders from one of the most bloodthirsty tyrants in history tore down a democratic order, or even the Bolsheviks who replaced the tsar's absolutism by something much more cruel. The imposition of communism upon Czechoslovakia was a disaster without any partial compensations. In Poland the communists may with some justification claim credit for forestalling the restoration of the pre-war rule by a selfish clique of dim-witted colonels, and for curbing the intolerant and obscurantist Church. On the other hand, for a decade they oppressed the people more systematically than the colonels ever did, did their best to deprave the youth by encouraging sychophancy and delation, and deprived the nation of the chance to build something better than either the pre-war or the present régime; which seemed possible just after the war, owing to the disappearance of social inequalities and divisions during the occupation. The imposition of a Castroist régime in Uruguay would have been a tragedy. Even in Chile, where there is more injustice and exploitation than in Uruguay, the destruction of the tradition of legality, of freedom of expression and of elective government would amount to a terrible loss; particularly as these factors create a possibility that reforms may be achieved through the electoral process. In Argentina, where few people suffer physically, a totalitarian police state would inflict worse sufferings than the present disorder and corruption, even if it were capable of eliminating the latter evils. But in comparison with the rapacious and terroristic dictatorships which still dominate the Caribbean area (and of which Batista's régime was the most brutal example) Castro's egalitarian and relatively conscientious totalitarianism does not appear to be without merit.

With the exception of Gomulka, no communist ruler has fewer killings on his conscience than Castro. Tito's partisans have killed perhaps a hundred times as many 'reactionaries'. As Stalin's viceroy in the Ukraine, Khrushchev supervised mass deportations, causing about as many deaths as the activities of Adolf Eichmann. While putting down the Hungarian uprising, Soviet troops killed more people in four days than the Fidelistas have from the beginning of their struggle to this day. What is very remarkable is that Cuba is the only communist country which allows the opponents of the régime to emigrate. Also, by releasing for ransom men who attempted to overthrow him by the force of arms, Castro has demonstrated, if not magnanimity, at least that he does not put vengeance above the prosperity of his realm, as was the case with Stalin and Rakosi. Bearing all these facts in mind, we must not, however, fall into the error of imagining that they prove that Cuba is not a police state; for there can be no doubt that the Cuban political system is a totalitarian dictatorship with the usual accoutrements of prison camps and omnipotent police force, and the usual practices of arbitrary arrests and delation, even though it belongs to a less sinister variant of the species.

From the ethical point of view the Cuban leaders seem greatly superior to most dictators. Peron and Mussolini, for instance, used ideologies simply as a means for duping the masses, and neither of them has shown any sincerity of conviction or readiness to risk his life or expose himself to privations. Mussolini started his theatrical march on Rome only after he made sure that neither the army nor the police would stop him. In contrast Fidel Castro gave a rousing speech on social injustices in Cuba at the court martial which was trying him for his first abortive rebellion, escaping death only because the Archbishop of Santiago interceded on his behalf.* This experience did not deter him from embarking upon his epic struggle a few years later. True, power corrupts and the youthful idealism of many *barbudos* has given way to self indulgence, while many unscrupulous opportunists and ruthless agents of the old communist party have wormed their way to the top of the hierarchy. Nevertheless, the fire of revolutionary idealism has not yet been completely extinguished by soulless bureaucrats.

What has the revolution accomplished? Let us begin with the economic side. In view of discrepant calculations and the arbitrary assumptions on which they are made, one cannot be very precise, but it seems that the average real income has declined, although not so much as might be inferred from the drab appearances of the shops and hotels. The rich have departed and the middle classes have experienced a major decline in their standard of living, but there are no paupers now and the previously worst paid workers have obtained some advantages. The

* And probably also because one of his relatives was close to Batista.

lower white-collar workers and the qualified manual workers probably earn less in real terms now than before the revolution but none of them have to endure unemployment or to live under its permanent threat. (5) Whether all this constitutes an improvement or deterioration is a debatable point, but it is clear that in economic matters the high hopes aroused at the inauguration of Castro's rule have been disappointed. Why?

The first part of the answer is that an economy (even of an unindustrialized country) is a highly complex system in which it is impossible to make fundamental changes quickly without reducing the performance temporarily. Even a small workshop has to restrict or even stop production when it is being reorganized; and, as everybody knows, a house which is being rearranged is uncomfortable. In Cuba's case the radical reforms were bound to be particularly painful as they involved the tearing off of an integral part of the Northamerican economy. Imagine how difficult it would be for Normandy or Brittany to cut itself off from the French economy and enter into the economic orbit of Japan. Even under the wisest management a radical reconstruction of the economic system combined with a reorientation of external trade would call for great sacrifices. To put it mildly, Cuba's management was not very wise and the blueprints for the new society not very good. Fighting in the wilderness is not the best training for managing banks and factories, and it would have been miraculous if without any preparation the *barbudos* had turned out to be efficient managers. Their miraculous victory, moreover, had imbued them with illusions of omnipotence and a scant respect for economic realities, which led them to imagine that to achieve desired results it is enough to pass a decree. Thus plans were made to change the pattern of cultivation without finding out what can be grown where – with the result that many (if not most) new ventures ended in failures. Factories were built without qualified personnel to run them or without ensuring the supply of raw materials. Until recently the new rulers regarded accountancy as a capitalist relic, and were glad to see most of the accountants leave – with results that can be imagined.

Unfortunately the liberality of the régime added to its difficulties. Many of the exiles allowed to leave freely were irreplaceable managers, technicians and other specialists whose counterparts in Russia had no option but to put all their skills at the disposal of the régime or to perish in the arctic forced-labour camps. The same applies to the treatment of the workers. By means of terrible punishments Stalin imposed upon the Russian workers an iron discipline, and squeezed out of them the last quantum of energy while reducing their consumption to the minimum compatible with bare survival. Castro and his lieutenants, in contrast, really thought that revolution and marxism meant good times for the workers and permitted a relaxation of labour discipline and rises in wages in consequence of which many collective farms and factories had wage bills exceeding the gross value of the product. With neither capitalist incentives nor proper communist discipline, the collective enthusiasm failed to elicit sufficiently sustained effort, and in combination with mismanagement, this has led to a serious drop in productivity, only partly compensated for by the disappearance of unemployment. (6)

The cardinal weakness, however, lies in the choice of a system which is completely unsuited to a small country dependent on foreign trade, and which could never become a self-sufficient industrial colossus. Indeed, if the masters of the Kremlin ceased to be interested in maintaining it as their foothold in Latin America, Cuba would be condemned to famine.

There are signs that, chastened by experience, Castro might like to adopt a more pragmatic approach in economic policy as well as in foreign relations, but the intransigent and vengeful attitude of the Northamericans leaves him little room for manœuvre and forces him to toe the Moscow line. Here seems to lie an opportunity for initiative on the part of the European allies of the USA.

In the field of education Castro's government has solid achievements to its credit. As was to be expected, many very serious errors were made and are being made: many courses are useless or nearly so; too much time is wasted on political indoctrination; politicians (including student politicians) meddle too much; expenditure is often governed by light-headedly established priorities, and so on. Nevertheless, even though largely wasted and misguided (and in which country is this not to a large extent the case?), the educational effort is very great and stands in a sharp contrast to what went on before the revolution and to what goes on in most countries of Latin America.

Perhaps even more important than the extension of formal

255

education is the example of a ruler and of most of his principal lieutenants who, though by no means free from the normal vices of pride and love of power, do show a sense of duty and a real concern for the fate of the governed, and who do not grab money. The more fortunate states have had such heads before but in Cuba this is an entirely new phenomenon, as also is the freedom from gangsterism and extortion, which is difficult to appreciate by those used to living under a law-abiding government. It is not therefore surprising that, in spite of his foibles and mistakes Castro still seems to command the loyalty of the majority of Cubans. The fact that he has a large and loyal militia – a body of part-time unprofessional soldiers who keep their weapons at home – proves that he has a large number of genuine supporters, because all generally hated régimes always take good care to prevent the dissemination of weapons beyond the confines of a regular force. The so-called militia in the communist countries of eastern Europe is simply a professional, well-paid police force.

On the whole it seems that, in spite of having embraced a harmful doctrine, Fidel Castro has laid some of the foundations for a better society by eliminating (or at least radically curtailing) graft, exploitation and contempt for work. He can hardly be blamed for not creating a truly democratic state: the economic and cultural conditions for a successful functioning of such a polity did not and do not yet exist in Cuba; and previous experiments in elective government have been bogged down in a morass of fraud. However, the undoubted benefits of his rule will not bear fruit – and may disappear very soon – if he persists in holding to the pernicious marxist dogmas, in which case the country will be taken over entirely by the grim *apparatchiki* of the communist machine.*

* Since this was written Cuba's ruling party has officially assumed the name of Communist and veteran communist agents have moved back into the controlling positions from which they were removed during Castro's brief burst of independence. As his dependence on Soviet goods and weapons is greater than that of many eastern European regimes, Castro may become one of the more docile satellites, despite his personal inclinations. The growing resentment against the unalleviated (though now more or less equally shared) indigence and the inefficient but all pervading and suffocating bureaucracy presents Castro with the choice of either retreating from totalitarianism and restoring some elements of private enterprise, as the Yugoslavs have been doing recently; or of applying increasingly severe doses of compulsion with the consequent terror and purges. Up till now he has been moving in the latter direction but the spread of corruption and bureaucratic parasitism will probably prevent him from erecting an efficient replica of the Soviet economic system.

CHAPTER NINE

CURES AND INCANTATIONS

External Aid

One of the greatest discoveries of Gaetano Mosca was what might be called the principle of alloy, according to which an ideology can inspire massive collective action only if it appeals to base and noble motives at the same time. This principle must be borne in mind when examining the working of the aid given to poor countries; because its effects are not unrelated to the motives which prompt it.

Only people with little knowledge of indigent societies can imagine that simply by pumping funds or goods into them we can ensure economic progress. The most obvious obstacle is graft, and the clamour for aid without strings often amounts to little more than demanding freedom to embezzle. Simple misappropriation, however, could be (and to some extent has been) reduced to modest proportions by channelling the aid into concrete projects such as dams or factories, and making it available in the form of goods and services required for the construction of these objects. Even in such cases there are considerable opportunities for graft in connection with awarding sub-contracts but at least the subsidy cannot be entirely wasted, and something concrete will remain.

It is more difficult to avoid the waste occasioned by inefficiency and bureaucratic parasitism. In societies severely afflicted by parasitism the number of parasites seems to be governed by the amount of surplus (surplus being defined as the stock of goods in excess of the minimum subsistence requirements of the producers). Any augmentation of the surplus tends to increase the numer of parasites and their consequent force in relation to the productive elements of society. An influx of funds from abroad usually stimulates the proliferation of superfluous administrative posts remunerated on a scale out of proportion to the economic possibilities of the receiving country, which whets the appetites and encourages the scramble for the spoils. This type of waste is seldom criticized because it brings commercial advantages to various interested groups in the donating countries and direct benefits to the parasitic elements in the international bureaucracies.

Not everybody who advocates aid to the poorer countries is prompted by altruism: when speaking about starving children, a man may be envisaging a new post with a large salary and an expense account, free trips, conferences in pleasant places, a pretty secretary and so on. Even in the best administered unilateral schemes of technical assistance a very substantial part of the funds is wasted on needless trips and conferences. In the international organizations the waste assumes gigantic proportions.

As any criticism of the international organizations is regarded as blasphemous by people who might otherwise have most sympathy with the judgments passed in the present book, I must digress for a moment from the present theme to point out that it is wrong to imagine that the venerable principles that 'power corrupts' and that 'the price of freedom is eternal vigilance' do not apply to bodies whose personnel is recruited from all over the world. Moreover, the hopes which induce so many people to entertain a highly idealized image of the United Nations Organization are vain: where frontiers are secure though unguarded (as between Sweden and Norway or Canada and the USA) this is due to the respect for bilateral treaties, and cordial relations between the nations in question, and not to any legislation by supra-national bodies. Peace between the giants, on the other hand, depends on the balance of terror. Furthermore, there is no reason to believe that even a strong world government would necessarily ensure peace because equally atrocious civil wars might replace wars between sovereign states if the sources of collective aggression retain their efficacy.* In view of the growing interdependence of the nations, UNO provides a needed forum for discussions but it can neither prevent wars nor rescue the poor nations from their plight.

* This problem is examined in my *Military Organization and Society* and in *Elements of Comparative Sociology*, Chapters 7, 8 and 9.

To be effective, technical aid must comprise an element of moral education. This does not mean that the members of the less fortunate nations are less moral in private matters or in any absolute sense; but, as pointed out repeatedly in the earlier chapters, the absence of customs conducive to efficient work and wise management constitutes at least as serious an impediment to economic progress as the lack of capital. For this reason, the aid can have good effects only if it is administered by people who can give a good example to the citizens of the receiving countries, and this condition rules out the agencies of the United Nations whose personnel does not rise above the average level for the member states. People learn each other's vices much more readily than their virtues, and once an institution becomes permeated by intrigues it attracts the intriguers and repels or expels upright individuals. In the agencies of the United Nations the manœuvres of clandestine pressure groups operating under a cloak of spurious impartiality, and the divergence of values and ethical standards, leave their personnel with no common interest other than the vested interest in their positions and salaries.

The aid administered directly by the more prosperous countries remains fruitless chiefly for two reasons. The first is sociological ignorance. Owing to the parlous state of the social sciences, the policy makers receive little guidance from them, and act upon uncritically accepted and unwarranted assumptions such as the view that industrialization must bring prosperity and social harmony, or that the rate of growth of an industry is governed solely by the supply of capital. These errors, however, appear trifling in comparison with the perversely obtuse determination to ignore the effects of the demographic explosion.

The faultiness of the aid is not surprising in view of the fact that the nations blessed with a relatively decent social order acquired it not through deliberate planning but in virtue of a fortunate and fortuitous combination of circumstances. Naturally, many beneficial piecemeal reforms have been planned and carried out more or less systematically but the basic underlying conditions – such as, for instance, the decline in the birth rate or the spread of religious tolerance – did not come into existence as products of a deliberate policy. The knowledge of how to engineer a good society does not exist and may very well be unattainable because of an ineradicable basic antimony: social engineering requires power over human beings, which because of its magnitude is inevitably turned to evil ends. The second reason for the scant fruitfulness of external aid is that in spite of noble phrases it remains subordinated to the goals of buying allies and cajoling customers. The subsidies given to the international organizations, with the aid of which numerous sinecures are created for well-connected persons from countries with exiguous resources, serve the same purpose. It seldom matters to the donors whether their gifts do any good so long as they secure compliance in diplomatic or commercial matters.

The good effects of well-administered aid are too obvious to require much comment, but on the negative side of the balance must be put its tendency to undermine self-confidence and the spirit of self-reliance, and in extreme cases to foster a beggar mentality anxious to evade difficult tasks. For this reason, measures designed to help the needy countries to sell their products would have a healthier psychological effect than outright gifts. In any case, what determines the wealth of nations is efficient organization and hard work, whereas aid from outside can play only a very subsidiary role.

As misery and strife cannot be eliminated without a slowing down of the population growth of the countries of Latin America (with the exception of Uruguay and partly of Argentina), enlightened aid would necessarily include a contribution to the spread of birth control. Nevertheless, although the donors are ready to spend vast sums on measures conducive to the multiplication of the sufferers, they refuse to do anything about the factor which makes widespread misery inevitable. In view of the fact that the two most powerful international pressure groups are the Catholic Church and the Communist Party, it is not surprising that UNO and its organs refuse even to contemplate this issue; but even the Scandinavian countries do nothing.*

* Since this was written UNO, at the insistent request of the Indian government and in the teeth of a bitter opposition from the Catholics and communists, has sent a mission to India to advise on the campaign for birth control which has been going on there for several years. Also the Swedish government has decided to include an offer of help in this matter in its programme of aid to the underdeveloped countries. All this, however, is a drop in the ocean and it does not affect Latin America.

One reason for this inaction is that aid in the form of free supply of contraceptive appliances, though more effective in reducing misery than steel mills and highways, cannot be equally spectacular. Moreover, as it concerns topics under a taboo, a discussion of this deadly serious matter often provokes levity which reflects on any reformer active in this field, who runs the danger of being cast into a comic role. And many people would rather risk death than ridicule. In addition to other deterrents, the very finality of this form of aid diminishes its attraction: for if children destined to starvation ceased to come into the world, the fortunate would lose the opportunity of making themselves feel virtuous by giving alms.

On the receiving side more often than not the preoccupation with economic development and the desire for foreign aid stem not so much from the concern for the fate of the poor as from the lust for the paraphernalia of power and glory. With a few honourable exceptions, what the rulers want are cars and aeroplanes, wide roads, elegant airports, big buildings and arms. Apart from the lack of altruism, sheer ignorance plays an important role. The connection between overpopulation and poverty cannot be seen in the literal sense, but only understood through moderately abstract reasoning which requires a certain amount of intelligence and the ability to free oneself from mental blinkers; and is, therefore, beyond the capacity of many politicians and their followers. Moreover, when the majority is plunged in deep ignorance, only an authoritarian government (provided that it is sufficiently enlightened) can push through a sensible demographic policy, because the voters lack the foresight to support it.*

If aid were really designed to alleviate suffering and injustice, the rational policy would be for the donors not only to include an abundant supply of goods and services needed for birth control, but also make the rest of the aid conditional upon the adoption on the part of the receiving governments of adequate measures of encouragement and propaganda. The concern for the susceptibilities of the receiving nations is overridden easily enough when commercial, military or diplomatic concessions are

* It must be remembered that obtuseness in this matter is as common in Europe as in Latin America, and that in Italy, Spain, Ireland and even France anybody giving instruction in birth control is liable to imprisonment.

at stake, and therefore should not be used as an excuse for inaction in this grave matter.

So long as the birth rate remains at the level prevalent in all countries of Latin America with the exception of Uruguay and to a lesser extent Argentina, the choice is not between democracy and social justice on one side and despotism and exploitation on the other, but between hostile and friendly tyrannies; and the only attainable goal of foreign aid can be the purchase of allies and customers.

Is Democracy Feasible?

A recent book by two distinguished students of Latin American affairs, *The Struggle for Democracy* by Robert J. Alexander and Charles O. Porter, opens with the assertion that 'Latin America is ready for democracy'. Unfortunately, however, the authors adduce no conclusive evidence that this indeed is the case. They describe with great acumen the struggle against the dictators, waged under the banner of democratic ideals, but they fall into the common error of assuming that to invoke an ideal is to prove a genuine attachment to it. Moreover, even if we assume that attachment to democratic ideals is not entirely superficial, we should realize that pursuit of a goal does not imply that the goal is attainable.

We can say little that is enlightening about the problem of the feasibility of democracy in Latin America if we limit ourselves to analyzing political struggles without taking into account the economic factors and the basic features of social structure. Furthermore, we must look at the wider problem of the conditions which are necessary for the functioning of a democratic political system.

Democracy can function only in an atmosphere of compromise, regard for fair play, and agreement on basic values. Once the hatreds become violent the verdict of the polls will not be accepted; and indeed it would be foolish for the rulers to hand over the reins to the winners at the polls who intend to slaughter them. As we saw earlier, there are many elements in Latin American culture which militate against democracy, but they are all of secondary importance in comparison with the curse of mass misery.

It is one of the best established principles of political sociology that democracy cannot function in the midst of misery. Though continuously disregarded, this principle was formulated by Malthus a hundred and fifty years ago in these words:

The pressure of distress on the lower classes of people, together with the habit of attributing this distress to their rulers, appears to me to be the rock of defence, the castle, the guardian spirit of despotism. It affords to the tyrant the fatal and unanswerable plea of necessity. It is the reason why every free government tends constantly to destruction; and that its appointed guardians become daily less jealous of the encroachments of power. It is the reason why so many noble efforts in the cause of freedom have failed; and why almost every revolution, after long and painful sacrifices, has terminated in a military despotism. While any dissatisfied man of talents has power to persuade the lower classes of people that all their poverty and distress arise solely from the iniquity of the government, though, perhaps, the greatest part of what they suffer is unconnected with this cause, it is evident that the seeds of fresh discontents and fresh revolutions are continually sowing. When an established government has been destroyed, finding that their poverty has not been removed, their resentment naturally falls upon the successors to power; and when these have been immolated without producing the desired effect, other sacrifices are called for, and so without end. Are we to be surprised that, under such circumstances, the majority of well-disposed people, finding that a government with proper restrictions is unable to support itself against the revolutionary spirit, and weary and exhausted with perpetual change to which they can see no end, should give up the struggle in despair, and throw themselves into the arms of the first power which can afford them protection against the horrors of anarchy?

Democracy has functioned for the longest time in the United States which, ever since it came into existence, was always the richest country in the world: even in the eighteenth century the wages were twice as high there as they were in England, not to speak of poorer countries. In Britain the extension of the franchise, which during the second half of the nineteenth century made the political system less oligarchic and more democratic, took place at the time of growing prosperity. The democratic constitution of the Third Republic in France could be maintained in the face of the poverty and discontent of the urban proletariat only because the peasants were prosperous and on the whole satisfied. And when the economic crisis of the thirties came, the republic nearly collapsed under the blows of fascist and communist movements. The connection between the rise of Hitler and the collapse of the German economy is also well known. The same world economic crisis brought about the demise of parliamentary governments in Argentina and Brazil. Even Uruguay – the model democracy of Latin America – experienced a short-lived dictatorship in 1930.

A democratic constitution implanted in the midst of poverty can escape violation only if the masses are so docile that they do not exercise their rights in order to press for improvements of their fate, and passively acquiesce in the rule of their social superiors, as is the case in India. The Hindu religion is the most powerful 'opium of the masses' yet invented: it induces submission of the masses by dividing them into a multitude of castes (thus impeding joint action) and by promising posthumous social ascent as the reward for keeping to one's status in this life. The weakening of religion in India cannot fail to make even this nominal democracy unworkable. In Latin America not even the Iberian variant of Roman Catholicism could induce similar resignation among the poor so that the rulers continuously had to resort to force to keep them down.

Once we realize that democracy in any real sense is not viable in desperately poor countries we can see it is absolutely futile to attempt to foist this type of government upon such countries unless we can expect a very quick inprovement of economic conditions. Such an improvement, however, cannot be effected by foreign aid alone, and it requires concerted efforts of the whole population. The question therefore is: can a democratic government lift a country out of a condition of abject and longstanding misery before it is destroyed by revolutionary forces? It seems doubtful, to say the least.

Thinking in terms of slogans is so common that few upholders of liberal and democratic values have dared to question the wisdom of foisting their ideal upon all countries regardless of their condition. One of the first who have dared to think on this topic was Hugh Seton-Watson from whose *Neither Peace Nor War* (London, 1960, pp. 451–2) comes the following quotation:

That Westerners should prefer to see democratic régimes in the underdeveloped societies is natural and right. Western influence should always be used in favour of freedom whenever there is a chance of success. But it is well to recognize that Western influence may be unsuccessful. Asians and Africans are rightly indignant when they hear from Westerners the argument (which may be phrased in a condescending or a sympathetic manner) that they are 'incapable of understanding liberty' or 'not yet fit for democracy'. But the same people will angrily insist that they must not be expected to accept slavish copies of Western institutions. It must be admitted that human ingenuity can devise a great variety of combinations of freedom and authority. Some Asian, African and Latin American régimes are and will be freer than others. Some are and will be dictatorships. But a government may be dictatorial without being totalitarian. Only a doctrinaire can deny that situations can arise in which the necessary economic and cultural progress requires dictatorial leadership ...

Totalitarian dogma is another matter. It may provide idealism and energy in the early stages of a revolutionary régime, but after a time it can only become an obstacle to progress. The Soviet Union has achieved magnificent successes by virtue of the great talents of the Russian people and the great wealth of the Russian soil and sub-soil, in spite of the dogma of Lenin and Stalin. Every sincere friend of the aspiring nations of Asia, Africa and Latin America must wish them escape from the pitfalls of totalitarianism. Yet even here a distinction must be made, from the standpoint of Western interests, between totalitarianism which makes a nation the instrument of the Sino-Soviet enemies of the West, and some other totalitarianism, at present unknown, which might not. The first priority for the West, the irreducible minimum, is that a given country should not become a satellite of the Sino-Soviet bloc, the second that it be not totalitarian, the third that it be not a dictatorship. Conversely, the ideal is that it should be a free and incorrupt democracy, second best that it be a comparatively progressive dictatorship, a bad third that it be totalitarian, but not hostile to the West, and worst of all that it be absorbed in the enemy camp.

It is important that Western leaders and public opinion should have clear ideas of the priorities of desirability, but it is also wise to distinguish between the desirable and the possible.

To the foregoing opinion it must be added (apart from a correction on the point of Sino-Soviet unity) that the acceptability of a régime from the point of view of the security of the democratic countries need not coincide with its desirability to those who live under it. A populist totalitarian government may be more attractive to the majority of the population than a non-totalitarian dictatorship whose sole concern is the defence of the rich against the poor, or a formally democratic régime based in reality on fraud and corruption, and the bolstering of parasitic exploitation.

In so far as strategic necessities permit, an authoritarian government which lays foundations for a decent and prosperous society in the future deserves more support than a regime which observes the democratic forms while perpetuating the social evils which make a real approximation to democratic and liberal ideals impossible.

Democracy is compatible with rapid economic growth only in countries which already have enough resources to make heavy investment a relatively painless process. There is no case of a democratic government breaking through a vicious circle of misery and parasitism. The danger to a government embarking on a programme of strenuous investment comes both from the suffering masses – which in any case could not be adequately fed and clothed even if all the wealth of the rich were distributed among them — and from the upper classes resenting the diminution of their wealth.

The intransigent defence of their privileges by the upper classes of the poor countries stems not only from their short-sightedness and predilection for idle existence but also from the magnitude of the sacrifice required of them: for whereas in the rich countries heavy investments and substantial improvements in the standard of living of the poorer classes necessitate a diversion of only a fairly small part of the income of the wealthy, in the very poor countries even a total confiscation of their possessions might not provide enough resources to ensure economic progress. In Bolivia, for instance, an expropriation of the landowners and capitalists brought no alleviation of general misery. It must be borne in mind, furthermore, that in a poor country a loss of a privileged position not only entails severe physical hardship but also involves a feeling of an acute moral degradation, owing to the great cultural gap between the classes. Thus the egoism of the privileged class is strengthened by the awareness of the enormity of the sacrifices they would have to make and the uncertainty of their fruits.

As many examples (ranging from Sulla in ancient Rome to Franco in contemporary Spain) show, the normal reaction of the privileged classes to the prospect of a sudden demotion is recourse to violence. The recent *cuartelazos* in Peru, the Dominican Republic and Brazil belong to the same category.

The Case for a Revolution

Many Latin Americans believe that no radical improvements can be achieved through gradual and peaceful reforms, and that revolution is the only remedy. Although this belief is rooted in traditional, partly magical, patterns of thinking and feeling, there are certain arguments put forth in its support which deserve examination. In strict logic the two parts of this contention are independent: even if it is true that gradual reforms are doomed to futility, it does not follow that a revolution would help; for the disease may be incurable. Such pessimism, however, is so unpalatable that a proof of futility of peaceful reforms will always be regarded as an argument for attempting revolution.

Clearly, there is little scope for peaceful reforms under the rule of a cruel despot; but unadulterated despositism is now rare in Latin America. Nevertheless it can be argued that the alliance between the land-owning and financial circles and the army officers is sufficiently strong to block the peaceful road to necessary reforms. In Peru, for instance, whenever the APRA won the elections, the army prevented it from assuming office and installed a military dictatorship. The last intervention of this kind took place in 1962, even although the APRA had by then shed most of its initial radicalism and become mildly reformist. In Brazil the military have lately forced Janio Quadros to relinquish the presidency, although the reforms which he tried to introduce were of a very limited nature. True, after the initial opposition the generals have agreed to the restoration of full presidential powers to the successor Quadros, Jao Goulart, notwithstanding his leftist connections and proclamations, but Goulart became a millionaire during his struggle for social justice, and shortly before he was deposed had bought his eighteenth estate. In Argentina the military have deposed president Frondizi for trying to reach some accommodation with the Peronists without whom no peaceful reform was possible. In Guatemala a slight gesture of reconcilation towards his leftist enemies on the part of the dictator Ydigoras brought about his overthrow by the army. It seems that only in Uruguay, Costa Rica and Chile could an opposition party advocating radical reforms win the elections and attempt to carry out its programme without immediately provoking a military coup.*

So long as the military are ready to nullify electoral victories by force, the road to peaceful reform is blocked, and the contention that a revolution ought to be tried appears to be justified. The argument that this therapy has been tried before without great benefit can be answered by saying that it was not applied with sufficient thoroughness.

The prevalence of electoral fraud constitutes the second argument in favour of desirability of a revolution. In rural districts dominated by a large estate the owner can usually rig the elections by making sure that his employees believe that he can find out how they have voted, or by arranging fraudulent counting. Where these methods are impracticable he can dissuade the suspected opponents from voting either by threats of dismissal or even of physical punishment by his retainers, who in the most backward areas constitute the only effective police force. This explains why many rural areas which are seething with discontent, or even plagued by armed uprisings, nevertheless return conservative deputies to parliament. However, political power based on the ownership of the soil is undergoing rapid diminution with the advance of urbanization. In the towns the election cannot be rigged by individual employers but only by the governmental machine; and even in rural areas the spread of literacy and improvements in communication facilitate penetration by political and trade-union organizers from the cities. Consequently, in the more urbanized countries, such as Chile, Argentina, Uruguay and southern Brazil, the concentration of property in land no longer constitutes an insuperable obstacle to an electoral victory of parties advocating radical reforms.

The proclivity of the leftist politicians to amass wealth and then to change sides provides another argument for revolution. There are numerable examples of politicians who have risen as defenders of the poor, and then quickly entered the ranks of the rich. In Chile, for instance Arturo Alessandri, nicknamed the Lion of Tarapaca, won the presidency in 1920 by advocating radical social reforms. He carried out a few of them but also acquired considerable wealth, and during his second presidency

---

* As has happened in Chile since this was written.

sided decisively with the rich against the poor. His wealthy son Jorge was the most conservative head of the state which Chile has had during the last forty years.

Crossing class lines is an extremely common phenomenon; and it is the height of naïveté to imagine that humble social origins ensure concern for the welfare of the poor. In Britain influential members of the Labour Party are enticed into the charmed circle by the bestowal of the titles of nobility – and then hasten to send their sons to the public schools (i.e. expensive private boarding schools) – but, as the class antagonisms in Britain are relatively mild, they are usually able to maintain some interest in the welfare of their former class. But where, as in Latin America, the classes are sharply divided by contempt, fear and hatred, it is very difficult to defend the poor while associating with the rich. Living in luxury while his former supporters are starving, an enriched ex-populist politician can escape the burden of guilt only by believing that the poor are contemptible.

It is arguable that in view of the seductiveness of the aristocratic way of life, only a complete destruction of the upper classes can save a populist movement from decapitation by suction. This argument is supported by the experience of the Mexican and Bolivian revolutions which – unlike the revolutions in Russia and China – did not destroy completely the pre-existing upper classes. It is a fact that the élites which emerged in consequence of the Mexican and Bolivian revolutions were far less industrious, disciplined and austere than the Russian or Chinese communists; but it is not clear that the superiority of the latter in this respect is due to the thoroughness with which they eliminated the pre-existing élites. Cromwell did not destroy the upper class, nevertheless his Ironsides were at least as frugal and conscientious as the Bolsheviks. On the other hand, many examples – ranging from the leaders of slave revolts in ancient Rome to Stenka Razin and the prophet of the T'ai ping rebellion in China – show that the mere acquisition of power and riches usually suffices to breed corruption among the revolutionaries even without closer contacts with the upper classes. It seems that it is the possession of a rigid doctrine ardently upheld, rather than the destruction of the pre-existing upper class, that restrains in the victorious revolutionaries the normal tendency towards sybaritism and peculation.

Given complete lack of faith in their rulers, it would certainly be difficult – if not impossible – to shake the masses out of their mood of apathy and political cynicism by piecemeal reform; and therefore in countries where the situation is very bad only a spectacular revolution could convince the people that things are really improving and spur them to effort. This view is not baseless; but, clearly, a revolution can be beneficial only if those who overthrow the old order know how to erect something better in its place, and at present the most popular blueprint is communism.

Totalitarianism

When the majority of the people are so poor that they cannot save while the rich spend all they get, the only method of finding funds for investment is to institute an authoritarian régime to compel by means of severe discipline the people to consume less than they produce. For this reason only an authoritarian government can undertake a task of modernizing a backward overpopulated country. Obviously, however, authoritarianism is not enough; for if it were, then poverty would have been banished from the world long ago. Indeed, the overwhelming majority of governments recorded by history were authoritarian, predatory and corrupt; and (as shown in detail in my *Elements of Comparative Sociology*) their parasitism constituted the chief obstacle to economic progress. A limited authoritarian government can promote economic progress by ensuring internal peace and refraining from intensive parasitism, if other conditions are propitious to the successful functioning of an economy based on private enterprise. A totalitarian government may bring about economic progress only if the ruling group is energetic, clever, disciplined and dedicated to the point of asceticism. The Chinese communists exhibit these characteristics most markedly.

In addition to being able to squeeze out of the people a large amount of wealth for investment, totalitarianism can slow the population growth even without war by massive conscription and exploitation of labour. Probably about 22 million men and two or three million women perished in Stalin's labour camps, and, if we add the number of births which did not take place because of these deaths, we can estimate that without his activities the population of the USSR would be larger than it is by 70 to 90 million. Being more sophisticated and less brutal than Stalin, and having obtained a firmer hold over the minds of their subjects, the Chinese communists have apparently succeeded in imposing postponement of marriage and pre-marital chastity. Clearly, no government based on consent could maintain this kind of pressure.

In the communist states of eastern Europe the impossibility of accumulating large wealth and investing it profitably prevents large-scale graft and parasitism, even though it does not rule out almost universal petty pilfering. What would be the impact of communist totalitarianism in this respect on Latin America is difficult to tell, as the Cuban régime – though reasonably successful in eliminating graft – has not lasted long enough for the effects of the initial enthusiasm to wear off and (what is even more important) is living largely on Soviet charity. However, the lack of traditions of dutiful obedience – which so markedly distinguished the Latin Americans as well as the Poles from the Russians or the Germans or the Chinese – must not be regarded as an insuperable obstacle to an establishment of an austere totalitarianism, because many examples show how the national character can be altered by a tenacious group of fanatical believers.

Assuming that graft could be reduced to manageable proportions, could a communist system cure the economic ills of Latin America? The answer is No – for the following reasons.

A totalitarian system can eliminate idleness and sumptuary consumption and mobilize energies and resources, but it is extremely wasteful, owing to the red-tape, overcentralization and other shortcomings of a top-heavy bureaucracy. Furthermore, unlike the Soviet empire or China, none of the countries of Latin America could become self-sufficient,* and all of them have to rely on exports for procurement of many most essential commodities; which means that they are exposed to the impact of fluctuation in world prices, and that they must be able to deliver goods to foreign customers' specifications and at competitive prices, which is a thing which none of the existing rigidly planned economies has as yet been able to achieve. The inability to alleviate the misery of the masses, however, need not render a régime unviable, for all the long-lived despotisms of the

* Except, perhaps, Brazil.

past have kept the majority in permanent degradation. So it is quite possible that, even without being able to improve the lot of the masses, communism or some other form of totalitarianism may put an end to the turmoil in Latin America by replacing the present ineffectual and disorganized ruling classes by a cohesive élite of experts in coercion and brain-washing.

The Prospects

As the countries of Latin America differ so much in so many respects, there is no reason to imagine that the same remedies would be equally likely to solve the difficulties of all of them, nor indeed that the same remedies would be tried everywhere. Let us then examine them briefly in succession, beginning with those which have the most chances of attaining the blessed condition of a democratic welfare state.

There can be little doubt that from this viewpoint Argentina is the most privileged country. It is the only country in Latin America where under-nourishment is uncommon, and which contains no large mass of apathetic peasantry. Its troubles are chiefly of political origin, and are due to the scant respect for law, the bickering about relative advantages between sectors and classes and the small ability of its leaders. It does not seem, however, that the antagonisms between the classes assume the proportions of deadly hatreds (as is the case in Central America) because even when the machinery of the state was in a condition of far-reaching disintegration no large-scale uprisings occurred. The course of mass demonstrations in Argentina has for many decades been very mild in comparison with the savage outbursts of vengeful violence which took place on various occasions in tropical America.

The rate of population growth remains (as we saw in the earlier chapters) considerable but it is at a level at which it could be overtaken by production if the latter grew at the speed attained in a number of countries in Europe. Apart from maladjustments which could be fairly quickly corrected by an enlightened government, the supply of skills is sufficient to ensure fast economic progress.

The influence of the Peronists and the communists, absentee landownership, military parasitism and other factors discussed in the previous chapters, make the task of governing Argentina very difficult but not beyond the capability of a group of able, hard-working and honest statesmen. Given a passably efficient government capable of putting the army in its place, the enormous resources of Argentina (in combination with a relatively low birth rate) would permit a rapid progress within the framework of capitalism and without any need for draconian measures.

The prospects of Uruguay are not much worse. Culturally it is on more or less the same level. Its chief disadvantages in comparison with Argentina are its small size which makes industrialization uneconomic, the ineffectual system of government and the even more serious hypertrophy of the bureaucratic class. On the other hand the lower birth rate permits a democratic system of government to continue even when the rate of economic growth is low. The absence of a heritage of divisive hatreds constitutes another important advantage.

Despite the larger proportion of miserable peasants in its population, Chile is not far (if at all) behind its eastern neighbours in the cultural level and the supply of skills. The land-owning class has been up till now more intransigent than in Uruguay, but, in comparison with its Argentinian counterpart, it has shown more skill and prudence in defending its privileges. It has not attempted to counteract by force the recent electoral victory of Eduardo Frei and the Christian Democratic Party, thus remaining faithful to the Chilean tradition of constitutional government. The rise of a truly reformist Christian Democratic Party constitutes an enormous boon to Chile, as it permits reforms to be carried out with the weight of the traditional religion behind them rather than against them – which is perhaps the most important factor which enabled the Protestant nations to build stable and democratic welfare states and which prevented the Catholic nations from achieving the same. It is to the great credit of the Chilean ecclesiastic hierarchy that it has at least partly broken with the habit of helping the rich to oppress the poor.

The political situation is more propitious in Chile than in any other Latin American country, but this advantage may very well be only momentary because the relation between the population and resources is much less favourable than in Argentina. Although there is still some room for a larger population, the agricultural possibilities are limited while the nature of the land and its geographical position give little reason to hope that Chile might become capable of paying for large imports of food and raw materials by exporting manufactured goods. The birth rate still remains very high and might even rise if the living conditions of the peasants improve. In view of the limited resources it seems very unlikely that the rate of growth of production could be maintained above the rate of population growth for a period sufficiently long to permit a substantial improvement in income per head. For this reason there is no hope that the birth rate might fall spontaneously in response to an enduring improvement in the standard of living, which means that without an extensive government-sponsored campaign for birth control the vicious circle cannot be broken. Actually such a campaign is indispensable merely for preventing further impoverishment. However, here the Christian Democratic Party finds itself in a blind alley: for it can enjoy the support (or even the mere neutrality) of the Church only so long as it does nothing about a population explosion which renders all reforms futile. Furthermore, like their counterparts in Europe, none of the Christian Democratic leaders have shown that they even understand the dilemma, and in all likelihood they will continue to refuse to face the demographic reality, thus ensuring that the hopes aroused by their advent to power will prove vain.

Despite greater peace on the surface the situation in Mexico is a great deal more explosive than in the southernmost countries of the continent, primarily owing to the much more widespread poverty and the stronger tradition of violence in public as well as private life. Unlike Chile, Mexico had no tradition of the rule of law and respect for the constitution, and the police are extremely brutal. No government by free and honest elections has yet been tried in Mexico; and a removal of the mono-party rule would release very explosive forces. As measured by the approximation to democracy, what Chile, Uruguay and even Argentina have to preserve, Mexico is still very far from attaining. What aggravates the situation is that whereas in Chile (and to a lesser extent Brazil) the Church has recently adopted a fairly enlightened attitude towards the question of social justice, in Mexico (mainly owing to the anti-clerical origins of the ruling party) the clergy are sponsoring semi-fascist movements inclined to subversion by violence. Whilst recruiting militants and sympathizers among the poor to whom anti-government religiosity is a form of protest against exploitation, these movements receive financial support from businessmen who find the bureaucracy with its trade-union appendages irksome, and hanker after government by the business-men for the businessmen so exuberantly exemplified in the neighbouring Texas.

The communists, of course, remain strong but their propaganda may appeal less to the Mexicans than to other Latin Americans because of the emasculation of the marxist phraseology by the ruling politicians who use marxist slogans to justify the status quo; which partly explains why so much popular discontent feeds the flame of clericalism. Had the birth rate not been so high, the fast growth of Mexico's production would have made gross poverty rare by now. Despite the anti-clerical antecedents of the present régime, however, nothing has been done about spreading birth control, and in consequence the condition of the poorest class has been aggravated during the last few years. So long as the ruling party retains its cohesion, it can continue to hold the dissatisfied down, but if its containing force weakens a great explosion might take place.

Despite its tempestuous politics, the widespread misery of the lower classes and the parlous condition of the middle classes due to the perpetual inflation, Brazil does not seem to be ripe for a great upheaval because the forces in the political arena do not seem to fall into well-polarized extremes and – as the effortless success of the last military coup has demonstrated – the masses remain rather apathetic politically. The communists were able to infiltrate thoroughly the educational institutions, many ministries, labour unions and, of course, Goulart's Labour Party, but they were not intransigent enough to fight and were unable to inspire the masses with enthusiasm for their cause. Two factors account to a large extent for this passivity: the first is the cultural, racial and regional differences and divisions which make a political integration of the lower classes extremely difficult: the second is the mercenary character of so-called revolutionary leaders whose sybaritism, peculation and lack of courage and conviction could not be concealed from the followers. The inequality of power between the classes persists in spite of surface turbulence because the same proclivities which make the Brazilian governments so defective incapacitate the revolutionary movements.

The new military government naturally claims that it has saved Brazil from communism and that it is sweeping away the old abuses; but although there may be some truth in the first part of the claim, there is none in the second. For although it is true that under Goulart Brazil was sinking deeper and deeper in disorder, his successors have so far done nothing about the deeper causes of economic and political difficulties. The coup has simply been just another application of the old remedy: when the masses are beginning to get out of hand the generals come out. The elimination of the communist danger seems to have been a secondary concern, as the persecution has more often than not been directed against non-communist intellectuals guilty of advocating serious reforms, whilst many communist agents remain unmolested. While there is no reason to imagine that the economic growth of Brazil will suddenly stop or that the country will be engulfed by a catastrophic upheaval, it seems very unlikely that any advances towards general welfare and democracy will be made in the near future. The giant of Latin America will probably continue to stagger on.

If a supply of money were an infallible cure for discord and strife – as many economic advisers on foreign aid seem to imagine – Venezuela would have reached the condition of a stable democratic welfare state long ago. Unfortunately the flow of effortlessly earned dollars aggravated inequality, stimulated cupidity and disinclination to work, directed energies into the struggle for shares rather than into the production of wealth, and discouraged industry by making imports cheap in relation to domestic products. However, we must not exaggerate: given the psychological heritage of exploitation, oppression and rebellion, the miraculous survival of Betancourt's government would have not been possible without the great financial resources which enabled the government to rely on rewards rather than punishments. The difference between the Venezuelan and the Bolivian attempts at social reform was primarily determined by the bounty of Venezuelan oil. Not that Accion Democratica have been able to lay the foundations for affluence and stability. The distribution of a substantial area to peasants has enabled the government to obtain some support from beneficiaries in its struggle against the Castroist guerrillas – and thus to avoid the necessity of a strictly military government – but it did not alter the basic features of Venezuelan society. Poised between the discontented and unruly populace on the one hand and the predatory army and parasitic upper class on the other, the position of the Accion Democratica remains very precarious. In Colombia, Peru and the smaller republics the old triumvirate of the army, the Church and the monied oligarchy continues to rule. A successful mass uprising is unlikely to succeed in any of these countries because the armies are too strong. What could more easily happen is a seizure of power by a group of 'Nasserist' officers; for by no means all the officers are satisfied with their role of the watchdogs of the plutocrats. Anti-communist indoctrination has drawn the attention of some of the younger officers to marxism and made them interested in social problems, in consequence of which they have developed technocratic inclinations.

In view of the Sino-Soviet split and the determination of the Northamerican government to prevent by force of arms the victory of any movement which enjoys communist support however small, the communists have no chance of taking over any Latin American country in addition to Cuba. Castro's admission or boast that he has deceived his capitalist enemies by concealing his marxist faith has ensured that he will have no imitators. But, as the communists have men in all parties striving for reforms, the Northamerican policy of taking no risks in respect of communist infiltration may very well lead to the entire Latin America falling under a rule of gangsters like those now ruling the most unfortunate states, whose sole title to membership of the 'free world' is their willingness to shoot or jail anybody accused of communism. An empire erected on this basis would be as bad as the Roman or the Turkish, and greatly more oppressive than the French and British colonial empires in Africa ever were.

In the poorest countries of America where the economic and cultural conditions condemn reformist democratic movements to helplessness, leading to communist infiltration or an overthrow by predatory generals allied with domestic and foreign plutocrats, some form of Nasserism may be the only kind of government which holds out any hope of reforms, however slight.

But a successful application of this remedy requires the prior existence of a group of officers who are honest, knowledgeable in economic matters and not content with remaining well-paid tools of oppression – in fact well above the level of their Egyptian prototypes. Unfortunately, it usually happens that those most in need of a medicine are the least able to make it for themselves: and so the countries where Nasserism may be the last hope have armies which are least able to evolve a useful specimen of the species.

The Northamerican government finds itself in a sad predicament: for obvious strategic and economic reasons it cannot let Latin America fall under communist domination, but the alternative course of backing bloodthirsty and rapacious tyrants offers no long-term security to the USA, while inflicting terrible sufferings on the peoples of Latin America. Indeed in cases like that of the Dominican republic at the moment of writing, it would be far better for the ordinary people (and perhaps even be welcomed by them) if the United States were to practise an old-fashioned and decent kind of imperialism, and incorporate the vassal state into its own territory. A direct Northamerican military or colonial administration would in every respect be better than a government by seasoned extortioners and torturers.

A POSTSCRIPT TO
THE NORTHAMERICAN EDITION

DURING the few months which have elapsed since the English edition went into press nothing has happened which would necessitate alterations to the theses advanced in the present book. On the contrary: the recent events provide additional confirmation. The military coup in Argentina constitutes one more turn of the old cycle. Argentina continues to enjoy the privileged position in respect of wealth, ethnic homogeneity and educational standards; and its new lapse into military dictatorship shows that a tradition of public vices may outweigh the economic and cultural advantages—and eventually even nullify them. Twenty years ago Argentina was by any of the usual standards far in front of all the other Latin American nations, but it has been rapidly losing its privileged position.

In many ways Argentina's recent evolution illustrates Montesquieu's view that a republic (that is to say, what we would call democracy) rests upon the virtue of its citizens. Where the elementary public virtues are lacking, democracy can only lead to chaos which will end in dictatorship. When a country is governed by a small wealthy class, while the populace is kept in its place by open or veiled coercion, the system can work without being supported by strong moral sentiments. The potentates need little will-power as they have everything they want, while the toilers have no choice but to work and obey. Such a system is unjust but perfectly viable and can persist indefinitely. An explosive situation arises when the apparatus of economic and political pressure loses its efficacity, and the masses begin to clamour for the bounties hitherto reserved for the few, while the wealth per head remains the same or even diminishes. The poorer the country, the more dedication and self-discipline is required if a system based on coercion of the many by the few is to be avoided.

The hardening of the Brazilian military regime need not surprise us. The ground has been prepared by the purge of the officers suspected of liberal or leftist leanings which has accompanied and followed the coup; and given widespread discontent with the result of their governance, the military rulers were faced with the choice between tightening the screw or giving up the supremacy. It must not be imagined, however, that all these repressive measures insure the perpetuation of the present regime. Without any ideology, without a leader capable of inspiring devotion in his subordinates, and increasingly permeated by graft engendered by its participation in economic administration, the army may easily split into warring factions or the present high command may be overthrown by a conspiracy of their juniors.

One point insufficiently emphasised in this book is that, apart from acting as watchdogs of the property-owning classes, the Brazilian military rulers have been furthering their own corporate interests and augmenting their incomes by taking over lucrative posts in civil service and nationalised banks and industries. In some ways the Brazilian situation offers curious parallels to Pilsudski's regime in Poland, but the element of true nationalism is lacking; and far from enjoying indulgence as defenders of the fatherland, the Brazilian generals are widely regarded as agents of foreign economic domination.

Despite the electoral victory of the de-contaminated and democratically reconditioned old comrade of Trujillo, nothing that has been said in this book about the position in the Dominican Republic needs to be taken back. If the defeated candidate had to surround his house by a wall of sandbags and literally did not dare to pop his head out, one can well imagine the freedom of expression and choice enjoyed by the peasants in outlying villages under the watchful eye of policemen well drilled by the late Benefactor in the arts of intimidation and torture. As an indication of popular preference, these elections are not worth much more than the recent victory at the polls of the South Vietnamese warlord Ky or the even more resounding successes of Walter Ulbricht.

The evolution of Castro's regime continues along the lines foreseen in the footnote on page 256; and as predicted, the economic dependence has forced Castro to toe the Moscow line and purge the pro-Chinese wing led by Che Guevara.

Some readers may be disappointed on finding that I have not said explicitly what I think ought to be done to help Latin America, even though a number of practical conclusions are implicit in the analysis. They should remember, however, that a correct diagnosis must precede an effective therapy; and that it might be more useful to try to improve our understanding rather than add another item to the already impressive array of ineffectual plans. Moreover, though immensely difficult, a correct diagnosis is still easier to give than a really good recipe for improvement, because for the latter we not only need to know which are the crucial factors but also how to manipulate them. Nevertheless, we might perhaps help to work out a better approach if instead of trying to produce a complete prescription, we consider only some of the conditions which (though definitely insufficient to insure success) must be fulfilled if any progress is to be made.

To begin with a negative statement, I must repeat that I do not see how any good can come out of foisting formally democratic constitutions upon countries where they cannot function. The liberal democratic welfare state is the highest political achievement of mankind up till now, but in many situations only an authoritarian government can function at all; and under such circumstances the ethico-political problem boils down to the question of which variant merits our acquiescence or perhaps even support. The most general principle which might guide us in this matter is that this authoritarian regime is best which is most decisively eliminating the circumstances which have made it inevitable.

More specifically, I would suggest the following criteria for assessing the value of governments which cannot operate in a liberal and democratic way. Naturally, this scale cannot be applied without modifications to cases like Czechoslovakia, where dictatorship has been imposed and is wantonly maintained out of sheer lust for power on the part of the party bureaucracy, despite the existence of conditions permitting a democratic order.

1. Honesty and a serious concern for the welfare of the subjects. On this score we must rate Nasser higher than Sukarno, and Castro infinitely higher than Duvalier or Somoza.

2. Rational outlook and freedom from an addiction to pernicious dogmas. On this point Castro is not too good but still better than Ulbricht and perhaps even Gomulka. Nasser, Tito, and the Mexican presidents, however, appear much better.

3. Curtailment of parasitism and waste. But it must be comprehensive, as it is no good eliminating landlords if they are replaced by parasitic soldiers or bureaucrats. On this point all the military presidents, including Nasser, score badly with the sole exception of Cardenas. It seems that in Cuba the party bureaucracy does not yet absorb as great a share of wealth as the parasitic elements of the previous regime did.

4. A vigorous policy of birth control which entails anti-clericalism so long as the attitude of the Church remains malevolent. On this score the highest praise must go to the Polish communists, although Mao Tse-tung also seems to have seen the light of reason, and the same has lately been dawning upon Nasser. It must be remembered,

however, that Japan's non-dictatorial rulers have achieved more in this respect than anybody else. Castro has so far done nothing about maintaining a demographic balance, but his system offers better prospects in this respect than the clericalist militocracies. Obscurantism in this matter will insure that political systems will grow increasingly more oppressive and the victims of internal violence more numerous.

5. Lessening the gulf between the rich and the poor. Apart from the founder of the Uruguayan democracy, Batllé y Ordoñez, the only Latin American leaders who deserve credit on this score are Lazaro Cardenas and, above all, Fidel Castro.

6. Efficient administration and inculcation of the elementary economic virtues. None of the Latin American dictators has left a beneficial legacy in this respect (least of all the pretorians) and even Castro has achieved little—very much less than his Russian comrades, let alone the early Prussian kings.

7. Restraint in the use of power as bloodthirsty oppression nullifies all incidental benefits. On this score the Latin American dictators do not appear bad in comparison with the sultans, khans, tzars and other oriental despots, although most of them were or are bad enough. In this matter our hero must be Lazaro Cardenas, who had almost absolute power but chose to give it up and thus put an end to military dictatorship in Mexico.

As some of the required dispositions tend to exclude one another, any leader or party who would score highly on all (or even most) of these criteria would be performing a magnificent feat.

BIBLIOGRAPHY

THE bulk of serious literature on Latin American affairs comes from the USA. The standard works are indicated in the bibliographies appended to the three excellent elementary introductions: Lewis Hanke, *Modern Latin America* (Princeton, N.J., 1959); Robert J. Alexander, *Today's Latin America* (New York, 1962); R. A. Gomez, *Government and Politics in Latin America* (New York, 1960). Frank Tannenbaum, *Ten Keys to Latin America* (New York, 1963), is an important recent addition. The most thorough and sophisticated introduction to sociological and political problems of Latin America is Jacques Lambert, *Amerique Latine: Structures Sociales et Institutions Politiques* (Paris, 1963) which contains an excellent bibliography.

Among the narratives of recent events from under the pen of Latin American writers, *Entre la Libertad y el Miedo* (translated as *The State of Latin America*), by German Arciniegas is outstanding, and provides a corrective to the national bias of the Northamerican writers.

Though superior in the extent of the coverage and reliability on points of fact, works by the Northamerican writers do not attain the depth of the insight of the best Latin American writers into the inner springs of their social order and national character. The indigenous social critics, moreover, are harsher. No foreigner has ever painted such a grim picture of a Latin American society as that given by Alcides Argüedas in *Pueblo Enfermo*. Some of the bitter remarks of Bolivar have not yet lost their validity, and the same is true of the thoughts of José Maria Luis Mora – a Mexican writer who died in exile in 1850. A selection of his writings was published in Mexico in 1941 under the title *Ensayos Ideas y Retratos*. Of great interest remains *Nuestra Inferioridad Economica* by Francisco Encina, written in 1911 and reprinted by Editorial Universitaria, Santiago de Chile, in 1955.

The famous works of Gilberto Freyre, translated as *The*

Masters and the Slaves (New York, 1956) and *The Mansions and the Shanties* (New York, 1963) are fundamental for understanding the genesis of all those societies in America which were based on slavery. In *Bandeirantes e Pionerios*, Vianna Moog compares the social evolution of Brazil with that of the USA and suggests possible explanations of differences in national character. Among the historiographic literature the richest in illuminating interpretative ideas seem to me to be the works of Alberto Edwards Vives (above all *La Organizacion Politica de Chile* and *La Fronda Aristocratica*) written at the beginning of the present century from the point of view of a Chilean conservative proud of his country's exceptional stability; and the equally old *Cesarismo Democratico* by the Venezuelan, Laureano Vallenilla Lanz, an apology for dictatorship of considerable weight; and *Siete Ensayos de Interpretacion de la Realidad Peruana* (many reprints) by José Carlos Mariategui, the founder of the Peruvian Communist Party, who died in 1930. In the recent literature there are two outstanding works by the Chilean writers: *Ensayo Critico del Desarrollo Economico-Social de Chile* by Julio Cesar Jobet (Santiago, 1955) written from a non-communist marxist point of view, and *Chile: un Caso de Desarrollo Frustrado* by Anibal Pinto Santa Gruz (Santiago, 1959), which is a brilliant application of economic theory and somewhat marxist sociology to history in order to give a genetic explanation of the present situation. Jesus Silva Herzog's *Nueve Estudios Mexicanos* (1953) also deviates from the pattern of nationalistic apologetics and superficiality to which the majority of the Latin American books on history conform, with the exception of those which fall into the opposite extreme of marxist orthodoxy. An intelligent marxist interpretation of Brazilian history is given by Caio Prado Junior in *Evolucao Politica do Brasil* (São Paulo, 1957) and *Historia Economica do Brasil* (São Paulo, 1959).

Of exceptional value is the little book *La Vida Familiar del Mexicano* by Maria Elvira Bermudez (Mexico, 1955), which should be read in conjunction with the shattering autobiographies edited by Oscar Lewis under the title *The Children of Sanchez* (Penguin Books).

The most penetrating analyses of economic mechanisms can be found in *Crecimiento Economico de America Latina* by Alberto Baltra Cortes (Santiago, 1959), in *En Vez de la Miseria* by Jorge

Ahumada (Santiago, 1960), and in the book by Santa Cruz just mentioned. *La Distribucion del Ingreso y el Desarrollo Economico de Mexico* by Ifigenia M. de Navarrete (Mexico, 1960) gives an analysis of this crucial factor.

The only book which gives conclusive evidence on the workings of economic imperialism is Romulo Betancourt's *Venezuela : Politica y Petroleo* (Mexico, 1956). The rest of the literature on this subject is too propagandist even when it contains some interesting pieces of information.

Among books on the genesis of Castro's revolution the most convincing was Claude Julien's *La Revolution Cubaine* (Paris, 1961) until the publication of Goldenberg's study listed below. The following are the most important recent additions to the literature:

Victor Alba, *Parasitos, Mitos y Sordomudos* (Mexico 5, 1964)

Victor Alba, *Historia del movimiento obrero en America Latina* (Mexico, 1964)

Rene Dumont, *Cuba, Socialisme et developpement* (Paris VIe, 1964).

Celso Furtado, *Le Bresil à l'heure du choix* (Paris, 1964)

Gino Germani, *Politica y Sociedad en una Epoca de Transicion* (Buenos Aires, 1962)

Mons. German Guzman, Orland Fals Borda, Eduardo Umana Luna, *La violencia en Colombia* (Colombia, 1962)

Santiago Ramirez, *El Mexicano psicologia de su Destructividad* (Mexico 1961)

Torcuato S. Di Tella, *El Sistema Politico Argentino y La Clase Obrera* (Buenos Aires, 1964)

Victor Villanueva, *El Militarismo en el Peru* (Lima, Peru, 1962)

NOTES

(1) The argument in favour of letting the international division of labour be entirely determined by commercial competition is valid if we can make the following assumptions:

1. That specialization guided by the comparative costs will not conjure up vicious and virtuous circles (i.e. positive feedbacks in the resulting system) which will perpetuate the initial advantages and disadvantages instead of levelling them.

2. That the population can move without hindrance in pursuance of the highest productivity of labour.

3. That the lines of specialization which are the most profitable at a given moment must also be promising in the long run.

4. That the military power gained in virtue of a specialization in heavy industry will not be used for obtaining economic advantages.

If migration is restricted then any region which has specialized in agriculture or extraction, or any other line of production which cannot be easily expanded owing to the scarcity of natural resources, will suffer if its population grows. According to the orthodox economic theory, this need not happen because as the population grows in relation to the resources the wages go down, which makes production cheaper and induces a flow of capital from abroad into the manufacturing industry. Unfortunately, 'the non-economic' factors often prevent this mechanism from operating. The flow of investments reacts much more violently to the danger of confiscation than to the differences in profitability, and as a downward movement of wages (or even their comparative stagnation) creates a danger of violent upheavals, it can not only deter foreign investors but can even induce a flight abroad of indigenous capital, regardless of the comparative costs of production and profit rates. We can see on this example why economic theory is not enough, and how unwise it is to rely on the advice of the economists alone in making development plans – especially if they are addicted to isolationism, and still believe that their theorems are self-contained, reliable and exact, despite the exclusion of non-economic variables.

(2) 'The economic development of Latin America is not only slow and irregular, it is also uneven, and this unevenness widens the gap between town and country, between rich and poor, between class and class.

286

The average family income in the city of Caracas in 1957 was estimated at $4,200 a year as compared with $430 in the rural areas of Venezuela.

UN experts estimate that the inequality of income distribution in Latin America is greater than in all other underdeveloped countries. A Latin American economist has calculated that during the last 150 years at the most 20 per cent of all Latin Americans received not less than 60 per cent of the total income of the region and other experts estimate that in Mexico for example, after ten years of progress only a tenth of the population is noticeably better off than before, a fifth is worse off and the situation of the remaining 70 per cent had remained almost unchanged.

But it would be an oversimplification to say that the "rich" have become richer and the "poor" poorer. Firstly because it is not simply a question of differences between "rich" and "poor", but also of growing contrasts between different economic interests existing side by side, secondly because it ignores the fact that a new class between "rich" and "poor" has developed in most South American towns, whose members are much better off than their fathers; and finally because it is important to point out that income differentials within the lower classes have also grown. In almost all countries the regularly employed part of the proletariat forms a minority — and there are very big differences in wages and salaries among workers and employees: there is a wide gulf between the wages of an oil worker in Venezuela and his colleague in other industries, and in Chile the weekly wage of a worker in the copper mines is $90 as compared with the average weekly wage of $14.'

(Boris Goldenberg, *The Cuban Revolution and Latin America*, p. 36).

(3) 'In 1960 there were 33,000 priests in Spain and 37,600 in South America: Spain has 30 million inhabitants and Latin America 200 million. In Chile, Ecuador and Colombia there is one priest for every 3,000–3,500 inhabitants: In Uruguay, Bolivia and Argentina one for every 4,000–4,500; in Venezuela, Mexico and Paru, one for every 5,000–6,000; in Brazil one for every 6,500; in Cuba one for every 9,500; in Guatemala one for 11,000 and in Honduras only one for every 12,000 inhabitants. It is important to note that in some countries most of the clergy are foreigners.

The Latin Americans are Catholics, but their "Catholicism is theatrical, sensual, superficial, in a word: childish". Many town dwellers go to Mass on Sundays and the women go to Confession. The upper and middle classes send their children to Catholic schools, often with unexpected results, as is shown by the example of Fidel Castro, who was educated at one of the biggest Jesuit schools in Cuba. But anti-clericalism has always existed among intellectuals, and the influence of the

287

Church on the urban proletariat has long been weak and is becoming progressively weaker.

In the countryside the Church was usually more powerful, although in Cuba and elsewhere most of the rural population were not under the influence of the Church, and there were large areas without priests. The Indians, in particular, are often fanatically religious, perhaps because their Christianity contains strong non-Christian elements. But the "revolution of growing expectations" has reached the rural population; outmoded ways of life are breaking down and the process of urbanization is undermining the power of the clergy. The growing masses in the towns are being "de-christianized" as social radicalism reinforces traditional anti-clerical tendencies.

(Boris Goldenberg, *The Cuban Revolution and Latin America*, pp. 49–50).

(4) According to James L. Payne: '. . . there is a scarcity of certain types of skilled workers in Peru. These workers can in effect stage a coercive economic strike, given the difficulty which their employers would experience in attempting to replace them. Examples of such groups are aviation mechanics and radio operators. Insofar as they rely on organized activity, these groups may successfully employ collective bargaining. But such groups of workers are very much the exception in Peru. The modal pattern of labor relations is determined by the method which most workers, who can be easily replaced, have been forced to adopt. . . . The presence of excess labor, in addition to facilitating replacement of striking workers, weakens collective bargaining in another way. In Peru industrial jobs are precious. The oversupply of labor has depressed "competitive" wages to extremely low levels, perhaps five or ten sols a day. But wages in industrial firms, maintained by trade union activity, are many times higher, varying between 40 and 80 sols per day. Even to assume that a discharged worker could gain employment at all is, given the fierce competition for jobs, extravagant.

The value of the job to the worker is significant in determining the solidarity of a strike. If the worker values his job as he does his life he will be reluctant to join a strike and anxious to return to work as soon as there is any indication that the strike will fail. Always in the forefront of his mind is the fear that he will be replaced. The economic strike requires, however, that a walk-off be nearly complete and that the strikers stay off the job even when the danger of partial replacement arises. If solidarity is low, as it is in Peru for the reason given above, an economic strike has less chance of success.

For Peruvian workers success lies in the method of political bargaining. Using this tactic the problems of solidarity and replacement become practically irrelevant. The strike does not need to be complete because it is not the firm which is being coerced but the executive. . . . The executive tends to see a decreed wage increase as the best, and perhaps only, way to avoid a military coup. Even though the Peruvian president fears inflation because it may eventually lead to a dangerous political climate as worker organizations protest against their declining real wage, he fears more the immediate danger which resides in the actual use of violence.'

(James L. Payne, *Labor and Politics in Peru*, pp. 14, 15–17, 23).

(5) This is how the author of the most thorough and penetrating study of the Cuban revolution describes its honeymoon which he has still been able to witness: 'The enthusiasm with which the masses supported Castro – whose revolution brought less official terror in its wake than similarly far-reaching and dynamic transformations usually require – an enthusiasm which fascinated so many foreign observers and which characterized the Cuban revolution, arose from the achievements, aims and promises of the government. Unlike other "socialist" revolutions the Cuban revolution *immediately* and without worrying about the cost or economic consequences of such a policy, provided material improvements for most members of the lower classes. It increased and extended their freedom (even if, as Erich Fromm and others have emphasized, in critical situations many people do not regard "individual freedom" as a blessing). It gave the poor new human dignity. It filled the young, who make up a large part of the Cuban people, with enthusiasm and it offered them an important ideology. With its grand primitive voluntarism it seemed to transcend painful realities and to open up new, unexpected perspectives. This revolution seemed to make little Cuba the centre of America, a thought which stirred the pride of Cubans.

For the masses the years 1959/60 were thus the dawn of happiness. The economic measures crushed the rich – a fact which alone produced understandable satisfaction in many hearts – and led to large-scale redistribution of the national income. For the majority of town dwellers living standards improved, because wages rose while prices and rents were reduced and new parks and places of entertainment or rest were created. But for most of the rural population a veritable heaven on earth seemed to have begun. Small tenant farmers no longer paid rent and many were given "title deeds" to the land which they farmed; for those who used to live in miserable huts thousands of new, attractive houses were built in the new co-opera ives, with tiled kitchens and bathrooms, built-in wardrobes, and front gardens. Schools were built and attractive streets and playgrounds laid out, people's shops sold goods more cheaply than the old private shops, and community centres and clinics were set up. Roads were made, lavatories were built, water and electricity were installed and doctors appeared where misery and under-nourishment had reigned before.

In spring 1960 the Institute for Social Research of Princeton University carried out a limited, unofficial opinion poll in Cuba. Of those asked, 43 per cent were enthusiastic supporters of Castro, a further 43 per cent were in favour of the government, and only 10 per cent were definitely in opposition. More women and young people were for Castro than men and people over 25, and his following was naturally greater among the lower than among the upper classes. The following were listed, in this order, as the greatest achievements of the revolution: land reform, honest government, educational advances and greater social justice. After a gap there was also mention of greater freedom. (It must be remembered that those questioned were comparing Castro with the Batista era.) Mentioned *last* were the "nationalist" achievements: greater national independence and growth of Cuba's international standing. The wishes for the future were mainly of a material nature: an increase in the standard of living was the most important. Sixty-five per cent thought that they were better off than in 1958. In conclusion the American investigators remarked: "The living standard and chances of work occupied the centre of national and personal worries and hopes. . . . The government will be judged by the public primarily on whether it will be able to raise the standard of living and to create more jobs."

A State Department representative said at a congressional committee meeting on February 18, 1960: "Well informed observers have reported that so far the Cuban people enjoy relatively more freedom than before. The people seem to have an honest government and enjoy a juster distribution of the national income. The revolutionary government seems to have brought the people political freedom and an improvement of its living standards."

After spending several weeks in Cuba Theodore Draper wrote with reference to the land reform: "No matter how the program turns out in practice there is no getting around the fact that for the poor, illiterate, landless outcast 'guajiros' the co-operatives represent a jump of centuries in living standards."

For the first time the poor (*los humildes*) felt that they were really being looked after and had become full "citizens". The old, feared army, the country gendarmerie and the police had disappeared and the new "army" – which was used to build houses, roads and schools – was part of the people. The people themselves were soon given arms and uniforms. The old luxury hotels, restaurants and clubs were thrown open to all. The new popular bathing establishments which sprang up all along the coast were spacious, elegant and comfortable, with cafés, restaurants and playgrounds; there were cabins and week-end cottages with air-conditioning and attractive furniture which could be rented for a small sum. The fact that many technicians and experts had fled gave the sons of the lower classes new chances of promotion.

White-collar workers, labourers, peasants' sons and unemployed or underemployed young intellectuals rose to responsible positions in the civil service and the economy. As directors of big sugar mills, which all employed over a thousand workers, a journalist found the following: a 33-year-old ex-employee of the public relations department of a big firm, who had earned £140 a month and who was now enthusiastically running a whole factory for a mere £30 (86 pesos): a 24-year-old former shop assistant; a boy barely 21 years old who used to help in his father's small cigar factory and a still younger boy who had been employed in a furniture factory. They had all volunteered some months earlier to be trained as teachers and because they were "able, dynamic and revolutionary" they had been entrusted by Fidel personally with the running of these factories.

Other opportunities and possibilities of advancement were provided, as we shall see later, by the cultural revolution which also brought foreign and native artists, often of world fame, to the co-operatives.

Many unemployed and underemployed joined the army, the militia and the "people's farms" where they found permanent employment. The little shoeshine boys who used to hang about the streets were given uniforms and fed in public kitchens by the Ministry of Welfare.

What could "political freedom" and "representative democracy" mean in comparison with all this? It was easy to do without them and to believe in the bearded leader who travelled from place to place, who appeared unexpectedly in the most outlandish parts, who spoke to everybody, advised everybody, gave hope to everybody and who for hours on end kept in touch with the people through television.'

(Boris Goldenberg, *The Cuban Revolution and Latin America*, pp. 210–213).

(6) As Theodore Draper says: The State farms were so badly run at the time, their chief administrator has revealed, that 80 per cent of the local administrators had to be removed. Later, Castro gave one reason for the trouble: 60 to 80 per cent of the sugar farms' administrators had had no more than a third- to fifth-grade elementary -school education. According to one pro-Castro writer, each dollar's worth of product on the state farms has cost approximately $1.20. . . .

Guevara's own program of 'accelerated industrialization' was the source of some of the worst disenchantment. The original conception was almost childishly simple. Its aim was the substitution of home made goods for those previously imported from the United States. Its method was the physical transplantation across half the globe of dozens of factories in the shortest possible time. Its financial basis was long-term credits or outright gifts from the Communist world.

By early 1962, Guevara knew that there was something radically wrong with the scheme. At that time, he analyzed the trouble as follows: 'We failed to put the proper emphasis on the utilization of our own resources; we worked with the fixed purpose of producing substitutes for finished imported articles, without clearly seeing that these articles are made with raw materials which must be had in order to manufacture them.'

In short, the Cuban industrializers thought solely in terms of factories, not in terms of raw materials for the factories. They were stunned to learn that, in many cases, the raw materials cost almost as much as the imported finished articles. In order to free themselves from dependence on the importation of finished articles, they had made themselves even more dependent on the importation of raw materials which they could not afford. Guevara subsequently explained: 'We began to acquire factories, but we did not think of the raw materials for them that we would have to import.' In this way, he said, two years had been lost 'installing factories for a series of articles which could be bought at almost the same price as the raw materials that we needed to produce them.'

(Theodore Draper, *Castroism : Theory and Practice*, pp. 140, 141).

INDEX

Luxembourg, 116
luxury goods, 59, 85–6, 236, 244

McCarthy, Joseph, 227
Madero, Francisco, 216, 219
Madrid, 42, 45
Mafia, Sicily, 66
Magloire, Paul, 76
Magon, Flores, 219
Malaya, 117
Malthus, 16, 263
mañana, 34–9
mano, 129
Mao-Tse Tung, 250
Mariategui, José Carlos, 280
market, 85, 107–15
marriage, 191, 194, 271
Marx, Karl, 12, 13, 85, 171, 197, 201, 212, 218
marxism, 92, 99, 123, 143, 144, 154, 186, 194, 212, 232, 245, 249, 255, 256, 277, 280, *see also* communism
Mas Haca, 129
matches, 69
materialism, 250
Maximilian, Emperor, 94, 189
Mayflower, 26
meat, 3, 118, 210, 223, 245
meat-packing, 223, 225
Medellin, 8
Melgarejo, 128
Mendeleyev, 210
mercantilism, 2
mercenaries, 216
mestizos, 32, 37, 46, 52, 54, 127, 155, 156, 157, 173, 174, 241
Mexico, 1, 2, 3, 4, 5, 6, 8, 9, 16, 19, 20, 24, 27, 39, 40, 41, 47–9, 54, 55, 56, 61–2, 65, 70, 73–7, 82, 83, 87, 91, 93, 94, 96, 101, 104, 108–9, 120, 122, 126, 127, 132, 133, 136, 140–5, 148, 150, 152, 153, 154, 156, 161, 162, 165, 166, 169, 174, 178, 179, 180, 182, 184, 189, 191–3, 199–200, 216–23, 244, 246, 247, 269, 274–5
Mexico City, 6, 8, 176, 191
Mexico Federal District, 167
Middle Ages, 121, 136, 187
middle class, 135, 136, 139, 144, 149, 154, 155, 163–70, 170–2, 177, 180, 185, 216, 223, 238–9, 245, 246, *see also* classes; population

migration, 109, *see also* immigrants
militarism, 180, *see also* pretorianism
Military Organization and Society, 15, 258
militia, 256
militocracy, 71–6
milk, 245
mines, 38, 67, 68, 83, 97, 100, 102, 218, 232, 233, 235
mining camps, 2, 56, 83, 98, 102, 232–3
miscegenation *see* interbreeding
Mission Economia y Humanismo, Bogota, 168
Mohammedans, 187
Molina, Humberto Sosa, 76
monarchy, 12, 37, 64, 125, 126, 135, 136, 145, 196
monoculture, 58
monoparty states, 140–5, 274
monopolies, 37, 45, 56, 77, 102, 115, 118, 127, 142, 149, 220, 231
monopsony, 81, 83
Montesquieu, 28
Montevideo, 6, 87, 164, 170, 206
Moog, Vianna, 52–3, 280
Moors, 30, 40, 157, 186
Mora, José Maria Luis, 279
Morelos, 191
Moreno, Gabriel Garcia, 131, 190
Mosca, Gaetano, 257
Moscow, 215
motor car, 43, 64, 118
Movimiento de Liberacion Nacional (Mexico), 144
Movimiento Nacionalista Revolucionario (Bolivia), 233, 234
Movimiento Social Democrata Cristiano (Mexico), 143
mulattoes, 32, 52, 53, 127, 152, 155, 174, 246, 247
Mussolini, 224–5, 228, 240, 253
mutinies, 184–5

Napoleon Bonaparte, 37, 135
Napoleon III, 94, 189
Nasser, 251
Nasserism, 277
National Guard (Dominican Republic), 128
nationalism, 20, 83, 94, 98, 102, 153, 186, 187, 189, 232, 234, 248